PHILIP MARSDEN is the author of *The Levelling Place* (winner of the Somerset Maugham Award), *The Bronski House*, *The Spirit-Wrestlers* (winner of the Thomas Cook Travel Book of the Year Award), *The Chains of Heaven* and *The Barefoot Emperor*. He is a fellow of the Royal Society of Literature and his work has been translated into more than a dozen languages. He lives near Falmouth in Cornwall.

From the reviews of *The Levelling Sea*:

'Had Philip Marsden simply used his travel-writing skills to create a hymn to our surrounding seas, and had he decorated it with this magical vocabulary alone, the book would have surely been a flawless triumph. But Marsden has done a great deal more than that …'

SIMON WINCHESTER, *We Love this Book*

'The best non-fiction expands the particular to the general, and perpetually discovers the marvellous in the ordinary. Marsden pulls this off every time. Read this book for a closer acquaintance with Falmouth … Read it for a good story and beautiful, unpretentious writing. Read it for its introduction, a brillant essay on seagoing, or for no particular reason. But read it'

SAM LLEWELLYN, *Marine Quarterly*

'Marsden's writing is delightfully honed as well as being profoundly well researched … convincing in its detail and exciting in its sweep, this portrait of a port sails deep into the reader's imagination'

Sunday Telegraph

'His pitch-perfect feel for a phrase, plus a gift as sublime as James Hamilton-Paterson or Jonathan Raban's for describing water, lifts *The Levelling Sea* far above ordinary history towards a state closer to poetry' *Sunday Times*

'Captivating ... Marsden has always had a knack of linking the local and the global' BOYD TONKIN, *Independent*

'The book is superb, by turns informative, inspirational and poetical ... a tour de force of marine meditation'
ALEX WADE, *Cornwall Today*

'Landlubbers will find much to be enthralled by in this biography of a port: a triumph of the author's deep learning combined with his passion for the sea'
HARRY RITCHIE, *Mail on Sunday*

'I feel as though I've been sitting at the feet of a master storyteller ... Philip Marsden knows and loves Falmouth, sailing and the sea, putting that love into this most satisfying of books' *Bookseller*

'An epic adventure, formed from the derring-do of Elizabethan sea-dogs, smugglers, Restoration speculators, and dashing naval officers ... a page-turning portrait of British identity in all its oddity, its thrust and diversity'
BARNABY ROGERSON, *Country Life*

'Delightful ... Marsden has unearthed some fascinating characters' *Literary Review*

Also by Philip Marsden:

The Crossing Place
The Bronski House
The Spirit-Wrestlers
The Main Cages
The Chains of Heaven
The Barefoot Emperor

PHILIP MARSDEN

The Levelling Sea

The Story of a Cornish Haven and the Age of Sail

Nor is his thought on harp or on ring-taking,
On woman's delight or on the world's hope,
Nor on aught else save the tossing of waves:
He ever has longing who hastens on water.

From The Seafarer

(Trans. from the Anglo-Saxon by Jonathan A. Glenn)

Harper
Press

Harper*Press*

An imprint of HarperCollins*Publishers*

77–85 Fulham Palace Road,
Hammersmith, London W6 8JB

This Harper*Press* paperback edition published 2012

1

First published by Harper*Press* in 2011

Copyright © Philip Marsden 2011

Philip Marsden asserts the moral right to
be identified as the author of this work

A catalogue record for this book
is available from the British Library

ISBN 978-0-00-717454-6

Typeset in Janson by G&M Designs Limited,
Raunds, Northamptonshire
Printed and bound in Great Britain by
Clays Ltd, St Ives plc

MIX
Paper from
responsible sources
FSC C007454

FSC™ is a non-profit international organisation established to promote
the responsible management of the world's forests. Products carrying the
FSC label are independently certified to assure customers that they come
from forests that are managed to meet the social, economic and
ecological needs of present and future generations,
and other controlled sources.

Find out more about HarperCollins and the environment at
www.harpercollins.co.uk/green

To Arthur
who already knows something of the sea

LIST OF CONTENTS

PART III

PART IV

LIST OF ILLUSTRATIONS

Map of Smithwick (1615). From H.M. Jeffrey, *Early topography of Falmouth*, JRIC vol. IX (1886). *Courtesy of Cornwall Centre*

The Lizard Light-houses, Cornwall, by William Daniell. © *Crown Copyright; UK Government Art Collection*

'*Sovereign of the Seas*', by John Payne (1637). © *National Maritime Museum, Greenwich, UK*

Thomas Killigrew, by William Sheppard (1650). © *National Portrait Gallery, London*

'A View of Falmouth Harbour', by Hendrick Danckerts (circa 1678). © *National Maritime Museum, Greenwich, UK*

Detail from 'Falmouth – To Sir Peter Killigrew, Baronet presented by Captain Greenville Collins (1693)', engraving, 47 x 58cms. © *Falmouth Art Gallery Collection. FAMAG:2003.13*

Peter Killigrew. Frontispiece from Susan E. Gay, *Old Falmouth: The Story of the Town from the Days of the Killigrews to the Earliest Part of the 19th Century* (Headly Brothers, 1903)

The Killigrew Monument (The Pyramid Arwenack), by Unknown artist (19th century), oil on canvas, 49.5 x 63cms. © *Falmouth Art Gallery Collection. FAMAG:1000.42*

'Fatte hogges, pretty oranges, strange crabs'. From Peter Mundy, *The Travels of Peter Mundy in Europe and Asia, 1608–1667*, vol. III, part I (Hakluyt Society, London 1919)

Avery the Pirate. *CRO J/2277. Courtesy of the Cornwall Record Office*

John Avery. From Captain Charles Johnson, *A General History of the Robberies & Murders of the Most Notorious Pirates* (Conway Maritime Press, 1998)

Armed guard for the Falmouth to London mail. © *Mary Evans Picture Library/Bruce Castle Museum*

Arwenacke House, Falmouth, Cornwall, by Unknown artist
(1786). Engraver: Sparrow. Publisher: Hooper, S.
Engraving, 15.3 x 20cms. © *Falmouth Art Gallery
Collection. FAMAG:1000.96*

Cover of Samuel Kelly's 'Life & Voyages', Vol. III. *CRO
X92. Courtesy of the Cornwall Record Office*

Ship-worm (*teredo navalis*). From Sir Charles Lyell, *The
Student's Elements of Geology* (Murray, 1871)

Jewish Cemetery, Falmouth. © *Philip Marsden*

Letter from George Croker Fox. *By permission of Charles Fox*

Books from the old G. C. Fox & Co. offices. © *Philip
Marsden*

'Sir Edward Pellew: Lord Exmouth' after Sir Thomas
Lawrence (*c.* 1797). © *Hulton Archive/Getty Images*

'View of Falmouth & Sir J Borlase Warren's prizes entering
the harbour', engraved by Thomas Medland (Bunney &
Co., 1800). *Courtesy of Cornwall Centre*

The *Indefatigable* capturing *La Virginie*, by C. Sheppard
(publisher) (1797). © *National Maritime Museum,
Greenwich, UK*

The wreck of the East Indiaman *Dutton* at Plymouth
Sound, 26 January 1796, by Thomas Luny (1821).
© *National Maritime Museum, Greenwich, UK*

Extract from *The Cornwall Gazette and Falmouth Packet*,
7 March, 1801. *Courtesy of the Courtney Libary (RIC), Truro*

Grave of Joseph Emidy. © *Philip Marsden*

A View of Falmouth and places adjacent, by H. Michell
(1806, published). Aquatint, 37 x 77cms. *Lent by Cornwall
Heritage Trust.* © *Falmouth Art Gallery Collection.
FAMAG:L2000.4*

'Encounter with Robbers Near Kengawar'. From J. S.
Buckingham, *Travels in Assyria, Media, and Persia* (Henry
Colburn and Richard Bentley, 1830)

James Silk Buckingham by George Thomas Doo, after
    Unknown artist (1855), stipple engraving. © *National
    Portrait Gallery, London*
Falmouth, by Joseph Mallord William Turner, engraved by
    T. Lupton. © *Tate, London 2011*
Liberty's bow. © *Philip Marsden*
From *Falmouth Guide 1815. Courtesy of Cornwall Centre*
Opening of the Falmouth and Truro railway (1863).
    © *Illustrated London News Ltd/Mary Evans*
Little Falmouth boatyard. © *Philip Marsden*

While every effort has been made to trace the owners of
copyright material reproduced herein, the publishers would
like to apologize for any omissions and would be pleased to
incorporate missing acknowledgements in future editions.

PART I

CHAPTER 1

For more than twenty years I have lived beside the sea, in Cornwall, in a house with a square of grass in front of it, a hedge, a road, a low cliff and then a shingle beach sloping to the water. To the north and west, I can see the whitewashed cluster of cottages around the arm of the quay. Out towards the headland, the houses grow larger: a facade of homes built during the great age of sail by trader-captains who exchanged shifting decks for solid ground, prize-money for building-stone, ship-life for a safe contemplation of the horizon. Beyond these are the newer buildings, villas from the 1930s and the 1960s in their rescued patches of land, built also for sea-contemplation but by those who never knew the dog-watch nor the terror of working the tops. On the point itself, like a high-plains beast come down to drink, its silhouette magnificent against the evening sky, stands one of Henry VIII's castles.

The headland opposite bears no buildings. A stand of pine covers its dipping entry into the sea. Gorse-spotted ground runs back from the point to a wood of holm and sessile oak. These two headlands, the one peopled and the other unpeopled, have been the borders of my life for two decades, open-ended, framing the vast-skied view from my studio window. Between them, stretching away into the distance, is the water.

During these years I have wasted weeks – months probably, when all added up – looking out at it. I have watched its constantly shifting shapes: the silvery slop after a blow, the sparkling mosaic in a winter sun, the slow swells of a southerly gale. I have listened to the rush of a week-long Atlantic storm, to the court of black-headed gulls, to the rummaging oystercatchers and roistering children. On windless nights, the air taut with expectation, I have woken to the rhythm of waves on the beach, each one hissing its message from centuries past, unintelligible and endlessly repeated. And during that time I have wondered this: what cumulative effect does such sea-proximity have? Does it offer anything more than a chance for idle gazing? Does it encourage a sense of restlessness, or complacency? Does it promote some spirit of equilibrium, a daily reminder that all things find their level? Or is its influence ultimately corrupting, creating the illusion of fulfilment always over the horizon, and in shipboard life an opportunity for living free from the constraints of the shore?

I have known this place since I was a child and although we came here for only a few weeks every year, it spurred an engagement with the world that nowhere inland could ever match. It was here that began a string of enthusiasms that filled my boyhood – first the beginnings of a rock collection (serpentine from the Lizard, quartzite pebbles from Samphire Island), then a passion for butterflies and moths (blues and commas and red admirals), birds, fishing and boats, always boats. Later, in my mid-twenties, in the wrong job and confounded by things I craved but could not name, I came here for a few weeks, to this house beside the Cornish sea, armed with one of those comforting and utterly useless phrases of intent – something like: *to try to find the calm to work things out.*

Calm! I remember the first morning. It was January. I had driven through the night and then watched dawn reshape the familiar form of the bay. I was used to it being full of boats, but there were none now. Instead the waters heaved in a grey easterly, bursting against the harbour wall and flopping back against the swells. Everything was in flux, the sea surface, the rushing clouds, the gulls flitting and arcing in the wind. By the next day, the sky was clear, the wind had gone and the sea was still. For weeks I wrote and walked and wallowed in the weather shifts and felt surprised by each one. But I was aware, too, of a growing sense of urgency, a sea-prompted rage against the rush of time. With the summer coming, I went off to East Africa before returning for another winter writing it up. That set up a pattern that continued for many years, a decade-long odyssey that followed its lone and dusty course through the Middle East and Eastern Europe. Sometimes I spent a whole year away, in Addis Ababa, Jerusalem and Moscow. But always I came back here, to this house beside the sea.

When I married, I thought it must be over, that solipsistic sea-life, but we stayed. We lived here for another ten years and now for various reasons we are moving inland (partly to do with a run-down farmhouse that has stolen our hearts). We are leaving this village, with its face turned to the water, and people say constantly: 'You will miss the sea.' And my instinct is to resist. I won't miss it. But how can I know? If I haven't been able to understand the presence of the sea, what chance is there of understanding its absence?

One October, in the brief decades between the wars, a young man arrived in this village. He was a Scot. With him was an English wife whose naval connections went back for gener-ations, but it was he who was the yachtsman, he who hired the boat and took it out into the harbour – between the twin headlands. So struck was he by that day, by the village and by the little boat, that he came back the next year, and the year after that, and each year for the next half a century. He brought his children every summer, to sail a small gaff-rigged sloop named *Ratona* ('female rat' in Spanish) and each evening wrote up the day in a series of leather-bound logs; embossed on their plain covers was the single word *Ratona*. If it was a particularly good day, or the first sail for one of his grandchildren, he would carefully flush the blue ink from his fountain pen and replace it with red.

In one of these logs, from the early 1960s, is this red-letter entry: '*Philip, two years old, left in the arms of his mother as we rowed aboard, wailed until we gave in.*' I was bundled with the storm-sails in the forepeak and although I do not remember that first time, I do recall the hours spent there later, half sleeping and half waking, looking up at the underside of the foredeck with its white gloss scattered with rosettes of black mould. I can still hear the lap of the water and smell the rough folds of the Egyptian cotton sail-cloth beneath me.

One golden evening when I was 9 or so, my grandfather and I were out alone in *Ratona*. He handed me the helm. As we beat back and forth across the Carrick Roads, heeling to one of those northerlies that often follows a hot day, he pointed up at the sails and for the first time explained the principle of sailing – the miracle of hull-shape and sail-set that enables a boat, obliquely, to sail *towards* the wind. I watched him in that moment, with his hand arced against the icing-white mainsail, describing the technique with a cracked softness in his voice that he used only when he spoke of certain people, and of certain periods in his life. I realised then, in a way I could not articulate, that this was as powerful as any human attachment, this love of the sea.

But I know, too, that 'love of the sea' is not strictly accurate. Mariners do not love the sea. Love for the sea is something you feel from the shore. You can admire the sea from a deck; you can be drawn to it, awed and terrified by it. If you are out on the water, your affection is not for the shifting mass all around the hull, but for the hull itself. What seamen feel for their vessel is something that elevates it high above the inanimate. It is, said Conrad, 'profoundly different from the love that men feel for every other work of their hands'.

No other arena of human endeavour has proved quite so challenging as the ocean. It has driven individuals and whole nations to do remarkable things – innovative, courageous and brutal. I have seen plenty of men, and it is almost always men, who are ill at ease on land, dazed, whose shore life is a mess; but put them on a boat, and they are transformed. They become athletes, commanders, strategists, heroes. The skills needed on a boat are unlike any on land, because everything is different at sea.

Take the language. Many think that nautical language is some dialect generated by cultural divergence long ago, in an age when mariners and landsmen rarely came into contact with each other. They think the modern sailor perpetuates it like some quaint outdated code, the lexical equivalent of dressing in eighteenth-century costume. But each sea-term has no translation in land language, because there is no equivalent on land. Every strange force the sea exerts, every quirk of tidal stream and every reef and twist of shoreline, every tackle-snapping, deck-swamping, broaching, pooping, pitch-poling and sinking, and every lone drowning, booms out the same warning: *you should not be out here!*

Yet it was the ability to build ships for passage, for oceanic voyages, to transport commodities and people, to line their sides with cannon, that shaped the modern world. More than any other agent, ships spread political power, ideas, goods and technology. Naval dominance – achieved first by the Spanish, then the Dutch and the British – decided whose ships went furthest, and who brought the greatest wealth home.

The maritime states' struggle was one of dominance *on* the ocean rather than *of* the ocean. Their success came not by taming the sea but by recognising its essential hostility, and working with its constraints. Basil Greenhill, chronicler of the end of wind-driven shipping, spoke of the age of sail as the 'the age of collaboration': the sailing ship represents 'the height of [man's] achievement in adapting the existing forces of nature … as opposed to the achievement of changing their direction and function'.

Sometimes reading the accounts of the sea battles of that time, the engagements involving privateers or ships-of-the-line, you have the sense less of the total war of the twentieth century than of some watery medieval tournament, a grand and deadly game in which each side, however pitiless, is bound by natural rules – the no-go areas to windward, the fatal advantage of the weather gage.

In the recent, post-industrial attraction to the wild, a yearning driven above all by the realisation of our distance from it, the sea is rarely mentioned. Yet it is perhaps the only true wilderness. You cannot manipulate the sea, you cannot cultivate it. Efforts to 'farm' its margins have in most cases proved disastrous. Fishermen are not agriculturalists; to find their equivalent on land you have to go back beyond written history, to hunter-gatherer groups of the Mesolithic age. The sea teaches the lesson every ecologist urges us to understand about the natural world: that it cares nothing for us, that it will survive us. Try to impose your will upon it and it will destroy you. Swim through it or pass over it in a boat, and you leave not a trace. In time it will, like sand over the works of Ozymandias, close over every brick, every avenue and every last relic of our civilisation.

That is the wisdom of the sea, its essential paradox. It quickens us, extends us, prompts feats of innovation and courage, then washes them all away. No trace remains; man and mountain yield to the levelling force of the sea. In its omnipotence, its beauty and its purity, the sea is the earthly manifestation of the divine. Building a vessel and crossing a body of water is a transcendent achievement, and afterwards nothing in this life quite compares.

During my first winter on the Fal estuary, my grandfather would telephone frequently from his home in Hampshire. He was now 90. He wanted to know exactly what the weather was doing, about the sea state, what ships had been going in and out of Falmouth. No detail was too trivial. Spring tides or neaps? Is the ferry running? He examined the weather maps and asked: has the wind backed yet down there? Has the cold front passed over you? He quizzed me about all those boats he knew, the people of the shore, the fishermen and part-time gardeners, the summer sailors and retired boat-builders. And then one storm-dark December afternoon, he rang and asked me: would I be kind enough to do something for him? Would I go up the river, have a look at *Ratona*?

In the dusk I walked through the cliff-top fields to where *Ratona* was wintering. She stood on legs at the rim of a tidal pool. Her bowsprit pushed up towards the serpentine roots of a group of Monterey pines; behind them was St Just churchyard, a mossy necropolis of slate and granite head-stones. Two mooring warps looped out from *Ratona*'s stern, down into the ebbing tide. Twice a day the water rose and fell around her, keeping her boards tight with moisture. The church clock's chimes rang out across the creek every quarter of an hour.

Climbing down to the muddy foreshore, I ran my hand along the curve of her waterline – the green topsides and scum-crusted red of her anti-fouling. I looked at the chain-plate, and the place where her mast should be and the winter cover stretched down tight over the ridge-pole, and was overwhelmed by a sense of the vanished past, of a hundred half-remembered scenes – squinting up the mast to check the lift of the cotton luff, gazing at the lee gunwale as the water rushed past it, rowing ashore in some hidden cove and looking at her at anchor, or lying again in the forepeak, cushioned by sail-cloth. With a squelch, I yanked my boots out of the mud, and climbed back up to the churchyard. The winter wind combed through the pines. It was almost dark.

I rang my grandfather that evening and told him *Ratona* was in fine shape. 'Good,' he said. 'That's splendid …' His words sounded distant. Just two weeks later, at his Hampshire home, he developed pneumonia and died.

When I was very young, I thought there were two grand-fathers, one in Hampshire, in woollen tie and leather-elbowed jacket, listening to music in his book-lined study. The other one lived in Cornwall, and was wilder, and more adventurous, and more appealing to a young boy. He wore sea-boots and salt-crusted trousers; he draped sails from the banisters to dry; he tinkered with tackle and rope, rowed his dinghy standing up. The memorial service for the first took place in a flint-walled church near the River Test, a dark-suited parade of family and surviving friends. It was several weeks later when there was a ceremony for the other grand-father. His ashes were brought to St Just. Only three of us stood with the vicar at the graveside. The wind sighed in the

Monterey pines. We placed his ashes among the roots. Just yards below him, as if he was some Norse hero buried with his boat, lay *Ratona*.

My grandfather.

CHAPTER 2

I have been away for a few weeks and now I go down to the water. Summer rain has left my upturned dinghy with green fur around the gunwales. I scrub it down, haul it to the beach and into the shallows. I sense the sudden lightness as the stern lifts and bobs free. The rowlocks *clunk-clunk* into the silence of the Percuil river. On the far side, beneath a flocculent strip of woods, lies the 21-foot harbour launch I bought some years ago with a friend. In the 1920s she was built as a liberty-boat, a solid workhorse of a naval craft, used to ferry men and supplies around Chatham harbour. Traditionally these launches took sailors ashore, from ship-bound service to shore-bound freedom – hence the name. For me, it has exactly the opposite meaning.

In the rounded clinker sides, the spade-like rudder, the steep and solid stem, I like to imagine centuries of maritime evolution. I picture the shipwright between the wars, circled by fresh-faced groms, instructing them in laying the keel, fixing the garboards, conjuring the lines outwards and upwards with each riveted strake, working as countless generations had before him, without plans, with no more than a practised eye and a couple of notions – to make the bilge a little deeper this time, the quarter a little fuller, and having the instinctive means to do it. A War Department registration is carved into the transom: WD 347. We call her *Liberty*.

Liberty's stern.

She is the last moored boat, at the far edge of a forest of spars. Beyond is a crescent of wooded shoreline and beach that now, towards the bottom of the tide, dries to mud. One or two punts lie on their sides, the sag of their painters hung with fronds of channelled wrack and eel grass. I am always amazed by the stillness of this place. Even in a rising gale, with gusts racing down from the slopes to scurry across the water, with the halyards beating out warnings from the masts in the river, the pool retains a calm so intense that I often sit here long after I have packed away the gear, engulfed by its presence.

It is thought that this small inlet was among the earliest-used anchorages of the Fal, the natural refuge of a ship groping in from the storms of the Western Approaches, running for the lee of St Mawes harbour, round into the mouth of the Percuil, then round again to settle on its side in this muddy cul-de-sac – tin ships from the Gironde, Breton traders, and those who brought no worldly goods, who kept within them no thought of return to their native ports. Long before the estuary's main shoreside settlements had appeared, monastic communities were measuring out their days here, with prayer and fishing and contemplation.

This then is how history begins on the shores of the Lower Fal, with groups of beehive huts and shaggy men half attached to the world, who immersed themselves up to the neck in the freezing water and pressed songs of devotion from their chattering lips. They were holy sea-wanderers, *peregrini*, who in the name of Christ took to the open water in the post-Roman centuries, trusting less to the rigours of seamanship than to divine providence. The sea was their desert, a blank alternative to the troubled world, and retreating to it an enactment of the reckless example of St Anthony. But the waters of north-western Europe are a harsher place by far than the wastes of Egypt. How many perished, drowned or starved in the great flat-horizoned emptiness, we shall never know. In the Fal, salvation was a labyrinth of wooded creeks, tidal waterways that pushed up far into the hinterland. They left their names in a series of creek-side churches. The one here is St Anthony's – the dedication honouring not the father of Christian monasticism, but the Cornish royal martyr, Entenius.

I work the mooring-chain over the samson post and watch it splash into the water. The weight of the chain as it sinks tugs the mooring buoy away from the boat. It is always a moment of anxiety, the severing of attachment. At the same time, *Liberty*'s bows are caught by the wind and blown further from the retreating buoy, down towards the shore. I jump inboard, jab the engine into gear, and head out of the river.

It is a bright day. A brisk westerly is driving gun-puffs of cloud across a clear sky. The water is flecked white, with short wind-turned seas that set up a barrelling motion in the boat. I lean back against the tiller. I can feel it in the small of my back. I can correct the lurch of the bows with the slightest movement. The village looks different from the water; all these years here and I'm still surprised by that: how seeing the land from the sea transforms it so completely.

Beyond St Mawes Castle, the estuary opens out, running several miles inland. I can see distant woods and fields and a few dot-clusters of white houses. Between them stretches the wide basin of the Carrick Roads, agreed by all who have written about it for hundreds of years to be one of the finest natural harbours in the world. I bring *Liberty* in past the town of Falmouth. The early sun lights up the town's terraces, each one following its own contour-line along the slopes, a stadium crowd of a thousand windows. Against the outer arm of the docks lies a rusting stone-barge named *Charlie Rock*. Towering over it is a Monrovia-registered tanker waiting for repairs. High up on the rail, a tiny figure raises its hand to wave down at me. As I pass in under the stern, the dock opens out. So close to the houses, the ships look out of scale.

Until as late as the seventeenth century, there was no town here. There was nothing – no docks, no quays. Where the wharves are were shingle beaches and mudflats. A sandbar enclosed a swampy lagoon where the National Maritime Museum Cornwall now stands. The slopes above the low cliff were open country, copsed and dotted with furze. The town centre itself was a bog. (It is still known as 'the Moor', a place where swampy land meets the tide.)

Yet within a century and a half, Falmouth was one of the great ports of the fast-expanding world – a global thoroughfare of war-news and innovation, whispered espionage and gold bullion, its quayside crowded with footsore explorers, high-worded gospellers bound for the New World. The view from the wharves was a pitch-pine, hempen jungle of yards and sheets, masts and ratlines. The decks were so numerous, it was said, that you could walk from one side of the harbour to the other on them.

The steep arc of Falmouth's growth reflects that of the era of sail, those ship-driven centuries that followed the Middle Ages. From the periphery of Europe, England emerged as a maritime power with such suddenness that it surprised her own people as much as it did her enemies. In the far south-west of the British Isles, Falmouth sprang from its bog with the same brash assurance. The Reformation prompted technical, political and cosmological changes that revolutionised mobility and fostered the restless urge to seek far-off lands. Falmouth itself was like a colony, an empty shoreline without a past, where the rootless and the hopeful could settle as equals.

Until that time, the Fal estuary had three ports. Each lay at the top of a long, tidal reach. Any settlement further downstream attracted the marauders who peopled the open seas and liked to burn the places they visited. Of the three, the most exposed was Penryn, a couple of miles up river from the site of Falmouth, where a chain could be stretched across the creek to repel incomers.

It is approaching high water when, later that day, I round the last bend in the Penryn river and see the ancient coinage town spread out over two valleys. Weekend yachts, day trawlers, houseboats and punts bob at the fringes of the creek. Alongside them lie semi-submerged hulks and wrecks, and the project-hulls of would be ocean-crossers, part-completed or long abandoned. I leave *Liberty* at Exchequer Quay and in sea-boots go up to the main road, standing to wait for the *beep-beep-beep* of the pedestrian lights before crossing. I follow the Antre river through the lower town and with the sun low find myself standing in the middle of an empty municipal field. The grass has just been cut. The trimmings lie in stripes at my feet, matted by the morning's rain.

In the thirteenth century the Bishop of Exeter was visited in a dream by Thomas à Becket. Come to this place, he was told, to the marsh known as Polthesow, Cornish for 'arrow-pool', so named because hunted beasts would flee into its waters and disappear. Build an altar there and in that place 'marvellous things' shall be seen. The bishop drained the swamp and raised Glasney church based on his cathedral at Exeter and a full two-thirds of its size. It helped that the land at Penryn, its woods and pastures, for some way inland and for miles south along the shore towards the open sea, belonged to the diocese of Exeter, as did all the money-spinning rights of the coast – the fundus, oysterage, shrimpage and right of wreck.

A college was established, and a constitution drawn up, a wise and prudent document that proposed a presiding council of '13 discreet persons of the more substantial sort'. Thereafter at night, and 'testified by the neighbours', a heavenly light was often seen at Glasney glowing high above the heads of the holy men of the college gathered to praise the name of God. Marvellous things indeed.

Glasney College was soon one of the largest ecclesiastical centres of Cornwall. As the English state pressed westwards, on the tide of its own language, the college became a great promoter of Cornish. Around it, the port of Penryn prospered. Tin and stone were loaded on its strand. Hogsheads of salted pilchard left for the Continent. The fortified walls of the college offered protection from the sea, as did the barrage of stakes and stone and chain put across the river.

Through the fourteenth and fifteenth centuries, as sea trade increased around the coast, and as the coastal peoples

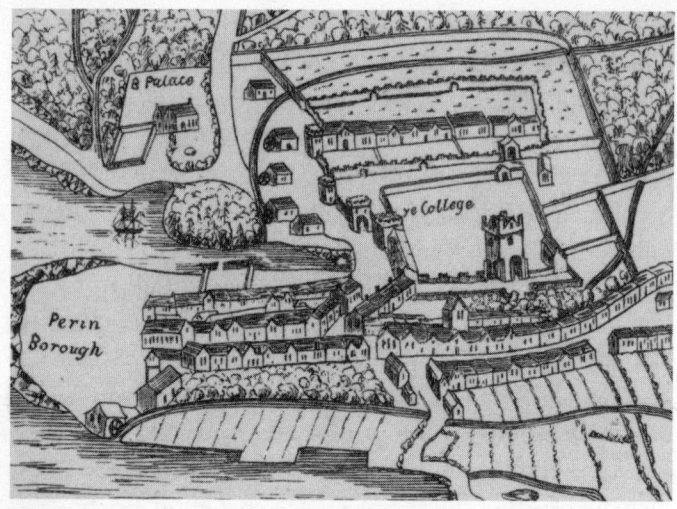

Glasney College.

of Atlantic Europe became more restless, so Penryn grew into one of the busiest ports in Cornwall. It was a frequent point of refuge. In 1506 King Philip and Queen Juana of Castile sheltered there for several weeks: 'We are in a very wild place,' wrote the nervous Venetian ambassador with them, 'in the midst of a most barbarous race.' Yet even in the Middle Ages, the sea had produced a cosmopolitan settlement. In 1327, half of Penryn's population was described as 'foreign', Breton for the most part. As a language, English was the third or fourth most used. The college and the port complemented each other perfectly – ships coming to the Fal for shelter were drawn to Glasney, while their victualling needs produced a thriving commercial centre.

But in time something of the worldly success of Penryn appeared to seep into Glasney College's inner rooms. By the sixteenth century its officials were being described as 'men of great pleasures, more like temporal men than spiritual'. The provost had little time for his ministry, preferring to 'drink and joust'. Henry VIII's Star Chamber was told how he 'doth slay and kill with his spaniels, some days two sheep, some days three and divers times five in a day'. The college's shoreside position, which had helped it to grow, now counted against it: 'By reason of the open standynge of the same on the sea,' gloated the Crown Commissioners shortly after Henry VIII's death, 'by tempest of weather felle into suche decaye.'

Yet it was Henry and not the weather that was to blame. Glasney College survived the dissolution of the monasteries, but was prey a few years later to the same covetous forces. Lead was peeled from its vaulted roofs and shipped to the Isles of Scilly to use in fortifications. Piece by piece the buildings were broken up. The bells were sold off. The stone was removed. For generations, vestments and treasures had been bequeathed to the college by wealthy men hoping for prayers in perpetuity. Now copes of green and crimson velvet were bundled up and taken off, as were bolts of cloth-of-gold, albs and chasubles, six altar-cloths of black, gold, green, blue and red velvet, and one of ivory satin, embroidered with images of roses and Our Lady, a bell with a handle of gold and red silk, breviaries, tabernacles and missals, and a piece of paper painted with the five wounds of the Saviour.

Standing alone in that playing field, I look around for traces of the college buildings. A panel-board shows the points at which archaeologists have recently conducted a series of digs. The dotted lines of their trenches are set against a plan of the church, and I am struck by its great size. Glancing away from the board, I picture the nave and aisles peopled by tiny figures, raising their heads and whispering – the grateful storm-survivors, passengers and merchants from the Low Countries, from France and Spain and Portugal.

Glasney was a part of that network of ports and havens and anchorages which for thousands of years had been not so much on the land-fringes of European countries, as on the edge of a loose nation linked by the sea. As they grew, sovereign states superseded many of those maritime links. Of centuries of ship-voyages, little evidence remains. Glasney's archaeological digs turned up floors and tiles and fragments of worked stone. But the digs themselves have now been covered up, the portable finds removed, and there is nothing on this late summer day, not a bump or hollow or mound, to break the green of the empty acre.

Afternoon is sliding into evening. I return to *Liberty* and head out into the river. The tide has turned, and with it the moored boats have swung round to face the ebb. Somewhere here – between the wharves and warehouses to starboard, the woods to port – stretched the barrier that had protected Penryn and Glasney. It was the chain, and the narrow approach to Penryn, that enabled its rise during the Middle Ages, but it was the chain too, the closing out of the sea, that helped shut Penryn off from the bold and expansive age that was coming.

CHAPTER 3

One day a few weeks later, I row out to *Liberty*, fold up the cover and pump the bilges. The summer yachts have thinned out, laid up in the sheltered corners of the creeks. The shore-side oaks are still green, but something tired now shows in their foliage. A few hundred yards to the south, the Victorian facade of Place Manor rises from its sweep of lawn and gravelled drive. Almost completely hidden behind it is the much older church of St Anthony's, its tower just clearing the manor's roof like the mast of a sunken ship.

I drop the mooring and head out towards St Mawes Castle. From the far headland rises Pendennis Castle, and the two stand guard over the estuary's approaches. When the religious community around St Anthony's church was dissolved during the Reformation, the buildings were pulled down and the stone barged across the harbour to build St Mawes Castle. With a neat circularity, the castle had been commissioned to oppose the threat of papal retribution that followed the Reformation and the Dissolution.

In Falmouth, I moor up at the pontoon and walk through the town, over the railway, through a just-ploughed field to the hilltop church of St Budock. According to the boast on the service board, the church was founded in AD 473–1,000 years before the first buildings of Falmouth appeared above the strand. Budoc himself was one of the greatest of the sea-soaked saints of the Celtic Church. Venerated in Ireland, Wales and Cornwall, his story was carried between them, embellished by a thousand tellings. On Brittany's hazardous shoreline, he has been called 'le patron de ces côtes' and in the miracles of his life, you can sense the particular licence of maritime myth: an adventure from the start, beginning in the middle of the English Channel, where Budoc was born in a bobbing barrel. Shaped by the winds, his earthly mission left him here for several years, above the Fal estuary, with his small group of monks, before he again took to the Channel, floating to Brittany in a stone coffin.

The church interior is damp and dark. Morning light falls through the high altar window, flashing on and off as clouds slide across the sun. A harvest tableau stands in a niche – bread rolls and a vase of poppies and cornflowers. Kneeling in front of the altar rail, I take the edge of the runner and roll it back beneath the chancel, revealing a grid of terracotta tiles. In the centre, set into stone, glints the panel I am looking for:

HERE LYETH IOHN KILLIGREW ESQVIER, OF ARWENACK ...
AND ELIZABETH TREWINNARD HIS WIFE ... GOD TOOK
HIM TO HIS MERCY THE YEARE OF OUR LORD 1567 ...

Above the inscription, mottled with age, lie the couple's brass images. I bend to examine them more closely. No trace of human softness crosses their faces, none of the flamboyance of the later Elizabethans. They are standing in prayer. Framed by a wimple, Elizabeth Killigrew's expression is stern and manly. John Killigrew's hair and beard are cropped short and he is dressed in armour – vambrace and breastplate, and sword trailing to the ground.

Yet these two can rightly be called the grandparents of the

port of Falmouth. With their ten children, they produced a dynasty that spread far beyond Cornwall, a line of mariners and politicians, pirates and felons, diplomats and courtiers who played a part in succesive royal courts, while here in their patch of shoreside territory, they carved a fief from open fields and cliffs, and from a minor estate a port connected to the furthest points of the known world.

HEERE LYETH IOHN KILLIGREW ESQVIER, OF ARWENACK, AND LORD OF Ŷ MANOR OF KILLIGREW IN CORNEWALL, AND ELIZABETH TREWINNARD HIS WIFE, HE WAS THE FIRST CAPTAINE OF PENDENNIS CASTLE, MADE BY KING HENRY THE EIGHT, & SO CONTINVED VNTILL THE NYNTH OF QVEENE ELIZABETH AT WHICH TIME GOD TOOKE HIM TO HIS MERCYE, BEING THE YEARE OF OVR LORD 1567.
S: IOHN KILLIGREW KNIGHT HIS SOŃE SVCCEEDED HIM IN Ŷ SAME PLACE BY THE GIFT OF QVEENE ELIZABETH.

John and Elizabeth Killigrew.

The family was not originally from the coast. The small farm of Killigrew – meaning 'nut-grove' (not 'grove of eagles' as is often supposed) – was located to the north of Truro, half a day's ride from the open sea. (Long after the Killigrews had gone from the town at Falmouth, the yard at Killigrew could still be seen. Not until the late 1990s was it finally destroyed, when teams of yellow earth-movers and diggers parked in it while they reshaped the land for the Trispen bypass.) It was through marriage, at about the turn of the fourteenth century, that the Killigrews became associated with the manor of Arwenack. From then on their name crops up in the records of Glasney College – as does that of John's wife, Trewinnard. But while Penryn and Glasney prospered, safe behind their chain-barrage, Arwenack remained of little importance.

For years, the Killigrews lived the provincial life of Cornwall's gentry, those families who owned land around the county, who married each other and visited each other in an atmosphere of leisure and conviviality. 'A gentlemen and his wife,' wrote Richard Carew, 'will ride to make merry with his next neighbour, and after a day or twain those two couples go to a third, in which progress they increase like snowballs.'

With the breaking-up of the church estates and the building of the two castles at St Mawes and Pendennis, power shifted on the shores of the Fal. Like a crab with a new shell, John Killigrew crept out from under his rock and snapped up much of Glasney's land. Soon he controlled the tithes of sixteen parishes. By buying up the south bank of the Helford, he controlled most of that river too. The land for Pendennis Castle was leased from him. Two of his sons received lucrative commissions for overseeing its building. When the castle was complete, John became its first captain and remained so for the rest of his life.

Pendennis Castle made a little king of John Killigrew, protecting Arwenack from marauding ships and fortifying his status with Crown bombards and perriers, pyramids of stone shot and keep-walls 11 feet thick. He joined that class of Tudor men who grew suddenly wealthy from the easy pickings of church land. Killigrew was particularly fortunate: not only did he have an enlarged estate and a brand-new castle, he also had the sea. The combination gave him control of one of the best anchorages in the land, and a power that was constrained by little more than the laws of wind and tide.

When Queen Mary came to the throne in 1554, and began to reverse the heretical advances of the Protestants, John Killigrew at once involved himself in the insurrection against her. Having no real authority as far west as the Fal, the new queen was forced to try to win him over. She reappointed him to his post at Pendennis. Her Privy Council confirmed his command of the castle, which he must 'diligently, faithfullie and truly kepe, save and defende with all his power, connyng and industrie'. He and his sons did nothing diligently, faithfully or truly. They continued to plot against the Queen. Two were implicated with Sir Peter Carew in Wyatt's rebellion. They fled to France where Henry II was happy to provide them with ships to attack the Spanish vessels of Mary's husband, Philip II. Along with a number of other families from the Cornish and Devon coasts, the Killigrews conducted an ongoing campaign against Philip's shipping in the Channel. Their small-time piracy, the habit of centuries among seafarers of Channel shores, became more political. The maritime historian Kenneth Andrews identifies a shift in motive at about this time: 'the gentry took the lead, especially the west country families connected with the sea, for whom Protestantism, patriotism and plunder became virtually synonymous ... the Cornish Tremaynes and Killigrews embarked on an unofficial war with Spain.'

Back and forth across the Channel the Killigrews sailed – harrying the Spanish and taking Protestant rebels into exile in France. During the hot summer of 1556 – heat which drove the frail queen to her bed – Mary's Privy Council lost patience with the pirates. At Arwenack, John Killigrew was arrested and with his heir, also John, brought up to London. The two were thrown into the Fleet Prison. At the same time, in the Queen's name, a small squadron was sent into the Channel to round up rebel ships. The force was commanded by the veteran pirate-hunter, Sir William Tyrell.

Tyrell had immediate success. Soon, just above the low-water mark at Wapping Stairs, six pirates swung from gibbets. He went to sea again and, according to the Acts of the Privy Council, captured 'ten English pirate vessels'. One of the commanders escaped to Ireland in a small boat, where he was killed by local men as he struggled ashore. Another – who had escaped Tyrell for years – was Peter Killigrew.

Of all the five sons of Arwenack Manor, Peter was the best-known sea-rover. The Venetian ambassador in London described him as 'an old pirate, whose name and exploits are most notorious, and he is therefore in great repute and favour with the French'. At first, Peter Killigrew escaped again, was recaptured, tried to stuff 150 crowns into the skirts 'of his woman' and was finally taken in chains to London. Twenty-four of the ordinary seamen were hanged at Southampton, and another seven at Wapping.

Peter was not killed at once. He and his brother were taken to the Tower where they later alleged they were tortured. From their confession comes a tale that resonates down the ages with an authenticity more convincing than the J. M. Barrie, dyed-in-the-wool brigand. Peter Killigrew was weary. He had known too many night chases, too many hostile landfalls, too many deceptions and betrayals. All he wished to do, he now explained, like any self-respecting mariner of the times, was to sail to the gold mines of Guinea and return with enough to retire on. He would then, he claimed, buy a house in Italy and never again put to sea.

By this time, his father had been released from the Fleet, and promised to pay compensation to anyone wronged by his miscreant sons. With their marine skills and position, the Killigrews were deemed 'useful'. Peter Killigrew was put in charge of the *Jerfalcon*, part of a naval squadron active in the war against France. John and his eldest son returned to Cornwall. Within a year Elizabeth was queen and John Killigrew's Protestant fiefdom, centred on Arwenack and Pendennis Castle, was once more in sympathy with the Crown. Pugnacious seamen like the Killigrews were no longer outlaws but set to become the very drivers of the new regime.

During the later years of his life, John Killigrew amassed a sizeable fortune. As governor of Pendennis, he continued to use the waters of the lower Fal to his advantage, in line with many of Elizabethan England's most colourful ventures, seizing chances as they came, exploiting the legal ambiguity and anonymity of the sea. Even so, his maverick methods infuriated the state. Throughout the mid-1560s they received reports of his piracy and 'evill usage in keeping of a castell'.

John's son Peter may genuinely have intended to retire, to reach Guinea, and buy a house in Italy. But it was easier to carry on doing what he did best, using the Killigrew lands on the Helford river as a base for his dubious trading. Helford – nicknamed Stealford – became known as a safe haven for pirates, a place to offload and distribute plunder without risk. The Killigrews operated their own mini-state around

Falmouth. When an envoy of the Privy Council was sent to Arwenack to claim 184 rubies stolen by Peter, John Killigrew – then in his seventies – reached for his sword and threatened to stick him.

With sea-gained bounty, the elderly John Killigrew set about rebuilding Arwenack Manor. Carts brought granite from Mabe quarry and, for ornament, barges of free stone from along the coast at Pentewan. Gables and high chimneys multiplied out from a three-storey central tower. A line of battlements ran along the top of the banqueting hall. A courtyard was enclosed on three sides, while on the fourth it opened onto a water-gate with a short canal dug out from the marshy ground of Bar Pool. John Killigrew's expansion of Arwenack, according to the family's chronicler, made it 'the finest and most costly house in Cornwall'. The bill rose towards £6,000. But just as the last fittings were put in place, in November 1567, John Killigrew died.

The sun flashes again on his brass likeness. Half-armoured, he looks every inch the late-Tudor strongman, his stance and expression set hard against the centuries between us. Opportunistic, fiercely Protestant, equating any sense of authority with the priestly rule of the past, he found in the sea an arena in which to exercise his will with impunity, a new breed of man, a semi-licensed rogue as yet untamed, clanking out of the Middle Ages to help lay the foundations of modern Britain.

CHAPTER 4

From the decades following John Killigrew's death comes one of the earliest and most striking images of Falmouth. Buried deep in the British Library, under 'highly restricted' access, the picture is bound into a volume of Christopher Saxton's maps of England's counties – known as the first English atlas. The volume was collated by Queen Elizabeth's secretary of state Lord Burghley during the 1570s – a period which happened also to see the most explosive progress in the history of English seafaring.

In the hush of the Manuscripts Room, I rest Burghley's volume on a foam cradle. I raise its pasteboard cover. The pages turn with a stiff and biblical crinkling. Saxton's *Atlas* reveals an England of crimson villages, rivers of heavenly blue, well-spaced market towns, lime-coloured hills and a jagged coastline back-shaded with gold. Its pretty pages, each showing its bordered shire, speak of the merits of regional order, and echo Burghley's own tireless efforts to achieve it.

Gathered in among them, Folio 9 is of a wholly different character, less stylised and much more exuberant. An inlay of vellum in a paper frame, the folio has on its reverse the title 'Map of Falmouth Haven'. The words are written in a curator's pencil, lightly marking the paper, like a whisper.

I turn the page and stand back. 'Map' is not right. Folio 9 is a painting, a wonderful vista of greens and yellows and browns, without symbol or key, without abstraction, with none of the functionality of Saxton's counties. A half-inch rim of black ink runs around the map's edge, sharpening its earthy tones. The image itself is a bird's-eye view of the familiar shoreline of the lower Fal – the view of a lark somewhere high above Feock. It is early summer. The hedges are full. Woods and copses are thick with new growth, mounds of fresh-cut hay dry in the fields. You can sense the air's fly-buzz and gorse-scent, follow the winding lanes, and feel beneath your feet the soft-grass ridge between the cart-furrows. But the image is really about the water: from almost every slope stretch the tidal tributaries and the pale-blue estuary of the Carrick Roads.

One of the first things you notice about the Burghley Map of Falmouth Haven is that it is upside down. The traditional south–north orientation is reversed. It does not, as you expect, start out at sea and guide you up from the Lizard

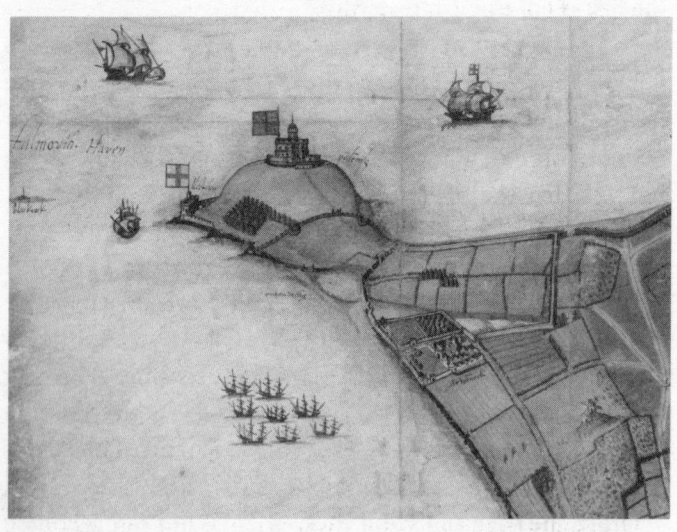

Detail from the Burghley Map of Falmouth Haven.

towards the sheltering channel of the Fal. Folio 9 brings you in from the north, from the land, leads the gaze up and outwards into open space. Falmouth is no longer merely a bolt-hole for ships, or a handy aperture for the kingdom's enemies. It is here presented as a conduit to the empty horizon. The overall effect is an urging, a siren cry: *leave behind the old terrestrial certainties! Join in the great sea-based bonanza!*

A glow of patriotism radiates from the manuscript. The castles appear jaunty and solid. Over the lower blockhouse of Pendennis rises a St George flag so large that it looks set to topple the little tower. From the castle itself flutters a Royal Standard of impossible size – peer closely and you can see the gilded symbols flashing like tiny jewels: the lions passant on a red field and the *fleurs de lis* on blue.

By contrast, the ancient town of Penryn, with its outdated, pre-Reformation dominance, is shunted to the bottom of the map. The cross-river chain is shown, and below it the remains of Glasney College. Years earlier, before the Norman Conquest, Penryn had been one of Cornwall's largest population centres, second only to the county town, Launceston. Here it is almost ignored, pressed to the margins, where four centuries of thumb-grasps and page-turnings have flaked the paint so that the town now looks to be in the midst of a snowstorm.

Where Falmouth will emerge during the coming century there is just shale and shingle in the very slight recess of Smithwick Creek, and on the cliff above, open ground. Only one building is drawn, a low shed marked *lym-kiln*. The great port has its lowly origins here: on an empty beach, in the swampy ground above, and in the cob-walls of a small lime-kiln.

Dominating the picture, dwarfing the ancient town of Penryn, is Arwenack Manor, the most opulent and expensive house in Cornwall. Placed between Pendennis Castle above and Penryn below, the house appears in style to be the child of both. With its battlements and towers, it has taken on the martial character of Pendennis. But in the courtyards, the mullioned windows and the long facade, the vast manor carries an ironic resemblance to Glasney College whose destruction allowed the Killigrews to create it. Aglow with Protestant triumphalism, surrounded by its neatly fenced demesne land, it fills the map with its worldly fortitude.

Such is the precedence given to Arwenack that the whole image suggests a piece of propaganda for the Killigrew family. It is usually assumed that Burghley himself commissioned the map, yet although he bound other manuscript maps into Saxton's *Atlas*, Falmouth is the only large-scale depiction of a harbour. Whether he asked for it or whether it was presented to him unsolicited is not clear.

The Killigrew family and Lord Burghley were certainly known to each other. Burghley would have been aware of old John, Pendennis's first governor, his sudden rise, his imprisonment, his pirate son Peter and all the nefarious sea-tales of the family. But he also knew more directly, from court, two of the sons who were rather better behaved. William Killigrew was an MP, who in his career represented Cornish constituencies in a total of seven Parliaments (no Cornish family of the time provided more MPs than the Killigrews). William was also Groom to Elizabeth I's Bed Chamber. His brother Henry Killigrew was even closer to the Queen's inner circle, by turns Teller of the Exchequer and Surveyor of the Armoury, and her chosen envoy on a number of vital missions to Scotland, France and the Netherlands. But the closest link was that Henry Killigrew and Lord Burghley were married to sisters, the famous daughters of Sir Anthony Cooke (a third was married to Sir Nicholas Bacon).

An upbringing in the rowdy atmosphere of Arwenack, with its visiting ships, its Huguenot rovers and Dutch sea-beggars, had prepared Henry Killigrew for an adventurous political career. He spent Mary's reign in exile and perfected his French and Italian. He was not a tall man and acquired a permanent limp from a wound picked up in the siege of Rouen in 1562. When he was released, and Rouen relieved, it seemed Elizabeth and England were in the ascendant. Henry Killigrew wrote to his wife's brother-in-law, Lord Burghley (then William Cecil): 'God prosper you as He has begun, and inspire her Majesty to build up the temple of Jerusalem.'

Burghley has annotated each of his county maps with a list of its 'justices'. There is a sense of him trying to order the kingdom, to catalogue it for better governance – or any governance. In Mortlake, the mystic John Dee was building a mythical Jerusalem for his queen, while Burghley, the great administrator, was assembling the more solid building-blocks for a civil state.

But Lord Burghley and the Killigrews of Arwenack were also at odds. In their respective attitudes to the sea, each represents a distinct thread of English interests which, when wound together, stretched taut through the coming centuries. One was legitimate, using the sea for the collective good; the other was illegal, exploiting it for private gain. One produced the Royal Navy, the other spun off into piracy. Each developed seamanship and a certain arrogance at sea, contributing in its own way to the victories of Drake, Cochrane and Nelson.

Burghley was among those who understood that the country's future – indeed its survival – lay in naval strength. He took personal control of the political aspects of the Royal Navy, and spent the 1560s and 1570s building up capacity, commissioning surveys of shipping and mobilising. He had a great love of geography and his copy of Saxton's Atlas also includes a map of the coast of Norway, Sweden and northern Russia. He was famous for his meticulous knowledge of the places of Europe. Yet he himself left British shores only once in his life, for a brief visit to the Low Countries.

The rise in piracy, represented by the Cornish Killigews, angered him; fish were the rightful yield of the seas, not plunder. Those who lived by the coast should spread nets to feed the people, not sail off on prize-grabbing adventures. But since the Reformation, and the relaxation of fast days, demand for fish had shrunk: to eat meat on a Friday, to roll your jaws over bloody slabs of beef, became an affirmation of Protestant faith, and it left fishermen with a shrinking market. They stowed their nets and joined privateers. To try to induce them back, Burghley – still William Cecil at the time – introduced a government bill to make twice-weekly fish-eating compulsory. His measure was jeered in the House for its Popish implications, and dubbed 'Cecil's Fast'.

The Killigrews on the other hand saw the sea as a source of personal gain. Arwenack became a hub for the illicit side of seaborne enterprise, for privateering, a practice which took off during the last decades of Tudor rule. Elizabethan 'privateering' was, strictly, distinct from the seventeenth- and eighteenth-century practice which spawned the term, but it offered the same dubious licence to attack foreign ships as redress for lost cargoes. In the sixteenth century, this licence was provided through a 'letter of marque'. If a merchant or captain was robbed of his goods by a foreign power, he was given a chit which allowed him to snatch compensation in kind from any ships of that power. Often the letters themselves were exchanged for money, and often not held at all. In practice, privateering was little more than semi-sanctioned piracy.

To Burghley, it made a mockery of the rule of law, and jeopardised relations with other nations, particularly Spain. But with hindsight, the spirit of privateering characterises the Elizabethan age – the ship as the vessel of the wildest hopes, the heady myth-making, the heroic sea voyages, the failure of the Spanish Armadas. Privateering also had one great practical benefit: it proved the nation's greatest school for maritime skills.

The countless and nameless figures who manned the privateers learned the advantages of the modern rig with its auxiliary sails. They learned to use the mesh of halyards and lifts and sheets. They learned how to charge the guns with volatile serpentine powder, and how to damp the recoil. And they learned something far more important, that despite the risks and discomforts, a successful foray into the Channel, or the taking of a Spanish prize, could bring greater reward than a lifetime of toil. The sea and quick wealth become part of a powerful association for coastal communities, brought together in the arts of seamanship.

Life on board a privateer was brutal and anarchic, lacking either the hierarchical order of Spanish ships or the fierce discipline of the later Royal Navy. Privateers were mutual enterprises, operated on the same basis as fishing boats, with the crew receiving no wages but reaping a third of the takings. They would coerce the captain if they disagreed with him – 'shite on thy commissions!' – or simply mutiny. There were open fights. The ships were often shockingly overmanned and under-victualled. Scurvy and the flux laid whole companies low; there were instances of starvation. But when a prize was sighted, all disputes were forgotten. The men took to their stations, gaining the weather-gage, firing on the prize not to sink it but to disable it. With small arms – fowlers and murderers, muskets and calivers – the ship was boarded. If booty was not revealed by searching, it was discovered by persuasion – wrapping ropes around the head, or bowstrings around the genitals.

As well as rewarding those with sea-skills, such enterprise encouraged private investment in ships. By the end of the century, the English merchant fleet outnumbered the Queen's own by twenty to one. The ships landed up to £200,000 a year in illicit prize money, establishing new fortunes, no longer tied up in land, as liquid as the sea that yielded them, a fund of robber capital that grew and grew, doubling by the decade, funding more ships and more ventures, and swelling through the seventeenth and eighteenth centuries into the prosperity on which Britain's global power was based.

On the Burghley Map, ships fill the blank sea-spaces with gleeful profusion. To the west of Pendennis an English three-master fires, rather gratuitously, on a caravel (its southern shape suggesting devious papist intentions). Another three-master waits to the south of Pendennis. In the Carrick Roads, marked by a couple of paddock-size St George's ensigns, a powerful squadron lies at anchor. But there are other ships, too, which fly no official flags. Mylor has a couple, St Mawes a couple more (Penryn has none); three more lie off St Methick's Point. But the greatest number, arranged in neat formation, lie off Killigrew land, a cluster of eight off Arwenack Manor.

Burghley's own handwriting has been identified on his map of Falmouth Haven and it is easy to imagine him during the dangerous years of the late sixteenth century, surveying his atlas and pausing to scrutinise Folio 9. He would have ignored the Killigrews' display of standard-waving from Pendennis Castle, seeing it for the sham it was, likewise the bellicose men-of-war. But he would have noticed, too, that anonymous group off Arwenack, their pack-like poise and confidence, and been reminded of the renegade threat of privateering.

Their rig is identical. Three masts, two bare yards on the fore and main, and a spar aft on the mizzen. A bumpkin juts from a high transom stern. The images are too small to see what guns they carry – typically a clutch of sakers, minions and falconets. They are not big, perhaps fifty or sixty tons burden, easily affordable for a private syndicate – but in the history of ship design they represented the most efficient vessels that had ever sailed.

During the fifteenth and sixteenth centuries, sailing ships had evolved more quickly than in the previous 5,000 years. Such was their success that they remained essentially unchanged for the next 200 or 300 years, until the coming of steam and ironclads began to make them obsolete. With only a little hyperbole, the maritime historian Alan McGowan equates the development of this type of rig with the discovery of fire and the invention of the wheel.

The standard sailing ship in most of Europe had, until well into the Middle Ages, tended to use a large, single sail, a very powerful driving force if the wind was steady, and moderate, and blowing from behind, or at least aft of the beam. Such a rig was pretty useless to windward and gave little scope for varying sail area in light airs or as the breeze freshened. So auxiliary sails were added – a maintop above the maincourse and ahead of them a foretop and forecourse. In time a spritsail appeared in the bows and lateen sails were set aft – which enabled the ship to manoeuvre through the wind with an ease never known before. A fourth mast and bonnets were sometimes added. Over time, sails grew upwards – top-gallants, royals and skysails – while the headsails pushed forward, out

From the Bayeux Tapestry.

along the bowsprit. Staysails filled the gaps ahead of and between the masts while, eventually, studding-sails stretched far out over the sides.

As to the hulls of northern European ships, they had tended to be clinker-built. The strength lay in the overlapping boards; an inner frame was added later, towards launching. When demands on ships grew, and voyages became longer and the risks from hostile ships increased (or rather, in the case of English privateers, the rewards from being hostile oneself), an alternative construction became popular, spreading from Spain and Portugal. Carvel building placed the boards of the hull flush against one another and relied for firmness and shape on an inner frame of ribs and crosspieces. (It is possible that, in Cornwall and Brittany, carvel construction had always been practised; the Veneti were reported to have used such ships against the Romans.)

Carvel building also helped solve one of the greatest problems of sixteenth-century fighting ships: how to mount heavy guns on board in a way that would be efficient in battle and not compromise seaworthiness. Having one large gun to fire from the bows suited the Venetians with their great galleys but in the waters of northern Europe, despite many attempts, galleys never really worked. Although bow-mounted guns and stern-chasers were fixed well into the seventeenth century, it was the broadside arrangement that decided the outcome of countless battles. The carvel structure allowed ports to be cut in the ship's sides without undermining their strength; in England, developments in iron-founding swept aside the constraints of expensive bronze barrels. Arming a ship, to the alarm of men like Burghley, became possible not only for the Crown but for privateers such as those of the Killigrews.

For want of a better model, early tactics at sea had followed the orthodoxies of land battle. The Spanish in particular took on board a military mentality based on strict rank, fortresses and close combat. They built ships with ever more elaborate upperworks. Soldiers would assemble for attack high in the floating arcades while sailors, with the status of water-carriers, performed their strange business with canvas and cordage. European kings were slow to see the strategic value of smaller, free-ranging fleets, preferring the ships they built to reflect their own magnificence. The Swedish king built the 230-foot *Elefant*. James IV of Scotland went one foot bigger with the *Great Michael*, which encouraged Henry VIII to join in and build the *Henry Grace à Dieu*. When he sailed to meet Francis I at the Field of the Cloth of Gold, the gilded sails glowed like the morning sky. Francis I himself took royal hubris further with the *Grand François*: a crew of 2,000, an onboard windmill, tennis court and chapel. Before even reaching the open sea, the *Grand François* was wrecked.

The success of English ships from the 1570s onwards stemmed in large part from leaving behind land-based hierarchies and abiding by the laws of the sea. Ventures were plotted in small harbours, in shoreside manors like Arwenack, not in court. Ships were self-contained, small-scale units of enterprise and power, and in Elizabethan England their design developed accordingly, producing compact and agile craft. Far from shore, and in the capricious hands of wind and waves, the spirit on board was more egalitarian than anywhere on land. 'I must have the gentleman to haul and draw with the mariner,' declared Drake on his circumnavigation, having just executed the troublesome courtier Doughty.

Even now, though, it is hard to glean very much about sixteenth-century ship design. The preserved boards of the *Mary Rose* are among the few actual relics. Otherwise there are only chance images – tapestries in Portugal, paintings in the Alhambra, the seal of Louis de Bourbon, Henry VI's psalter, chest designs, or manuscripts like that of Anthony Anthony or Burghley's folio of Falmouth Haven. From these sources, a vague outline of development can be traced. Masts grow in number along the deck, yards sprout from them. A bow-rigged flagstaff in one period has mutated into a spritsail in the next. Sometimes a ship will be shown with an experimental spar, which then disappears like some redundant limb. Rarely has the growth of a technology so closely mirrored biological evolution.

The vessels themselves have long since vanished, wrecked or destroyed by fire, or after countless gravings and rebuildings and re-riggings, the cutting down of decks, stripped of all blocks and fittings, then taken up some muddy creek to settle slowly back to nature, their timbers broken down by the drilling shell of shipworms. Like some race of aquatic dinosaurs, Tudor ships have been reassembled from the faintest of traces. But in the Pepys Library at Magdalene College, Cambridge is a set of papers that gives the only detailed glimpse of the process and thinking behind their construction, and of this decisive moment in man's relationship with the sea.

CHAPTER 5

Storm-clouds press down dark and close above the Fens. I scuttle across Magdalene's quads just as the first patter of rain rises to a crescendo. It is the day after seeing the Burghley Map, and now in the upper room of the Pepys Library, with the same thrill of expectation, and to the sound of approaching thunder, I lay out another ancient volume, between another pair of pasteboard covers.

When he died, Samuel Pepys left a collection of some 3,000 books. Among the large number concerning maritime history was a series of loose folios which he had bound into a volume, naming it *Fragments of Ancient English Shipwrightry*. They include the country's earliest record of paper plans for building ships. Looking at them, you can sense the process of experimentation, with the dividers' prick-marks still visible, and the arcane grids of hull curves framed with marginal calculations. Other folios place the art of shipbuilding in a much wider context. Included by Pepys is a painted image of Noah's Ark – 'Noah did according unto all that God commanded him even so did he make thee an arke of pine trees …' Another page has jottings about Jason's voyage to Colchis, and the invention of ships in the Hellespont. The overall impression is less of an inquiry into a practical problem than a quest to rediscover some lost secret – closer to the spirit of the Renaissance than the Enlightenment.

The papers are attributed to Matthew Baker, greatest of Elizabethan shipwrights. Baker was the first to leave a record of the abstraction of hull design into numerical proportions, the first to have a ship built from his blueprints (the private warship *Galleon*). It was he who built the *Revenge*, Drake's flagship in 1588, from whose decks Grenville later fought the most famous rearguard action in English history. Martin Frobisher's three Baffin Island expeditions used Baker's ships. In his *Seaman's Secrets* John Davis said that as a shipwright Baker 'hath not in any nation his equall'. To many of his contemporaries, Baker's craft put him on a par with Vitruvius and Dürer.

Among his bound papers in the Pepys Library is what is believed to be a self-portrait. Baker is shown standing at his plan table which is spread with instruments of drawing and mensuration. He holds a pair of dividers and is marching them over the drawing of a hull. The dividers are exaggerated, some three feet high, and there is something faintly comic about the image. Though Baker's head is bent in earnest concentration, his left leg is kicked up behind him, giving the impression that he is skipping as he works.

It is Baker who is credited with the design that revolutionised English shipping. Rejecting the cumbersome, castellated upperworks that compromised ships' seaworthiness, he helped develop a much lower, sleeker form, recognisable in the shapes of those on the Burghley Map lying off Arwenack Manor. Initial resistance to the new hull shape came, it seems, from Queen Elizabeth and Lord Burghley (as well as possibly from John Hawkins, the Navy's treasurer to whom, paradoxically, Baker's innovation is often attributed). Baker had a battle to fight in gaining approval for his revolutionary design, a battle that produced the most unusual image in his collection.

Baker has used a fish. He has transposed the profile of an Atlantic cod below the waterline of his ship. The curve of the fish's belly gives the distinctive 'crescent' shape to the keel. The long upward slope towards the tail represents the pinching of the floor that produces the sharp and narrow after-keel section. (The convention of good ship design was long framed in the expression 'cod's head and mackerel tail', which persisted for yachts right up to the 1960s, when the convention was suddenly reversed, the sleek tail in the bows, and the bulk of the beam aft.)

Baker's cod is not an exact fit, the cod's distinctive fat lips stick through the stem while the flukes of the tail do not correspond to very much. But that makes its use more interesting. Clearly, the cod was persuasive.

Such animism has always been a part of seafaring. So much is unknown, so much goes on unseen beneath the surface, and such are the uncertainties and risks of being on the water that pure reason rarely survives very far from the shore. A certain imitative instinct is in the name of the high-bowed West Country boat, the balinger (*balaena* – Latin for 'whale').

From Fragments of Ancient English Shipwrightry.

Likewise, the forces of the sea should be absorbed rather than resisted. It was believed that a ship that flexed with the water was a good one, and there were instances of pirates who removed some of the ship's frames to make it even more flexible. Whatever the exact thinking behind Baker's cod, it represented an alternative to building ships like castles, a recognition that the best way to prosper away from land was not by transposing terrestrial forms but by realising that the sea operates by its own set of rules.

In 1588, when Elizabeth's fleet (made up in large part of privately owned craft) at last engaged with the Spanish Armada, observers said that the English ships could tack six times to the Spanish galleons' one. The clash was one of diverging maritime cultures, the apostate newcomer against the lords of the old order, the English in their nimble, cod-bellied ships manned by freebooting mariners, against the great floating fortresses of papal Spain.

More than a generation later, Thomas Fuller wrote about the verbal sparring of William Shakespeare and Ben Jonson. The skit gives a sense of how much ship design had entered the thinking of the age:

> Many were the wit-combats between [Shakespeare] and Ben Jonson: which two I behold like a Spanish great galleon and an English man-of-war. Mister Jonson like the former, was built far higher in learning; solid, but slow in his performances. Shakespeare with the English man-of-war, lesser in bulk but lighter in sailing, could turn with all tides, tack about and take advantage of all winds, by the quickness of his wit and invention.

During the late 1560s and the 1570s, when Matthew Baker was at work, something of a watery revolution was taking place. Until then, English mariners had lagged far behind their European counterparts. They were coast-bound, ill-equipped, ignorant and unambitious. The Navy consisted of no more than a couple of dozen serviceable ships. Navigation charts were imported from Lisbon. In 1568, months after the completion of Arwenack Manor, it was said that only one Englishman was capable of sailing a ship to the West Indies without a foreign pilot. Yet within ten years Francis Drake was sailing around the globe. Another decade on, the Venetian ambassador to France wrote that the English were, 'above all Western nations, expert and active in all naval operations, and great sea dogs'.

Like all such revolutions, this one was a result of the coincidence of means and motivation. As ships became more efficient and more affordable, so there was a rush to use them, not only for plunder in the Channel, but for more distant ventures. Riches were one incentive; the glittering promise of El Dorado, the bullion-filled holds of the Spanish *Flota* or the route to Cathay drove many an oceanic crossing. But there were others, equally persuasive: patriotism, curiosity and sheer restlessness.

The work of Richard Hakluyt reveals the questing spirit of the times. So shamed was he by the French view of the stay-at-home English and their 'sluggish security' that he began to collate records of English overseas adventures. Hakluyt's own epiphany took place right at the beginning of this period, in the late 1560s, with a visit to his cousin's office in the Middle Temple. Lying open on the table were an atlas and several books of cosmography. As he watched, his cousin took up a staff and guided the young Richard through the atlas, pointing 'to all the knowen Seas, Gulfs, Bayes, Straights, Capes, Rivers, Empires, Kingdomes, Dukedomes and Territories'. With each wand-struck feature, each tapped length of coastline, each sweep of open ocean, Hakluyt grew more excited. His cousin then reached for the Bible, flicking through its pages to the oft-quoted verses 23 and 24 in Psalm 107: 'They that go downe to the sea in ships, and occupy by the great waters, see the works of the Lord, and his wonders in the deep ...'

Hakluyt did not go to sea himself but spent the rest of his life gathering accounts of those who had. *The Principal Navigations, Voyages and Discoveries of the English Nation* was published some years after the Middle Temple meeting, and opens with an account of King Arthur (taken from the pseudo-Zeni document): 'This kingdom was too little for him, and his mind was not contented with it. He therefore valiantly subdued Scandinavia.' There then follows a long list of all the other territories that Arthur valiantly subdued.

After the first volume, Hakluyt added another two, and a further million words of stirring quests and sea battles. By the time of his death, ten more volumes had been produced while his unpublished papers were edited and added to by Samuel Purchas in twenty further volumes. Since 1846, the Hakluyt Society has published two volumes of voyages every year. It would be impossible to assess the legacy of that encounter in the Middle Temple during the reign of Elizabeth I – the contagion that spread from it through English literature, or the number of sea-miles it generated, or the fortunes it helped create – but it is easy to measure it on library shelves.

As Hakluyt began his great page-odyssey, prodding less book-bound souls than himself into roaming the world, advances in scientific literature helped them on their way. In 1570 the first English translation of Euclid was published. 'No other work in the English tongue,' wrote the historian of Tudor science D.W. Waters, 'has been so influential in stimulating the growth in England of the arts of mathematics, navigation, and hydrography.' Perhaps even more important at the time than Euclid's text was the introduction to it written by John Dee, Elizabeth I's favourite philosopher and astrologer.

Dee's introduction applies Euclidian method to seamanship. He provides the first English definition of navigation, stressing the range of sciences it relies on – 'hydrographie, astronomie, astrologie and horometrie' – as well as the basics of arithmetic and geometry. At the time the word 'navigation' referred to all aspects of seamanship and Dee could not restrain himself from presenting maritime skills not just as a practical discipline but as some sort of transcendent communion. Be attentive, he urged ships' masters, be attuned to all things, for in their changes lie both threats and opportunities. If signs were noted 'of Moon, Sterres, Water, Ayre, Fire, Wood, Stones, Birdes, and Beastes, and of many thynges els, a certain Sympatheticall forewarning may be had'. Such attentiveness, he added, could lead to 'pleasure and profit'.

His essay emboldened a generation of seafarers, particularly those in the West Country, for whom patriotism, adventure and greed were beginning to coalesce in maritime enterprise. Going to sea, reaping its rewards (by any means), was both the right and the destiny of the English people. 'What privilege,' wrote Dee, 'God had endued this Iland with, by reason of situation, most commodious for *Navigation*, to Places most Famous and Riche.' Dee was much taken with rebuilding an English mythology, and like Hakluyt was drawn to the Arthurian cycles (he called his own son Arthur). He, too, celebrated the far and ancient wanderings of the English, quoting Geoffrey of Monmouth as well as his own collection of esoteric texts. Such was the importance of his task for the nation that it was sometimes necessary for Dee to embellish them with his own inventions. It was Dee who first coined the term 'British Impire' in his 1577 book *General and Rare Memorial Pertaining to the Perfect Art of Navigation*, and a few years later, Burghley and Queen Elizabeth were presented with Dee's two voluminous rolls explaining the English queen's extensive rights to the world's territories.

The 1570s also saw great advances in cosmology, adding to expanding perceptions and the range of geometrical techniques. In 1576, John Dee's pupil Thomas Digges published *Pantometria*, the ground-breaking work of his father, Leonard. At the same time, Thomas Digges was the first advocate in England of Copernicus's strange idea that the Earth revolved round the Sun. Thomas Digges even extended the Copernican vision: the stars you see at night, he suggested, are just a fraction of them all, running off from our sight in numbers unimaginable, into eternity. Awareness of a tiny Earth in a celestial infinity found an equivalent in the sense of a rapidly expanding terrestrial world. Closer to home, Digges applied his science to harbour engineering and an overhaul of the art of navigation using mathematical methods. Unlike Hakluyt and Dee, Digges validated his theories – for himself, and in the eyes of mariners – by testing them during a fifteen-week stint at sea.

CHAPTER 6

In Cornwall, the Killigrews were perfectly placed to take advantage of the new age – Protestant, proficient at sea and in control of one of the best anchorages in the country. Emphasis had shifted away from the east coast, away from the Narrow Seas towards the Western Approaches, the Atlantic and the adventure of the New World. Plymouth was already the springboard both for Crown-sponsored missions and for fleets defending the Channel; Drake, Hawkins, Raleigh and Grenville had all sailed from Plymouth on their heroic voyages.

In many ways Falmouth had even greater natural advantages than its rival up the coast. Comparing the two havens, Richard Carew found much to favour the Cornish one. Falmouth 'lieth farther out in the trade way, and so offereth a sooner opportunity to wind-driven shipping than Plymouth'. Where Plymouth had 'fairer towns', Falmouth had the great asset of secrecy – 'a hundred sail may anchor within his circuit, and no one of them see the other's top, which Plymouth cannot equal'. Whichever is the better, he concluded, they each have 'precedence over all other havens in England'.

Heir to the harbour's entrance, during these heady years of maritime progress, was the second John Killigrew. Succeeding from his father in 1567, he inherited not only the

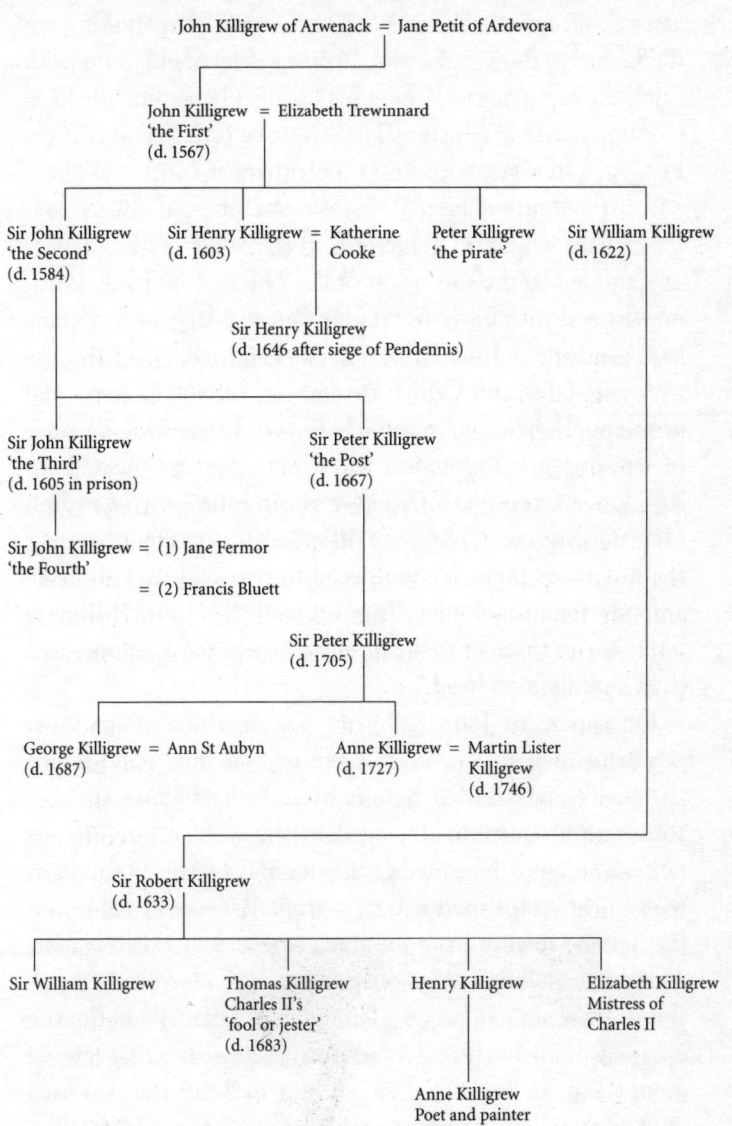

The Killigrew family.

just-rebuilt Arwenack but a lucrative scroll of freeholds from the Lizard to Penryn, fee simple farms as far afield as Penwith – and the captaincy of Pendennis Castle. He became the local Commissioner of Musters. He was twice returned as MP for Penryn, and along with his two brothers at court – William and little limping Henry – was a member of the crucial Parliament which rid Queen Elizabeth of her Catholic plotters and led to the execution of the Duke of Norfolk. Once imprisoned with his father under Queen Mary, twenty years later – in 1576 – John Killigrew was knighted.

A year later, the Crown turned to deal with a perennial problem. To help purge the Channel of its growing number of bandits, a Commission for Piracy was established. In London, its receiver of fines was Sir John's own brother, Henry Killigrew. Among the offenders was another brother, the notorious pirate Peter, forced to part with £25 to make amends for his felonies. In Cornwall, Sir John Killigrew himself – no stranger to the business of piracy – was appointed the Commission's head.

On paper, Sir John Killigrew was now one of the most powerful men in the West Country, but his name is not among the far-sighted figures of the Elizabethan age. Sir John was a consummate, dyed-in-the-wool rogue. To his father's bullying, he added profligacy and a taste for southern wines. He established a family trait that would push him further and further from the track of the law – extravagance. Among those he owed money to was the convict Anthony Bourne, holed up in his own Pendennis Castle. When Bourne escaped, Cornwall's vice-admiral accused Killigrew of complicity. Sir John challenged him to fight; the two men clashed swords at Truro but without resolution. Arbitration found in the vice-admiral's favour, but Killigrew still refused to pay the £100 fine.

The limitations of Tudor sources, and the reluctance of lawless privateers to commit their adventures to paper, have left little but glimpses of the second John Killigrew and his affairs. (One contemporary described him 'as proud as Ammon, as covetous as Ahab and as cruel as Nero'.) But from the proceedings of the Privy Council come details of a particular incident.

It was the winter of 1582. A Spanish ship, the *Marie*, some 140 tons burden, had been struggling down the Channel. Days of gales had left her rigging badly damaged. Rather than tack south into the weather, towards her home port of San Sebastian, the *Marie* did what any stricken ship would have done: sought shelter in Falmouth. She bore away to the north, loosening sheets for St Anthony's Head, past Pendennis Castle and Black Rock, and into the flat waters of the Penryn river. There her master commissioned repairs.

On shore, the people of Penryn watched the *Marie*. They watched the pinnaces come and go and in the evening they watched her crew at the inn of Ambrose Cox. The days passed. The gales fell away and the swells flattened; the waters of the Carrick Roads became glassy. Now the *Marie* could not leave for want of wind and so she sat there still, her masts restepped, her new sails bent, while her anchor chain dropped vertically into the flat winter water.

At Arwenack, Sir John Killigrew, too, had been watching the *Marie*. Together with his wife and a number of his men, he put together a plan. Having set it in motion, Sir John – Cornwall's Crown Commissioner for Piracy – saddled his horse and rode far away from any taint of involvement. At nine in the evening, a couple of Killigrew's men appeared at Cox's inn and told the Spaniards: there is illness on the *Marie*, you must board at once. Bess Moore agreed to tell anyone who might ask that two more of Killigrew's servants, Kendall and Hawkins, were with her that evening and tarried until midnight while one had his shirt dried.

In fact they and the others hurried out to Arwenack, launched Killigrew's pinnace, and rowed across the moonlit water to the *Marie*. Among the *Marie*'s crew were two Flemings who had secretly agreed to hide the ship's weapons. The boarding party had little difficulty in tying up the Spaniards. Inspection of the holds, though, proved a disappointment – all they found was holland cloth and some nice leather chairs. They would have to rely on the ship itself for a return; they set sail for Ireland and, as the Privy Council was later told, 'most of the men cast overboarde'.

When a London merchant, with a venture of his own aboard the *Marie*, called for an investigation, the Commissioner for Piracy in Cornwall strangely failed to muster any evidence. But in this case the Privy Council made one or two of their own inquiries and managed to breach the local cordon of alliance and alibi. Soon Killigrew himself was being sought as a suspect. He fled Arwenack. He travelled to London 'where he secretlie lurked in some place'. When he was discovered, he was held at Greenwich, bound before the Earl of Bedford for sureties of £1,000.

The case against Sir John Killigrew for the ransacking of the *Marie* was still outstanding when he died a year or so later, in 1584. In seventeen years as master of Arwenack, Sir John had managed to outdo his father in extravagance, the wanton exploitation of official appointments, and impunity. Now with Europe slipping into war, the Channel becoming ever more dangerous, the next John Killigrew sailed back to Cornwall, leaving behind the court of Elizabeth where he had been living under the wing of his uncle Henry. He promised not merely to 'make large satisfaction for his father's faults', but to correct the wrongs of all his other freebooting uncles. He pledged to honour Her Majesty by doing everything in his power to protect, during these dark days, the strategic part of her realm that was his charge. He took over Arwenack Manor and the governorship of Pendennis Castle, and in due course, was elevated to the position of vice-admiral of Cornwall.

But the third John Killigrew, according to a later charge-sheet, 'kept not within the compass of any law, as his father now and then, from fear of punishment, did'. To try to stem his growing debts, he sold off land, parts of Penryn and farms in the hundreds of Penwith and Kerrier. He managed, though, to cling to his house at Arwenack and also the wooded-off creeks of the Helford river where the plunder-mart provided income. Looted ships slipped with ease in and out of the river, swelling his shoreside cellars with cloth and metal and wines. He had his supporters in the surrounding area, those with little regard for the English state, who decorated their houses and their person with the pickings of pirated cargoes. The clamour of creditors and writs did not stop Killigrew filling the banqueting hall at Arwenack with a host of high-living merchants and privateers. He lived a life of risk and sudden reward, of brazen ship-ventures, and in the interludes between them recreated their spirit at his own gaming table. Of all the Killigrews, the third John Killigrew of Arwenack was by far the most dissolute.

The Privy Council became used to petitions for his debts. They summoned him frequently from Cornwall, but he never appeared. In 1588 they received a complaint from a Danish merchant: Killigrew had ransacked his ship. The Council was furious, not least to learn that he was still at large: 'for as much as divers messingers have been sent for the said Killegrew ... he goeth up and down the countrey accompanied with divers and lewde and disordered persons for his gard, armed with unlawfull weapons'.

All available force should be used, they urged, to apprehend him, even if he was in the keep of Pendennis Castle. Only the following year, still uncaptured, was he deemed not a 'fytt man to beare anie office of authoritie'. He was removed as vice-admiral (yet remained governor of Pendennis). A few months later, the Privy Council went further. They requested a writ of rebellion to be raised against Killigrew.

But he survived. His case was swamped by the great tide of Spanish-invasion fear. And within a few years, with a common enemy, he was trumpeting his loyalty. He asked the Council for money to fortify Pendennis: £1,400 or £1,500, he wrote, should cover it. He himself would provide for half the garrison. There was no response. He wrote again: he understood, of course, that with his record, they might have reservations about giving him money, but the Council may award it through a third party. Still nothing.

In 1595 a force of a couple of hundred Spanish landed near Penzance and burned the villages of Mousehole and Paul. They were driven back, but the people of Cornwall remained terrified of the next attempt. John Killigrew's pleas became more shrill. He urged Hannibal Vyvyan, governor of St Mawes Castle, to try to convince the Council on his behalf. Vyvyan excelled. Killigrew, he explained to the authorities, had diligently repaired the castle when required and 'used her majesties money (yea rather more) for mounting of his great ordnance'. (A lie – the courses of Pendennis Castle were sprouting with fern and only one gun in the entire castle was serviceable.)

The following month, Killigrew himself wrote, saying he was ready to sacrifice his own life and those of his men to protect the castle: 'better 1000 as good as myselfe should loose theire lives, rather than the enemy should possese the place'. The threat, he pleaded, was becoming ever more urgent, and in this he was perfectly correct.

In Spain, a plan had resurfaced, one that had first been presented by Pedro Menendez de Aviles long before the 1588 Armada. To invade England, it was not necessary to sail up the Channel and risk interception. Instead, a fleet could head straight into Falmouth, take Pendennis Castle and cut its link to the land. Then as many ships as were required could be brought into the Carrick Roads. Sea-surrounded Cornwall would be easy to defend from Crown forces. Ten thousand men could march to Plymouth, and from a western bridge-head, the errant land be rescued from its godless rulers.

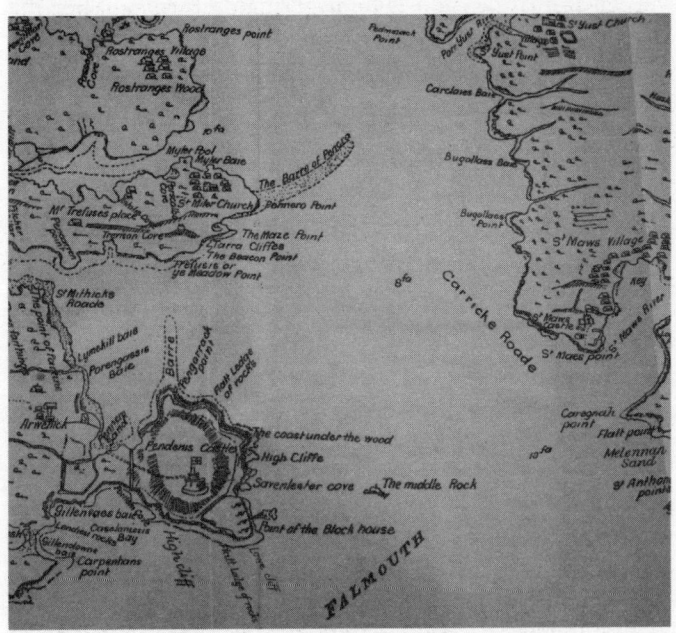

From the Boazio map of Falmouth.

In order to illustrate the danger, Killigrew cited a recent incident. A Spanish force had landed at Arwenack at midnight, and laid barrels of gunpowder around the house. Only one charge went off and the raiding party fled, taking a fisherman and a local boy with them back to Spain. The intention, said Killigrew, had been to kidnap his own wife and children. When they reached King Philip the Spanish detail tried to cover their failure by dressing the boy up in fine clothes and telling the King that they 'burnt Mr Kyllegrews house to the grounde being the finest house of one of the finest cavaliers in all the weste partes'. Pointing to the boy, they told Philip that he was a younger son of Killigrew. King Philip made him the page of his own younger son, and rewarded the captain with a gold chain of 200 ducats and an annual pension. The fisherman returned, reporting the intention of more raids.

But there was a much easier way for the Spanish to secure Pendennis Castle. It was common knowledge in coastal ports, 'table talk'. A Spanish prisoner, captured at Calais, confessed that he had been 'feasted, entertained and lodged' at Arwenack. He was then secretly sent to Spain with an offer from the Englishman Killigrew: when he saw the approach of Spanish ships, he would hand the castle to them without a fight.

On 8 October 1597 another Spanish Armada left La Coruña for Falmouth. There was, this time, no fleet to stop them. The English fighting ships, under Essex, were far to the south, in the Azores. One hundred and thirty Spanish vessels pushed north across the Bay of Biscay. On board were crammed 10,000 troops, along with chests of booty to establish themselves in Falmouth and the West Country. On the great *St Bartholomew* alone were 100,000 ducats and sheaves of printed posters proclaiming in English: *Peace and immunity for all who turn Catholic! Devastation to apostates!* The country lay like a ripe fruit before them. But twenty leagues short of the Isles of Scilly, the winds veered and strengthened, coming out of the worst and also the rarest direction, east-north-east. The fleet was scattered and the *St Bartholomew* lost with all its treasure.

Once it became known that the Adelantado's plan was to capture Pendennis and the Fal, Killigrew's pleas were answered. A high-ranking delegation was sent to Pendennis to survey its defences. It included Sir Walter Raleigh and Sir Ferdinando Gorges. They were horrified by what they found. 'It is now,' spluttered Raleigh as he inspected the headland, 'the most dangerous place that I ever saw and the worst provided for.' Only a few months separated the realm from disaster – with better weather in the coming spring, the Spanish would try again. Hundreds were drafted to dig earthworks and erect around the headland a series of 200 wooden perches. As the men trenched the slopes of Pendennis Point, and the order went through to the foundries for more guns, so in Castile, Philip II lay dying. Thoughts of invading England receded. As for John Killigrew, he was summoned to London when the true state of Pendennis was revealed. He was thrown into a cell in the Gatehouse at Westminster.

For England, the Elizabethan era had been shaped by the sea, with its bounty, its threats and its natural cordon. It had also shaped the fortunes of the Killigrews. Just over fifty years earlier, they had been minor gentry, living in a modest house in a far-off province. Within decades, they had land and money, command of a castle, family members in Parliament and among the Queen's ministers, and the highest offices locally. Now there was nothing to show for it. The line between villainy and heroism in Elizabethan England was always a fine one. Perhaps it was their own fault that the Killigrews found themselves on the wrong side of it, unable to resist the temptations that the sea offered them. Or maybe it was just bad luck.

CHAPTER 7

The uncanny failure of the Spanish to land their forces, repeated again and again, stamped itself on English identity for centuries to come. The weather had played its part in 1588 and had helped turn back two subsequent Armadas. What it took away from the English in terms of naval might, it gave back to them in mystique. But to speak of luck is to fail to understand the divine hand half hidden in the breeze and in the mysterious folds of the sea. A.L. Rowse was echoing a widely held belief when he wrote of the 'anti-Catholic, anti-Spanish winds of the Channel'.

The moment in 1591 when Sir Richard Grenville died off the Azores, with his crippled *Revenge* surrounded by enemy ships, the winds freshened to a gale. Soon fish were being hurled against the Spanish topsides. Grenville, muttered the watching Spanish (according to the Dutch traveller and historian Van Linschoten), 'was raising all the Devils of Hell from the bottom of the sea'. Van Linschoten also reported that, after all these years of war between Elizabeth I and Philip II, the Spanish believed that 'fortune or rather God was wholly against them' while the English, 'seeing all their enterprises do take so good effect, that thereby they are become lords and masters of the sea'.

The same spirit fills the second volume of Richard Hakluyt's anthology. Amidst the epic tales of sea fights, the

PHILIP MARSDEN

taking of Spanish prizes and the firing of their carracks, is a
strange presumption of eventual triumph. 'It is evident in all
the writings of that period,' wrote the literary historian Anne
Treneer, 'that English sailors relied consciously or uncon-
sciously on a force external to themselves, which made them
invincible.'

That English seafaring emerged so suddenly and so effectively contributed to the sense of destiny. From the high
ground of the 1890s the jingoistic historian James Froude
pointed to the early Elizabethan years: 'the bark of the
English water-dogs had scarcely been heard beyond their
own fishing-grounds, and the largest merchant vessel sailing
from the port of London was scarce bigger than a modern
coasting collier'. But within a couple of decades, 'these insig-
nificant islanders had struck the sceptre from the Spaniards'
grasp and placed the ocean crown on the brow of their own
sovereign'. For puff-chested British imperialists, the improb-
ability of Elizabethan sea victories helped explain the improb-
ability of Victorian global supremacy.

Conceptions of the sea itself shifted during the late
sixteenth century. In the early years it remained something
unimaginably vast, a watery infinity, the most visible example
of God's power. But by the death of Elizabeth I, some of that
power had been brought to earth. Those men who crossed
the ocean removed a little of its dread, as they returned with
worldly wonders, strange new plants, sparkling jewels and
silver, and wondrous tales of golden cities.

In the work of Shakespeare, which coincided with
England's maritime blooming, references to the sea increase
over the years. To begin with, it was used simply to convey
great size. In the early poem *Lucrece*: '"Thou art," quoth she,
"a sea, a sovereign king"', or in *Romeo and Juliet*: 'My bounty
is as boundless as the sea / My love as deep.'

Whether Shakespeare went to sea or not is a question that has been much discussed. In 1910 a professional seaman Captain Whall trawled the plays for technical language and published his thoughts in *Shakespeare's Sea-Terms Explained*. Amazed at Shakespeare's accuracy, he was persuaded that the playwright spent time at sea (possibly during the seven years of his adult life for which there is no biographical material). How else, wonders Whall, could he have learned such a supple command of terms if not aboard ship?

While much of his sea imagery is sophisticated, there are phrases in the plays that do not suggest sustained experience at sea: 'He, that hath the steerage of my course, / Direct my sail!' (from *Romeo and Juliet*) is not how a mariner would use language. Describing the fleet in the prologue of the third act of *Henry V*, he reports that the sails 'Draw the huge bottomes through the furrowed sea' – ignoring the intricate mechanics of sailing apparent to those on board; and those agricultural 'furrows' suggest swells seen not from on deck but looking down from a cliff-top.

Shakespeare's precise use of sea-terms, where they occur, probably came by the same route as everything else in his writing, via an astonishing ear for language. As the port of London became a-bustle with ships and sailors and talk of voyages and far-off places, so his work filled with the drama of the sea, with wharfside tales of storms and distant shores, and the briny spirit of the age. All his foreign towns were ports. According to G. Wilson Knight's intricate study of marine reference in Shakespeare, 'his one general rule was that all distant towns are by the sea side; and if not they should be.' By the time of *The Tempest*, written in the last decade of Elizabeth's rule, the sea is not just a source of metaphor, but a conduit for the exotic. Ships come back with reports of 'men of Ind', the 'Arabian Phoenix', Tunis and

Carthage. Wilson Knight concluded that, in Shakespeare's work, 'fate is to be equated with the elements, any human enterprise with the ship'. In the plays, ocean-going craft tend to be hapless pawns of the weather, and storms and shipwreck their frequent lot. Putting yourself in a ship on the sea is the same as embarking on a course of worldly power: those who do each are risking tragedy.

John Killigrew sat in his cell in the Westminster Gatehouse, a tragic character left alone to contemplate the wreck of his own life. It was June 1598. He had been there for over four months and was already suffering. The damp stone stiffened his joints. He had pawned his horse and his clothes for food, and there was little left. He had glimpsed his wife and some of his eleven children at the prison window but now they had returned to Cornwall. His only distraction, as he wrote in the surviving letters, was to dwell on all 'his past vanities'.

Fifteen years had passed since he left Elizabeth's court. For several decades before that, under the protection of his uncles Henry and William, he had played an anonymous part in the Queen's wider circle. Even there his reckless greed helped him through a large part of his wife's estate, forcing her to sell £3,500 worth of her land. But it was at Arwenack, as governor of Pendennis, during the great rise in privateering in the 1580s, that the sea spread its glitter before him.

'It is true', he reflected from prison, 'that a golden prey enticeth many a man.'

Locked in the Gatehouse, he wrote a petition, outlining a plan to settle his debts. Gather a committee, he pleaded, call my Lord Anderson, Sir Anthony Mildmay, Sir Edward Dyer, the old friends from his days at court – Sergeant Heale, Mr Poynes (clerk of the Queen's Kitchen) and Mr Moore (sheriff of London). Ask them to tot up the amounts owed, then he would mortgage his remaining estates. Given time, he could meet all legitimate demands. Had he not already settled the £1,000 he owed Her Majesty?

But forty years of bullying and coercion were catching up with him. Tenants were refusing to pay rent. The sheriffs of Cornwall, in gathering debt from his property, had helped themselves to another £1,000. 'My enemies and creditors,' he complained, 'are malicious towards me.' He was unable to defend either his estates or his reputation. Down on the Galician coast, in La Coruña, no one was surprised to hear the false rumour that, following Killigrew's arrest, he had been executed as a traitor. They were convinced like many others that Killigrew, desperate and renegade, had secretly turned Pendennis Castle for the Spanish.

Whether he had can never now be proved. But like his forebears, he was a proud Protestant. Only weeks before his arrest, a pirated ship from Waterford had fallen into his hands. When its cargo was discovered by Killigrew's agent to be Catholic missals, beads and relics bound for England, they were publicly burned in Penryn market. The Killigrews had, in their own wayward manner, upheld principles – like Shakespeare's 'sanctimonious pirate' in *Measure for Measure* who takes a wooden board to sea with the Ten Commandments written on it, or rather nine, as he has scrubbed out *Thou shalt not steal*.

John Killigrew remained in prison while officials picked at the bones of his Arwenack estates. He grew more and more concerned for the upkeep of his wife and children. In 1600 Queen Elizabeth 'most graciously pyttieng the extremities whereunto the said John Killigrew hathe of late fallen' allowed him home for three months.

So he went back once more to Arwenack. In forty years, through its high-ceilinged rooms and banqueting hall, had passed countless adventurers and riches. But the estate now lacked the land to support itself. On the headland to seaward of Arwenack, and visible from the curtilage, Pendennis Castle was, for the first time, not governed by a Killigrew. As it had once been the agent of their rise, so its neglect had marked their downfall. The new governor, Sir Nicholas Parker, was immune to the temptations of the sea. He was a soldier, veteran of campaigns in the Low Countries. As soon as John Killigrew was removed, he hastened to restore the castle. Falmouth was regarded as one of the country's most vulnerable corners. 'There are two places in these western parts,' Sir Francis Godolphin wrote to Burghley, 'where, if not fortified, the enemy may prevail; the harbours of Falmouth and Scilly.' Elizabeth addressed Sir Nicholas Parker directly, suggesting in a letter that he was having to start from scratch: 'We committed to you the charge of our fortifications intended to be built upon the haven of Falmouth.'

Parker took to his duties with zeal. He employed 400 men to dig ditches, curtaining the castle with earthworks and look-out posts. He applied for new guns to add to the one that remained in the castle. In examining the castle grounds, he spotted a more effective land boundary and annexed fifty acres of Arwenack land. Short of timber, he felled 1,700 of Killigrew's trees.

John Killigrew complained, but he could do little. Parker was a proven hero. Richard Carew considered that Pendennis's 'greatest strength consisteth in Sir Nicholas Parker, the governor'. Tacitly Carew admonished the Killigrews' years of local bullying, in contrast to Parker 'who demeaning himself no less kindly and frankly towards his neighbours ... than he did resolutely and valiantly against the enemy when he followed the wars'. His presence and leadership were exemplary. At Pendennis he had two companies of 100 men, as well as being colonel-general of all forces in Cornwall. He commanded, gushed Carew, 'not only their bodies by his authority, but also their hearts by his love'.

John Killigrew died in prison in 1605. His heir – the fourth John Killigrew – inherited the house and little else. He had married a lively woman named Jane Fermor whose inheritance managed to give a little respite from his father's debts. But according to all accounts, she caused him much misery. At Pendennis Castle, succession had a new heredity. When Sir Nicholas Parker died, his son became governor and added a further humiliation to the fallen Killigrews. It was this man, according to the Killigrew chronicle, who 'first debauched' Jane Killigrew.

With the death of Elizabeth I and the arrival of James I in England, travelling overland from Scotland in his great cavalcade, came a radical shift in official policy to the sea. Gone was support for those who pursued sail-driven adventure. The state would no longer tolerate mavericks like the West Country sea-barons for whom the Channel was a free-for-all, who made a grab for whatever ships passed within their reach. King James appeased the Spanish with an instant treaty, locked up Sir Walter Raleigh, banned the practice of privateering, and presided over a Navy that, though generously funded, rotted like some diseased shrub from the top down. The number of admirals, who rarely went near the water, soon exceeded that of serviceable ships, while crews went unpaid.

James had little understanding of the sea, finding that his attempts to bring order to it had exactly the opposite effect. Released from naval service, unable to sail on privateers, tens of thousands of seamen were now idle. Nothing ashore could match the returns of their life at sea, so they went back. The first years of James's rule witnessed a rise in English piracy never seen before or since. By 1608 an estimated 500 English pirate ships were at large, ten times as many as in the time of Elizabeth. Brutalised by war, emboldened by their nautical skills, the bandit mariners – the finest pirates in Europe – infested the seas, spreading the spirit of lawlessness from the English Channel, out across the North Atlantic and down into the Mediterranean.

The seamen of the West Country were well represented in this great flowering of robber enterprise. In Plymouth, the mayor complained of the 'great number of sailors, mariners and masterless men, that heretofore have been at sea in men of war [and their] intolerable outrages'. In 1605 the *Jonas* was seized off the Isle of Wight with £10,000 of lawns and cambrics. Over the coming months, the *Jonas* was sailed westward, stopping off to flog its cargo, a travelling bazaar of looted cloth. At Helford, numerous bales were taken ashore, carried to Penryn and sold openly in the market.

In Devon and Cornwall the pirates had nothing to fear from the authorities. Richard Hawkins, son of Sir John, and Hannibal Vyvyan – respectively vice-admirals of Devon and South Cornwall – themselves benefited from piracy. They sold pardons to the leaders and took generous bribes for allowing plundered goods to be sold. Tolerance of piracy spread beyond the West Country, along the coast and right up the hierarchy of the Navy, to the Lord High Admiral, the Earl of Nottingham.

If piracy and privateering were the principal blemishes in the emergence of England as a maritime power, naval corruption came a close second. In the final years of Elizabeth's reign some ingenious scams appeared in the service. Finding no check, they multiplied. James's regime of official profligacy encouraged naval leaders like Sir Robert Mansell (treasurer of the Navy) and Sir John Trevor (surveyor of the Navy) to help themselves to Crown supplies, and their example was imitated down through the ranks. Everything, from cordage and spars, canvas and crews, to ships themselves, was written in the books at vastly inflated quantities. As the actual fleet shrank, so the Navy's ledgers recorded a phantom version of itself, growing larger with each passing month. When at last the Earl of Northampton forced a public inquiry – at which the full extent of corruption was revealed – the King did little more than wag a beringed finger at Mansell and Trevor. Likewise, when Hannibal Vyvyan was summoned from Cornwall, he too was let off. Holding pirates like Captain Jennings to ransom in the Helford river, allowing the release of Robert Duncomb at Falmouth, merited a summons, but no penalty.

Strangely, among all the complaints of wrongdoing in the early years of James's reign, in the State Papers and Acts of the Privy Council and Star Chamber, even the extensive account of reformed pirate Sir Henry Mainwaring, the name of Killigrew is nowhere to be seen. The fourth John Killigrew, it turned out, was a stickler for the law. The picture of his own father dying bankrupt and alone in prison convinced this John that it was worth following the path of legality. He spent a great deal of time in litigation – riding up and down to London, attending courts first for his divorce from Jane, then lobbying for a scheme that he hoped would re-establish his family's position.

On the northern boundary of what little land remained to Arwenack – just half a mile along the coast from the manor – lay Smithwick Creek. There above the low cliff, where a stream cut back into the soil and splashed to the shingle, stood the lime-kiln. A small inn had been built there, too, to provide for visiting crews – the single seed from which the port was about to grow.

According to the Killigrew family chronicle, the idea had been Walter Raleigh's. Returning from the Caribbean in 1595, he put into Falmouth. His ships carried none of the journey's hoped-for treasure, but he did bring tales of glittering cities on the Orinoco and the promise of future expeditions to discover them. In Falmouth, he sent his men to the single inn at Smithwick while he himself dined just along the shore with the Killigrews.

Raleigh was a mariner at heart and he had an instinctive attraction to Falmouth's natural merits, its sheltering headlands and network of deep-water creeks, its position far out towards the Western Approaches. Now he spoke of Arwenack's potential as a staging-post in the coming age. Old John Killigrew was in no position to pursue it – an outlaw, laden with a lifetime of debt and felony. But his son picked up on it. The chronicler, who wrote with scorn about his forebears, spoke of the fourth John Killigrew as 'a sober good man'. His misfortune was the legacy of his father and grandfather. He had been forced into an 'unfortunate' marriage with Jane Fermor who had brought £6,000 to the family. But her adultery and the ensuing divorce made it a costly dowry. Countless trips to the archbishop's court in London did little for Killigrew's health and 'quite ruined his estate'.

John Killigrew poured his energies into making money. He was the first at Arwenack to understand the basic rule of business, that it is better to offer people a service than rob them, better to victual ships than plunder them. And he knew that, by dint of geography, inheritance and timing, he was sitting on something priceless. For despite the piracy and corruption of King James's court-bound regime, peace with Spain had led not only to a rapid increase in overseas trade

but to a revival of the question of colonisation. Traffic through
the Channel – Dutch and English, commercial and colonial,
legal and illegal – was growing rapidly. John Killigrew seized
his chance. He presented a petition that, with the Killigrews
still well represented at court, was approved by King James.
It was a modest beginning for a great port: permission to
build four inns on what remained of his land.

The scheme was not without its critics, at least locally.
The burghers of Penryn had nurtured a hatred for the
Killigrews ever since the destruction of Glasney College.
More and more ships took shelter off Arwenack land, rather
than sailing up to Penryn. So when Jane Killigrew sought
sanctuary from her estranged husband, Penryn was where
she fled. She in turn presented the town with a 2-foot-high,
silver loving-cup which is still borne around the town streets
as part of the mayor's parade. Jane Killigrew's grateful
message can be seen running around its rim: *To the town of
Penryn when they received mee that was in great misery.*

A map survives from the early years of Killigrew's settlement. The original has disappeared but in the *Journal of the
Royal Institution of Cornwall* (1886) it is reproduced: 'Map of
Smithwick c1615'. The name Smithwick (Falmouth only
came into use for the town some fifty years later) derived
probably from the Celtic saint Methick – 'St Methick' thickening easily into 'Smithwick'. (Another anglicised name of
the time was Penny-come-quick which may be topographical: *'pen-y-cum-cuic'*, 'head of the valley'. The story of an
innkeeper running out of beer – the pennies coming so quick
– also persisted, with its pejorative hint of commercial greed
and drink.)

Drawn just a few years after King James approved the
petition, the map already shows a busy little place. Several
buildings have been added to the one already there. A road

Map of Smithwick.

has been built across the top of the creek, and the stream diverted. A line of pilchard cellars – the essential land-works for the coast's most lucrative legal pursuit – runs up the north side of the valley. On the shingle lie three punts (looking somewhat like beached bananas). A four-rung wooden ladder leads up from the beach (you can almost feel the mossy hand-rail, hear the drip of fresh water down the undercliff). At the top of the ladder stands Fforde's house, with its inn sign hanging outside. The whole settlement – all on Killigrew land – has something businesslike about it, something invit-ing, something that would have satisfied the vision of Walter Raleigh (who by now languished in the Fleet Prison).

In little more than fifty years, seafaring had become, for the peoples of north-western Europe, one of the high earthly callings, combining the questing spirit of the Crusades with the proving of medieval battle. Each of its arts, from hull-design to rig and navigation, sail-trimming to mooring, took on a significance that raised it far above the functional. In a letter written at about this time, John Killigrew showed that, unlike his impulsive forebears, he had reflected on the nature of his birthright: 'An ancient philosopher recounting the joyes of this worlde affirmeth none so greate as after a dangerous storme to have a sodayne and safe arivall in a secure port.' Like a church with ever-open doors, his little haven at Falmouth was a place of hope, of relief from those dark perils that more and more people were discovering on the oceans. From then on, John Killigrew's trips to London, in which he continued to pursue his divorce, gained new purpose. Offering sanctuary and sustenance at Smithwick was one thing, but now he began to work towards a greater ambition. He wanted to build a lighthouse, not at Falmouth itself, but on Britain's most southerly head – on the Lizard Point.

PART II

CHAPTER 8

One night in October, about 2 a.m., I am woken by the wind. I go to the bedroom window and look out on a scene of such drama that all traces of sleep vanish. The moon flashes through rushing clouds, lighting up the bay and its silvery swells and white crests. All around the water's edge – on the rocks below St Mawes Castle, along the foot of the sea wall, on the reefs beyond Long Lodge, runs a wild border of surf. On the beach below me, the tide has scattered ribbons of kelp over the sand – and a boat. Leaning to one side, high and dry in the half-darkness, lies a 20-ton, 55-foot motor-yacht.

Over the years, I have seen a number of boats washed up here – several fin-keeled sloops, a couple of fishing boats and a beautiful teak-decked motor-launch that was turned to kindling in a matter of hours. This is the largest. I phone the coastguard and they ask if there is anyone on board. I say, no: I know the boat, the *Lady Adrienne*. She has sat untended on her mooring for weeks.

But I can't be certain. Pulling on coat and sea-boots, I hurry down to the beach. The tide is low, the wind still gale force. The noise of it and the breaking waves dashes at my ears. In the moonlight, the boat's topsides rise high above the sand. Following them down towards the stern I find the lowest point, haul myself up by the stanchions and slide in over the scuppers. The cabin doors are locked; no one is on board. On the foredeck a few links of mooring chain are still attached to the cleat. It has broken; the boat has been driven back on to the lee shore. At high water the hull has been left firm on a shaley outcrop of rock. The surf has softened the sand and, as I jump back down, my boots push deep into its spongy surface. I flash a torch in underneath and I can see where the keel and the stabilisers have dug into the rock, flaking it off in shards. But the bottom looks intact. When the tide rises again, she will float.

In the morning, at high water, she is pulled off and towed to Falmouth for inspection. Little damage has been done. But for days afterwards I am haunted by the image of the stranded hull high on the rock, and the sense of the natural order of things being overturned.

On calmer nights, I look out from my window towards Henry VIII's two floodlit castles at the entrance of the Fal estuary – St Mawes and Pendennis – and the orange glow of Falmouth beyond them. Further south, the sky darkens above a five-mile stretch of open water which glitters in the moonlight and extends to a velvety point of land. Every three seconds, with a slow metronomic rhythm, the loom of the Lizard lighthouse swivels round, 800,000 candelas of brightness filling the sky and marking the Lizard Point.

By day, you can see the fields and the rounded headlands of this stretch of land. Sometimes, with the wind in the south, the rays of the sun break through and light up the fields and hedges with an intense green; seen from across the water, it looks like a promised land. In winter, when the easterlies blow for days and the sky clears, you can see the swells rising in slow motion against the rocks, distant fountains of water which create a yearning in me that I cannot explain.

But this is dangerous country. To the south, the land drops to the water in a reef known as the Shark's Fin – clearly visible from ten miles away. Just out from the Shark's Fin, also visible at low water, are the Manacles, among the deadliest rocks along Britain's 5,000 miles of coast.

The Lizard peninsula is a boneyard, a wreck coast. Look at a map of Cornwall, one of those maps of lost ships that hang on the walls of countless pubs, and you can see the names crowd and busy themselves at the county's headlands. Around the Lizard they become so thick it looks as if someone has trodden on an ants' nest.

On the western side is a perfectly designed ship-trap. In the age of sail, countless craft ended up here, locked in by the headlands, embayed. What happens is this. You make landfall after a long crossing from America or India, from the Groyne or the Canaries. You find that you are, by dead reckoning, somewhere west of the Lizard and east of Land's End. The wind is blowing, likely as not, hard towards the cliffs, from within the south-west quadrant. For the first time in many weeks you know exactly where you are – but it is no comfort. For now you must come round quick towards the wind. You listen to the creak of ocean-weary tackle as the sails are hauled and the blocks pounded for every inch. You watch the bows pan along the land, slowing as they do so, stopping short of the open horizon. So you go onto the other tack, and find that you cannot clear the land on that side either. Thirty miles of coastline in your lee but not one safe anchorage, not one haven or port. What you have sought through a thousand miles of ocean has at once become a threat. You beat back and forth across the bay. Your ship makes some five or ten points of leeway, so rather than bringing you out, each tack pushes you deeper into the bay. You ready the anchor but it is hopeless. Whether the cable snaps or the anchor drags makes no difference, the result will be the same.

On the eastern shore of the Lizard peninsula, the wrecks are just as numerous. By the merciless law of averages, from the vast number of ships putting in and out of Falmouth, a proportion end up driven onto this coast or onto the Manacles rocks. The Lizard Point itself offers its own hazards. Instructions to returning ships were issued from the cliffs; but trying to read the signal flags drew many too close in, and they also were lost.

I have walked this coastline dozens of times, and evidence of its perils is everywhere. A window in the village of St Keverne's church commemorates the 106 passengers who died when the *Mohegan* struck the Manacles in 1898. In the same churchyard were buried the 104 who died aboard the *Dispatch* on 14 January 1809, while in the church is a brass gudgeon from the *Primrose*, lost on the same night with only one survivor out of some 150. In cliff-top hamlets all along the coast are cottages built from washed-up ships' timbers; electric cable for export encloses fields, stapled to railway sleepers intended for the Patagonian prairies. In Coverack, you sit in the bar of the shoreside Paris hotel, named after a liner that was washed up in a fog on Lowland Point. Local people who climbed on board were so taken by the luxury of the state rooms that when the hotel was completed the following year, it seemed natural to name it after the ship in this way. In the belfry of Manaccan church is the ship's bell from *The Bay of Panama*, driven ashore during the great blizzard of 1891. People recalled seeing from the cliffs survivors scrambling up the rat-lines to escape the rising water, only to freeze solid in the rigging.

The English Channel, *La Manche*, *Engelse Kanaal*, is northern Europe's gateway, and the Lizard peninsula its much-knocked gatepost. The Lizard was the starting point of William Bourne's hydrographical guide to Cathay, of the

Lizard Point.

Great Circle and Rhumb Line Tracks, the courses in Norwood's *Trigonometrie* and *The Seamans Practice*. It was the last fixed point, the shrinking cliff that dropped away as you sailed south and west into the ocean bound for the New World, for the Mediterranean, for the Cape of Good Hope. It is the most important landfall on the British coast, heralded for hours before by the shortening of soundings and by the loom of the lighthouse which was lit, for the first time, by the fourth John Killigrew of Arwenack.

Until the Reformation, and the wedge it drove between the sacred and the secular, many cliff-top beacons were kept burning by monks and hermits, and were thus both votive and functional. The wild-eyed anchorite, squatting on his far-off rocky cape, muttering the name of a saint beneath a flickering brazier, was keeping a vigil for visitors who by day would trek out to his remote spot on the edge of the tangible world, and hand him supplications. At the same time the light would perform its own ministry, easing ships into harbour.

At the mouth of the Humber, a hermit named Richard Reedbarrow received a grant for maintaining a light. Hermits probably kept a light at St Edmund's Point near King's Lynn. The entrance to the Gironde river was marked by a hermit-maintained light on the island of Cordouan. Nuns tended a light on the Hebridean island of Shillay, as they did off Youghal on the southern Irish coast. It was said that the monks of St Anthony-in-Roseland kept a flame burning on St Anthony's Head, at the eastern entrance to the Fal estuary.

John Killigrew was one of the first laymen to try to build a lighthouse, and the saga of his efforts now shines out across the centuries, as lonely and valiant as the light itself. If he faced the fury of Penryn for his shoreside inns, opposition to Killigrew's Lizard light was much more formidable – and involved a great many more journeys to London. Fiercest of the scheme's critics were members of the Brotherhood of Trinity House of Deptford Strand.

Trinity House remains responsible to this day for every one of Britain's lighthouses and its thousands of navigation buoys. Despite its name it was neither monastic nor ecclesiastical. Its origins lay instead in a guild of Thames mariners who took their name from their local church. Successive Tudor monarchs confirmed Trinity House's exclusive right to 'make erecte and set up suche and so many Beakons, Markes and Signes for the Sea, in such Place or Places of the Sea Shore and Uplandes near the Sea Costes or Forelands of the Sea'.

But it was not until 1609 that they bothered to build their first lighthouse, near Lowestoft. At the same time, private applications for lighthouses began to appear, from individuals like Killigrew. Although Trinity House was hardly dotting the coast with new marks, it defended its charter vigorously. King James was equally keen to keep his prerogative for granting patents. To settle the three-sided dispute, he sought the counsel of Sir Francis Bacon. Bacon examined the case carefully and found against the King and individual schemes – and in favour of Trinity House. Safety at sea, Bacon decided, was too important a matter to leave to private schemes. The requisite trust could only be sustained by an institution like Trinity House. In a persuasive and poetic statement, Bacon stressed that keeping beacons was 'a matter of an high and precious nature, in respect of salvation of ships and lives, and a kind of starlight in that element'.

Within months, Bacon's principled ruling had been countered. Trinity House might be entitled to erect marks but where they failed to do so, the King had every right to allow others to protect mariners. Killigrew was the first to take advantage. He rode to London with his plan. His stated motives were the 'Safety of Mariners' and 'Comfort to the Distressed' – though it is clear that Killigrew stood to make a good deal of money not only from the levies he could impose but also from ships picking up the light and calling in at his little settlement at Smithwick.

Trinity House at once raised objections to Killigrew's plan. There was no need for a Lizard light. The Channel was a hundred miles wide at this point; ships could pass up it without any assistance. Besides, they claimed, a light would only assist pirates and the state's enemies.

In his own handwriting, and in response to the reservations of Trinity House, Killigrew wrote a compelling defence of his scheme. Concerning its necessity, he cited the vast loss of life, shipping and goods around the Lizard, suggesting that no sea-captain would ever trust completely to his navigation when making a landfall: 'I would ask the best marryner that ever lived, if he will presume soe much upon his Arte.' He compared a ship coming to the night-shrouded coast of Cornwall – with the Wolf Rock, the Longships, the embaying sweep of coast west of the Lizard – to a blind man trying to cross the Thames. If such a man were to step off the bank, the chances of his feet finding a bridge were tiny, and the poor man thus 'is drownd and perisheth'. Thousands of mariners would meet the same end, urged Killigrew, and 'must be helped ... by no means (as I have said) but by a fire'.

To the suggestion that such a light would assist the country's enemies, Killigrew made an assurance that in time of war, or threat of invasion, the light would be extinguished. As to the question of pirates, in all his long document he made no mention of them (any reminder of the links between the Killigrew name and piracy might perhaps undermine his case). One of his supporters, a Thomas Locke, was not optimistic. It had stood a good chance, he explained, until Trinity House put their oar in. Locke warned Killigrew that in King James's courts such lawsuits were now as numerous as 'budds in March or the children of Paris'. Few were passed: 'for every one that hitts, ten misse'.

But the Killigrews still had connections at court. With the support of his cousin Sir Robert Killigrew, John had received a knighthood in 1617. Sir Robert was also a friend of the new Lord High Admiral, the Earl of Buckingham. 'Killigrew,' wrote the earl, 'is a gentleman I love.' Within weeks of advocating the need for a Lizard light, John received a patent from Buckingham, with glowing support:

Whereas it is most notoriously known by wofull experience that by reason of Sundry rockes, sandes and other places lying near the Lizarde in the Sea upon the coaste of Cornwall, shippes, barkes & other vessells sayling & traffiqueing along that coaste, have in former tymes in great numbers perished & been utterly lost & are dayly in the like imminent danger of shipwracke for want of sea marks and beacons ...

The project was a noble one, continued Buckingham, and he who pressed for it was deserving of the highest admiration: 'Sir John Killegrewe of Arwennecke in the said Countye of Cornwall Knight having entered into a Christian and charitable consideration for the avoyding & preventing of future losses in that kinde'. The gentlemen of the court 'very much comend the said purpose and intente of the said Sir John Killegrewe & do think him worthie'. After several paragraphs of such gush, the patent was declared: that Killigrew had the right to erect on the Lizard 'for the terme of fifty years one convenient and sufficient beacon or lighthouse with a light in it continually burning in the night season'.

CHAPTER 9

In the summer of 1619 Sir John Killigrew sailed back to
Cornwall with permission for his light. From Arwenack, and
the growing harbour at Smithwick, he took the patent southwards, with all its authority and optimism, on past the
Helford river, towards the 'uttermost cape of Cornwall'.

North of the Lizard peninsula lie Cornwall's badlands.
Isolation and the rocky dangers of the coastline have
combined to breed a fierce spirit of independence. The
parish of St Keverne in particular saw some lively unrest in
1538, and again in 1548, and again the following year during
the Cornish Prayer-book rebellion. And it was St Keverne
which produced Michael An Gof, Cornwall's greatest rebel,
who helped lead a force of 15,000 to London in 1497, for
which he was hanged, drawn and quartered.

Killigrew now presented his plan to the people of the
Lizard. The building of the light and its maintenance would
bring work and prosperity to the area. But the inhabitants did
not share Killigrew's enthusiasm. They had long profited
from wrecked ships – or 'God's Grace', as they called it.
Killigrew reacted with fury. His project also had its divine
support. 'It must be granted,' he wrote, 'that the Light is
under God.' These people, he fumed, in a letter later that
summer, live by the calamity of stricken ships. They come to
him 'hourly' complaining of his work and the strange ills it

was bringing them. He told them that rather than profit from the ruin of others, they should see to 'their land which their former idle life has omitted'.

Nothing sours so swiftly as thwarted idealism, and it is clear that for all John Killigrew's far-sighted schemes, the efforts to achieve them were now wearing him down. On the Lizard that summer he picked a row with one of his own colleagues, a Captain Lambert. He himself had invited Lambert to come from Rotterdam to watch the building of the light, in order to relay its benefits to wealthy Dutch ship-owners. But Killigrew was soon bristling at the captain's High Church musings: the man's an Arminian! he barked. When the captain took up with a local woman, Killigrew raged: 'I will send his whoor from Falmouth to Rotterdam to his wyffe who I hope will pull out his eyes.'

Nor did the light, once it was lit, provide any relief. The beacon's brick tower, pointed with lime, stood proud on the Lizard's cliffs. Coal could be landed in a small cove below and brought up by cart. But on a blowy night, with the brazier hissing with rain, the fire could consume ten shillings' worth of coal. By April the following year, with building and running costs, it had already cost John Killigrew some £500. For all the support for him and his light, Buckingham's patent had one omission. It lacked provision for the levying of dues. But with the light now burning, cleaving the darkness of the Western Approaches, Killigrew managed to win a conces-sion: a ha'penny per ton on every passing ship.

The levy only renewed general hostility to the light. From Penryn to Poole, from Portsmouth to the Thames, seamen and officials refused to pay, dismissing the beacon as 'need-less ... very unnecessary ... more burdensome than commo-dious'. Killigrew was back on his horse, London-bound, to argue his case. He enlisted the great naval hero Sir William

Monson, and the plea offers a glimpse of what it meant to go to sea at that time: 'What a comfort a ship in distress shall find by this light it is to be imagined by example of a traveller on land losing his way in a dark cold night and espying a light in a cottage.' Monson recalled the many times he had sailed past the Point and the assistance such a light would have given him, in particular the saving of a Spanish prize lost to him – and the country – in Mount's Bay: 'A light from the Lizard at that time would have saved a hundred men's lives and £100,000 of wealth.'

But Monson was ignored. The future of Killigrew's light, like its inception and so much else in Jacobean England, was decided not on practical grounds but by the currents of fear and favour that ran through King James's court. Likewise Killigrew's request for further inns at Smithwick: *refused*. He continued to hope for assent, continued to ride to London and wait in numerous anterooms for rulings.

But the years passed and nothing was granted on either front. All that his London journeys yielded now, after two decades, was his divorce. The tight-faced clerics of the archbishop's court recoiled at the evidence against Jane Killigrew – 'this wretched woman's flagrant prostitution' – and bound John Killigrew to pay her just £20 per annum. By that time, he was an old man. Sir John never managed to expand Smithwick, nor to relight the brazier on the Lizard, that vital pinprick of light in the ocean's vastness.

During the 1620s the English Channel became a sorry reflection of King James's neglect of the sea. Trade was dominated by the Dutch. The peace that began his reign had collapsed. The Navy was useless. Buckingham presided over a series of disastrous operations. Little sign remained of the great days of Elizabethan seafaring. According to the naval historian

N. A. M. Rodger, English ships and sailors now 'aroused amusement and contempt rather than respect'. Even the supremacy of England's maritime brigands was challenged.

In 1625, immediately after King James's death, a sudden rash of piracy broke out around Devon and Cornwall and for once local mariners were not perpetrators but victims. Hundreds of fishermen were plucked from their boats that summer. In April three Cornish boats were seized at Plymouth. The Newfoundland fishing fleet was attacked off Falmouth. The coastal villagers, as they had in earlier centuries, watched the approach of every alien sail with a sense of dread. The following year a desperate report from Pendennis spoke of thirty marauding 'Turkish' ships headed for Cornwall – one of them even flying an English flag.

Jacobean piracy had come full circle. Many of the seamen laid off in James's early years, who chose a life of freebooting, had ended up in the Mediterranean harrying Venetians and Spanish, French, Flemish and English. Some worked with – or were captured by – the galley-pirates of the Maghreb, from Mamora, Tunis and Algiers. These men, the Barbary corsairs, at once recognised the advantages of English ships. The seaworthy hulls allowed long spells away from harbour; their rig proved weatherly and adaptable, but best of all their topsides were studded with rows of ports not for paddles, but guns. Sometimes the corsairs placed the northern pirates in command of these ships or even of small fleets, until the corsairs themselves perfected their handling, abandoned their galleys, and began to roam beyond the Mediterranean. Soon they were competing with English pirates in the Atlantic, then in a sudden flurry along the south coast of England.

It became a common sight to see deserted ships drifting off the Cornish coast. The corsairs were targeting people rather than cargoes. Terrified of being ransomed, or sold as slaves in some dusty market, West Country fishermen and mariners remained in port. 'The boldness and insolence of those pirates,' lamented the vice-admiral of Devon (a region that had done more than any other to spread piracy), 'was beyond all comparison.' He estimated that in 1625 alone, the West Country lost 1,200 men.

The shoreside communities of the Fal went into decline; then in 1626 an outbreak of the plague swept through Smithwick's tight-packed houses. With fishermen fearful of the corsairs, revenues dwindled. Sir John Killigrew was isolated by the corruptions and hostility both of the governor of Pendennis and of Cornwall's vice-admiral. He called on his old patron, now the Duke of Buckingham, but still Lord High Admiral, to help. Killigrew in turn promised to 'dedi-cate [his] life and fortune to obey your Grace's commands'. When Killigrew identified one of Buckingham's own ships among the prizes of a notorious Dutch pirate, he did all he could to rescue its £3,000 cargo. But Killigrew's campaign came to nothing. In 1628 Buckingham was stabbed to death by a subaltern in the Greyhound Inn, Portsmouth.

Killigrew himself died a few years later, alone and without issue. His ex-wife Jane moved back from Penryn to claim her jointure. She took up residence at Arwenack with her new husband, Francis Bluett. For the first time in hundreds of years, there was no Killigrew at Arwenack. As to their great wealth, their golden position, their grand schemes, only the house remained, a small parcel of shoreline, and the plague-scarred settlement at Smithwick.

In December I am down at the Lizard Point, part of an early winter hike around the coast. I walk through the Lizard village late one night, passing closed-up shops and serpentine workshops. The current lighthouse stands squat on the cliffs, sweeping its tube of whiteness so far out into the night that it appears to dust the clouds. It is thought that Killigrew's original light was built more or less on the same site. After it went out for the last time, no one did anything to replace it, neither the remaining Killigrews nor the hostile Trinity House. More than a hundred years passed before the next light shone from the Lizard. Now a sign at the gate reads: *No Unauthorised Access – Trinity House*.

I take the path down towards the cliff. The full moon shines through a row of tamarisks, painting the ground ahead with a silvery mesh of shadows. The sound of the sea fills the darkness. I follow the last bend down to the small cove and see the roof of the old lifeboat station and the pale swells shouldering in from the Atlantic.

Some years after the end of Sir John Killigrew's Lizard light, a report reached the Privy Council that suggests that he was not above a little coercion, that he was, at heart, a Killigrew. During the building of his light a ship had been wrecked near this point, scattering a substantial cargo of silver bars. Killigrew sent his men to try to recover what they could, and let it be known locally that if anyone else tried to do the same, he would have them killed.

It is after midnight. I pull my hat down against the cold and stand there watching the waves in the moonlight. Surging around the cliffs and the low-tide reefs, the white surf looks luminous, as if lit from within.

CHAPTER 10

During the mid-1630s, in a bid to express his authority, Charles I turned to the sea. Barbary pirates assailed the West Country, navies from warring Europe were growing bolder, and Charles calculated that what his people needed more than anything was a reminder of their good fortune in having such a mighty monarch. He insisted that all ships – English or otherwise – dip their colours on seeing any of his own. In 1635 he also approved publication of *Mare Clausum* ('closed sea') by John Selden, a provocative treatise that even his own father had banned. Selden presented the legal case for the rightful extension of England far out from the coast. To do so, to play the role of mythic father of English maritime claims, Selden resurrected the strange figure of King Edgar.

The tenth-century rule of Edgar is conveniently short on actual sources, but what there is suggests great prowess at sea. Edgar had already grown in stature thanks to the work of later chroniclers; manuscripts of the twelfth and thirteenth centuries embellished his story with tales of the seven kings who submitted to him, and the summers he spent travelling the entire way around the British Isles, by boat, sailing the bounds of his realm, followed by a fleet of 4,500 ships.

Selden's case rested in part on Edgar's claim of '*Marium Brit. Domini*', a clause that embodied the eternal right of

Sovereign of the Seas.

England to the seas around her, but in fact was only the label for a box containing one of the later manuscripts about Edgar. Yet it was enough to encourage King Charles: 'We, and our progenitors Kings of England,' he wrote, 'have always been master of the aforesaid sea, and it would be very irksome unto us if that princely honour in our times should be lost.' To ensure nothing so irksome took place, Charles did what so many European rulers had done to prove their potency: he built a very large ship.

The *Sovereign of the Seas* revealed in her very name the tragic presumption of the King. She was the most powerful ship ever built, her ninety guns arranged for the first time over three gun-decks. Hearing of the plan, Trinity House put in their jealous and exaggerated warning – as they had with Killigrew's light. Cleverly flattering King Charles as they did so, they wrote a cautionary letter. Reading it now, it is hard not to see in their warning an unconscious parallel between the ship and the King's own fate: 'There is no port in the kingdome that can harbour this shipp. The wild sea must bee her port, her anchors and cables her safety; if either fayle, the shipp must perish ...' Charles ignored them, and personally pushed up the number of guns to 102.

At the same time, the King commissioned Thomas Heywood to spread the good news of his ship around the realm. The resulting pamphlet has survived: *A True Description of His Majesties Royall Ship ... To the great glory of our English Nation, and not paraleld in the whole Christian World*. Heywood begins by placing royal seafaring in its proper context, citing God's chosen sailor, the first ship-wright – Noah. He then continues, taking a full fifth of the pamphlet, with a long discourse on the achievements of King Edgar, to 'give the World a true and authentick expression, that whatsoever his sacred Majesty challengeth concerning his absolute Title claimeth from this King Edgar, being his true and lawfull hereditary Successor'.

A much-reproduced painting of the *Sovereign of the Seas*'s designer, Phineas Pett, shows the ship in the background. She is presented stern-on, in order to reveal the splendour of her decoration. The high and gilded transom looks less like a piece of the vessel's structure than some lofty altar-screen. The decoration was the ship's most obvious feature, extending over the entire hull, a pantheon of figures filling the upperworks like a mythical crew. In the foremost position, adorning the beakhead, and amidst a glittering cast of heraldic and classical characters was King Edgar himself, busily trampling the seven kings beneath the hooves of his horse. (Such was the cult of Edgar that at one time the *Sovereign of the Seas* was to be called Edgar, and the name was given to Charles's grandson, the child of James, Duke of York.) Back along the beakhead rails, with the bow-waters dashing beneath them, ran the ageless emblems of Charles's throne – the lion, the unicorn, England's roses, Henry VII's greyhounds, Cadwaladr's dragon, the fleur-de-lis and the Irish harp.

Dozens of statues, figurines and caryatids – finished entirely in gold and black – rippled around the ship and crossed the transom in tiers, each involved in the eternal struggle between power and disorder: Cupid on a lion, Jupiter on an eagle, Care with a compass, Virtue with a globe, Mars with a fox, Neptune on a sea horse, Aeolus on a chameleon, Hercules pointing to Aeolus, Jason pointing to Neptune and Victory pointing to Jason. Even Heywood tires of recording them: 'It would bee too tedious to insist upon every Ornament belonging to this incomparable Vessel.'

One curious feature of the ship which only became apparent when she was finished, and which somehow confirmed her divine right, was that her tons in burden came to exactly 1637, the number of years between the birth of Christ and her launching. 'A most happy Omen,' wrote loyal Thomas Heywood, and one 'for the World to take especiall notice of'.

Charles's full-blown entry into maritime matters in the 1630s had led him, like many others, into folly and extravagance. Heywood ends his pamphlet with a call to Charles's people that the *Sovereign of the Seas* 'should bee a great spur and incouragement to all his faithful and loving Subjects to bee liberall and willing Contributaries towards the Shipmoney'. To begin with, the King's faithful and loving subjects paid up, and one of the results was the victory of a small fleet against the Sallee pirates of the Maghreb.

But Ship Money was a clumsy tax, while the cost of the *Sovereign of the Seas* exceeded the original estimate by more than three times. Her carving and gilding cost fifteen times that of King James I's own showy ship the *Prince Royal*, and was roughly equivalent to the price of a complete, two-decked man-of-war. The *Sovereign of the Seas* succeeded in conveying the nature of his majesty to the world – but not in the way he intended. Such extravagance contributed as much as anything to his downfall. At her launch, it was discovered that the *Sovereign*'s gilded upperworks were so weighty that, when sailing in anything more than a light breeze, the ship heeled and rendered an entire row of lee gunports useless. In 1642 the fleet defected, Phineas Pett hastily handed Chatham dockyard to Parliament, the *Sovereign of the Seas* was laid up and Charles began the struggle that would lead him to the scaffold.

In Falmouth, Pendennis Castle served both as a stronghold for the Stuarts and as a back door. In July 1644 Queen Henrietta Maria fled to Cornwall and after a night at Pendennis hurried down to the beach, to take a ship for France. One man who witnessed her flight wrote about it in a letter home: 'Dear wiffe, here is the woefullest spectacle my eyes yet ever look'd on: the most worne and weak pitifull creature in ye world, the poore queen shifting for one hour's life longer.' A year and a half later, her son, Prince Charles, chased ever westwards, reached Pendennis and remained there a couple of weeks while he received daily news of the collapse of Royalist forces. Warned about the loyalty of those around him, he left Pendennis at ten o'clock one evening to be rowed out to a ship, and exile.

The Parliamentary forces of Sir Thomas Fairfax were not far behind, taking Lord Hopton's surrender at Tresillian Bridge, at the tidal top of one of the Fal's tributaries. What happened next has been a matter of some confusion, but in the Public Record Office are papers that give a plausible account. On 11 March 1646 Fairfax's army was at Truro; Cornwall was under his control and only Pendennis Castle and its elderly governor Colonel Arundel were holding out. One Parliamentary correspondent confidently declared on that day that Arundel 'will not be so mad as to see the whole Gentry at liberty, injoying their owne, and himself as it were in prison'. Fairfax's men marched down to Pendennis to take his surrender.

Hearing of their approach, Arundel sent out a detachment. First they set light to Arwenack Manor, then carried on to Smithwick. Arundel had no intention of surrendering. Preparing for a siege, he sought to remove any material support from around the castle. But before they were able to torch the new-built inns and cottages of Smithwick, the enemy was spotted. The Royalists fled, back out to Pendennis Point and the protection of the castle walls.

The Parliamentarians pursued them, taking Smithwick and dousing the flames at Arwenack as best they could. Fairfax himself moved into its smoking ruins, having issued an ultimatum to Arundel: 'I demand you to deliver up the Castle at Pendennis ... I expect your answer in two hours.'

Arundel despatched a reply: 'Having taken less than two minutes' resolution, I resolve that I will here bury myself before I give up this Castle.' He was now 70 years old, he said, and did not wish to live out his few remaining days under the shame of such a treason. With him were more than a thousand men, arms and powder, victuals for nine months and 200 tuns of wine. Among the Cornish gentry in the castle was a Killigrew, Sir Henry, son of Elizabeth's limping ambassador.

Over the coming weeks, the ring around Pendennis grew tighter. To begin with, the Royalists had a man-of-war of forty guns which menaced any ship coming near Falmouth harbour, as well as firing on the two regiments dug in at Smithwick and Arwenack. But soon she was taken, and a Captain Batten sent down to blockade the castle from sea as it was from land. Each night he posted a small flotilla at the entrance to the Carrick Roads and in Falmouth Bay. The Royalists kept beacons burning for any approaching relief; in April a shallop did manage to slip through the cordon. There was little on board, except more wine.

The open sea was their only hope, and one of those inside wrote some verses, likening the castle to Penelope waiting for the return of Ulysses while holding off a flock of suitors:

> Weepe not as one forsaken and forlone;
> Thine own Ulysses will, in time, returne,
> Embrace, and hugge, thee in his Royall Armes,
> Ne'er conquered yet by force, nor won by charmes –
> Brave Governor, be still but what thou art,
> England may be subdued erse thy great heart.

In June a ship was spotted sailing for the castle. Before it could even moor, it was intercepted and a cache of ciphered letters captured. A few days later, another appeared, its hold rumoured to be full of supplies; when that, too. was captured in the sight of the garrison, spirits in the castle began to slide.

On one of those long midsummer days, with the besieged loyalists enfeebled by hunger, word reached them that at last a whole squadron had left France. With so many ships on their way, most believed that some at least would get through. Yet not one of those sails even came within sight; republican winds from the north sent them running back into Morlaix. By July supplies were running low. In desperation, a party broke out from the shore but were driven back with much loss of life. A couple of weeks later, the order was given in the castle to kill the horses 'for beefe'.

In mid-August, with their food reduced to a few barrels of salted horse, and with hundreds now too weak and ill to move, the Royalists opened negotiations. So effective was their feigned nonchalance that the besiegers were convinced they had months of supply. The garrison extracted good terms, securing agreement for free passage to wherever each wanted to go and, in an extraordinary *coup de théâtre*, managed also to dictate the manner of their surrender.

Twelve weeks after King Charles had given himself up in the north of England, Pendennis Castle's gates flew open and, after five months of siege – the longest of the war – the survivors marched out. Under the agreement, they had been allowed to keep their arms, to fly their colours, to sound their trumpets and beat their drums. They clutched spills lit at both ends, and clenched between their teeth were bullets. Like some biblical horde, they strode down into the enemy camp, where it is said that more died from over-eating than during the entire siege. Behind them, inside the castle, the besiegers found hundreds more, starving, lying immobile. To their amazement they also discovered just twenty-four hours' supplies.

A century had passed since Pendennis Castle's completion and the appointment of John Killigrew as the first governor. In that time, the fortress had benefited the Killigrews much more than it ever had the Crown. Now one of the family, Sir Henry Killigrew, emerged from its gates as defiant as all the others. With Killigrew flamboyance, he raised the barrel of his musket and fired it. The musket exploded and wounded Sir Henry so badly that he had to be carried on board the ship that took him into exile. Several days later at St Malo, he died.

The siege's anonymous poet added to his verse and, as the Royalists' Ulysses failed to arrive, wrote: '*Penelope ipsam, perstes modo, tempore vinces*' ('If you only persist, you shall eventually conquer Penelope herself').

CHAPTER 11

Arwenack lay in ruins. What had been saved from the flames at the start of the siege had then been stripped bare by months of occupation. Earthworks scarred the grounds and everywhere lay the ruts and rot of the military camp, the smear of several hundred bodies living, sleeping, waiting. Shortly after the end of the siege, the former Jane Killigrew – now Jane Bluett – moved back in to the manor's shell with her husband. But they had so little money and their position became so dismal that the people of Budock parish issued a plea for the poor inhabitants of the manor. Like the country's ruling body, Arwenack Manor had lost its head. Jane Bluett died two years later.

Yet it was during the coming years, the grey years of the Commonwealth, that the Killigrew settlement at Smithwick at last took root, and it was a Killigrew who profited from it. With Jane's death, the estate passed to Peter Killigrew, brother of her ex-husband. Peter had always been a Royalist. In 1623 he had acted as courier during the disastrous 'Spanish Match' journey of Prince Charles and Buckingham. He was an emotional man, a composer of verses in his youth, and tears would fill his eyes when he spoke of the executed king and the night he himself had almost enabled him to escape, waiting with horses to hurry him to a ship on the Sussex coast. But when the time came, he found no difficulty in switching his loyalties to Parliament. During the war he served as a courier for Cromwell and afterwards the House of Commons generously awarded him £2,000, combining payment for his swift service with compensation for damage to his Cornish property at Arwenack.

A few years later Peter Killigrew used his good favour to press for concessions for Smithwick. He was spectacularly successful: legislation was granted to hold a Thursday market there, two annual fairs, a regular ferry across the river and, most significant of all, a 1,000-year lease for a Custom House – formerly at Penryn (thus fulfilling the borough's worst fears of its downriver rival).

Peter was an opportunist, clearly, but he lacked the recklessness of his sea-crazed forebears. Unlike each of Arwenack's previous masters, he had been brought up hundreds of miles inland, in Madrid, in the house of John Digby, Earl of Bristol. His career had been spent in court and in the field. He was known as Peter the Post for his extraordinary speed over the land and had, famously, once ridden from Madrid to London in seven days. The Killigrew chronicle picks him out for rare praise: 'a fine gentleman, a gamester in his youth, when he had nothing to lose, and ever a merry and desirable companion'.

With the Restoration secure, Peter Killigrew again unfurled his Royalist colours and Charles II made him governor of Pendennis Castle. He also provided him with the legal backing, a royal charter no less, to give Killigrew's Smithwick official endorsement:

Whereas our village of Smithwick, in the county of Cornwall, is an ancient and populous village situate upon the Sea Coast, and near adjoining to our Port of Falmouth, which is a most safe and capacious Harbour for Ships, in so far as Merchants and Mariners, as well Natives as Foreigners,

have need to assemble and do now assemble from divers
parts, to the village and port aforesaid, with their Ships,
Goods and Merchandize ...

Although the small cluster of buildings at Smithwick was
neither ancient nor populous, the charter did recognise that,
in an age of increasing maritime activity and contact with
'divers parts', its importance would grow. With Killigrew
presumption, Peter inserted into the charter a paragraph
giving royal backing for a new name. The village would
henceforth be known as Falmouth, a name that until then
had been used not only for the miles and miles of the estuary's creeks and anchorages but as a generic name for its few
older and much larger ports. With royal backing, Smithwick
leapfrogged them all.

For one who had swung so easily to Cromwell, it appears
strange that Peter Killigrew should have received such immediate reward from Charles II, and that a small village on the
edge of the kingdom should be granted such a fulsome charter. The place itself had unhappy associations for Charles.
Not only had his mother fled the country from there, but
later he too – hurrying at night aboard the *Phoenix*, whose
Cornish crew at once managed to rob the prince and his
party of £300 of silver and lace.

Equally, though, Pendennis had proved the most stubborn
of all Royalist strongholds. Peter Killigrew had also played
his own swift-footed part in Charles's Restoration, riding
back and forth between the various factions. Nor was the
wider clan of Killigrew unknown to the King; he was on good
terms with many of them. As with the Burghley Map, inserted
into an atlas of the entire kingdom, the colourful Killigrews
again made sure that their remote corner of Cornwall was
well promoted in the circle of court.

Peter's cousin, Elizabeth Killigrew – described later as 'too much and too long versed in amours' – left her husband for Charles's court-in-exile, and in 1650 bore the prince his second child. Elizabeth was the favourite sister of Tom Killigrew, one of Charles's constant companions. In exile, Charles had sent Tom Killigrew as his Resident to Venice for two years (until he was dismissed for smuggling and 'riotous behaviour'). Tom Killigrew spent the years in exile writing a great many plays – though his wit was said to be rather more obvious in person than on the page. The King awarded him, with Sir Charles Davenant, a monopoly on theatres in London. Tom Killigrew established the King's Players, introduced women to the stage (whose parts had until then been played by boys), revived the plays of Shakespeare and built the first theatre at Drury Lane.

Many of Tom's family held positions at court. His wife became Keeper of the Queen's Sweet Coffer while Tom himself was both Groom of the Bedchamber and Master of the Revels. He was given a salary of £400 per year. He also developed a lucrative line in selling invented posts for others – the 'King's Physic-taster', the royal 'Curtain-drawer'. As Groom to the Bedchamber, he spent a great deal of time with the King and was known to be the only man who could stand up to him, who would chastise him to his face for allowing pleasure to come before duty. He once appeared before Charles in the ragged garb of a pilgrim.

'What now, Killigrew?' asked the King. 'Where are you going?'

'To Hell, sir! To fetch Oliver Cromwell. The country was governed badly enough in his time, but infinitely better than it is now.'

On another occasion he was said to have boasted that he could come up with a pun on any subject. 'All right,' said the King. 'Make one up about me.'

Tom Killigrew.

Killigrew fell silent.

'Well?' prompted the King.

'I cannot, sir – as the King is no subject.'

Tom's son Henry, Groom to the Bedchamber of the Duke of York, lurched in and out of favour. He and his gang of 'young blades' were, according to Pepys, 'ready to take hold of every young woman that come by them'. He helped a certain Rose Gwyn free herself from Newgate Prison, and it is likely that this is how her sister, Nell, reached the stage and royal circles. Henry was banished from court for claiming that the King's mistress Lady Castlemaine was 'a little lecherous girl when she was young, and used to rub her thing with her fingers or against the end of forms'. He was sent to the Tower for fighting with the Duke of Buckingham, fled to France, returned and was soon in trouble again. He spoke openly about an affair with Lady Shrewsbury. 'Mr Killigrew's carriage towards her,' wrote the King to his sister, 'has been worse than I will repeate.' One night, Lady Shrewsbury's men attacked Killigrew as he travelled home, killing his servant and leaving him on the road to Turnham Green, bleeding from nine wounds.

But it wasn't all scandal. Tom's brother Henry was chaplain to the Duke of York and Henry's children were respectively a naval captain (killed in action), a vice-admiral and the much-admired poet and painter Anne. When she died in her mid-twenties, Anne became the subject of a famous pindaric by John Dryden – *To the Pious Memory of the Accomplished Young Lady Mrs Anne Killigrew, Excellent in the Two Sister-arts of Poesie and Painting*. Dr Johnson later judged it to be 'the noblest ode our language has produced':

> Though much excellence she did show,
> And many qualities did know,

Yet this alone, she could not tell,
To wit, *how much she did excell.*

Such panache provided fleeting distraction in the salons of
Restoration London; back in Cornwall, it was being put to
more commercial use. Peter Killigrew's new town was
blooming. He filled its governing council, the Corporation,
with his own tenants. He arranged a special Act of Parliament
to create a new parish, sliced from the rump of old Budock.
He built a church, midway between the half-ruined manor
and the new settlement and, with a flourish of sentimental
loyalty, dedicated it to the figure whose memory so often
misted his eyes. Falmouth's church was the first in the country to be given the title King Charles the Martyr. In 1662,
when its population had risen to some 700, a visitor described
the town as 'now a great place ... it consists chiefly of
alehouses' (though the beer, moaned another, was 'not fitting
for any Christians to drink').

A painting of the time, by Hendrick Danckerts, shows the
harbour entrance filled with a southern glow, borrowed from
scenes of Renaissance Italy, and giving Falmouth and its
waters not only a sense of light and hopefulness, but a hint of
all those hot and distant shores with which it was now
connected. Another contemporary image, an engraving, by
Walter Schellinks, reveals a spread of useful-looking buildings. Luggers and punts criss-cross the harbour. Casks are
rolled along the beach and a delivery of deals is checked in
the foreground. Lying on her side, like a fallen elephant, is a
large ship with smoke rising from her port quarter. A graving
team is burning the weed from her hull. Dutch privateers
paid Falmouth Corporation £100 for such a service – burning
off the weed and crustacea, before applying a treacly blend of
tallow, hair, sulphur and tar to delay its return.

Falmouth Harbour by Hendrick Danckerts.

Port books and written records confirm the flood of activity at Falmouth during the 1660s. From France came ships laden with salt, which was then packed into hogsheads of pilchards (already pressed and cured) and loaded back for passage to the Canaries and the Mediterranean. Tin went to London in ever larger quantities. Household goods and medicines returned: soap, glue, dyes, haberdashery, saucepans, books, pewter and shot – some for local consumption and some to be assembled for the Atlantic crossing to Virginia, where in turn bundles of tobacco leaves were packed for the trip home. The overworked ships needed their own tending and in the lanes around Arwenack, ropemakers' donkeys hauled and twisted plies of cordage. In new-built stores, chandlers built up stock of lanyard and blocks, caulking tools and adzes, while lengths of Baltic timber lay in the water at Bar Pool, waiting to be hauled over the saw-pits and fashioned into spars.

During the reign of Charles II, England's overseas trade doubled. The King involved himself in maritime affairs in a way that his father and grandfather had considered beneath them. Years later, after the King's death, Pepys reflected how lucky it was, at that time, to have been granted 'a king who understood the sea'. In exile Charles had learned to sail and at the Restoration, the Dutch gave him a yacht. He and his brother, the Duke of York, built two more – *Catherine* and *Anne* – and could often be seen racing each other along the Thames, thus introducing the new sport of sailing into the country.

Charles himself burrowed into the mysteries of oceanic navigation. He commissioned the observatory at Greenwich, and passed the Laws of Trade and Navigation which remained the legal framework for British overseas commerce for 170 years. He created a similar code for the Navy, binding the Articles of War, the Fighting Instructions and a set of flags, pennants and ensigns whose cantons, groundwork and monotones made clear to each squadron every wish of their commanding officer.

Charles II is often seen as father of the Royal Navy. But just as the crucial concessions for Falmouth were gained in the kingless years of the 1650s, so Charles merely built on the huge maritime expansion of the Commonwealth. Between the reign of Charles I and the Restoration the number of ships had more than trebled, while spending had risen so steeply that the Navy soon accounted for more than half the entire national budget.

Yet the culture of the Navy still suffered from the neglect and corruption perfected during the reign of James I. Sailors were treated like slaves, savagely punished, short-rationed and rarely paid. State shipbuilding was riddled with scams. For most of the century, the chief shipwrights had been the

Pett family. Between them the Petts had built the *Prince Royal*, *Sovereign of the Seas* and the *Naseby*, the largest ships of three successive regimes. But like the Killigrews, the Petts, who had become prominent under Elizabeth I, followed a path that flickered between glory and scandal.

Peter Pett, a master shipwright at Deptford, began the succession. His son Phineas Pett briefly studied under Matthew Baker. Phineas later said he owed a great deal of his skill to Baker – but Baker became critical of both the younger man's ability and his integrity. As purveyor of naval timber under James I, Phineas Pett helped himself to what he needed for his own lodgings, and sold a good deal of the rest. When he let the topmast of the *Repulse* go to a private buyer and pocketed the proceeds, the controller of the Navy hit him with a cudgel.

Phineas's son Peter built the triple-decked *Naseby* during the Commonwealth. Refitted and renamed the *Royal Charles*, the ship fetched Charles II back to England. Peter Pett eased himself into the new regime. As Resident Commissioner of Chatham dockyard, he was the senior Master Shipwright and filled the best posts of the royal shipyards with his own family. He sold naval timber for private gain and drove both the King and the Duke of York to fury for the chaos of the fleet. Pepys talks of Pett's 'villainy ... false dealing ... as very a knave as lives upon earth ...'

Peter Pett was also blamed for what one naval historian has called 'the most shameful incident in the history of the fleet'. In 1667 the Dutch sailed into the Medway, penetrated the very heart of British naval power at Chatham and sailed off with Pett's *Royal Charles* in tow. He was ridiculed for rescuing his shipwrights' half-models while ignoring the loss of the ship – but, he claimed to laughter in the court, they were more valuable. In fact it was English sailors who, after years of maltreatment, had guided the Dutch into Chatham. Peter Pett was made a scapegoat, as Andrew Marvell showed:

> After this loss, to relish discontent,
> Someone must be accused by punishment.
> All our miscarriages on Pett must fall:
> His name alone seems fit to answer all.

Pett was sent to the Tower, and later released to obscurity.

The first two Stuart kings regarded ships as an extension of their land-based power, gilding them and swelling their dimensions like palaces. But the sea has no regard for worldly pomp, and of the funds and largesse they poured into the Navy, a great deal was squandered. As a yachtsman, with an enthusiasm for marine science, Charles II's more respectful attitude to the sea was much more successful.

One afternoon in the summer of 1668 the shoreline at Falmouth filled with people. It was just seven years since the town's incorporation. Now 2,000 had gathered on the beach and on the low cliff. They had come to watch the launch of the first sizeable ship to be built at Falmouth – seventy tons burden, six guns. Falmouth was never a large shipbuilding town, not like Belfast or Hull. It was a place for repairs and supplies. Yet the launch of this ship can be seen as the moment that Falmouth came of age. Twenty years later, the burgeoning port was selected as the most westerly station for the Packet service.

Peter Killigrew lived to see neither the launching of the first ship nor Falmouth's sudden growth. He died as he had lived so much of his life, on the road, riding to Exeter. The year was 1667, exactly a century since the death of his great-grandfather, and the completion of the manor at Arwenack.

Much of that was now destroyed, but in its place the spreading settlement offered a more secure enterprise. A hundred years of banditry had been served. The Killigrews were now legitimate players in the great global expansion of trade, their port a hub of its ever-quickening activity.

CHAPTER 12

A low mist caps Pendennis Point and covers all but the lower courses of the castle. It is the week before Christmas and the air is still. One or two ships wallow in the grey lake of the Carrick Roads and *Liberty*'s bows slice the flat water without a sound. I moor up at Custom House quay. In Arwenack Street, bag-flanked shoppers struggle through the crowds; an electric, life-size Father Christmas waves from the window of Trago Mills. After the shops, the road runs south, emptying of people and entering something of an urban backwater. Beyond its own car park rises the new oak-clad development around the National Maritime Museum, occupying several acres of reclaimed land. The road itself pushes on towards a mini-roundabout.

But it is here that it began, in front of Arwenack Manor's mullioned facade, where the grounds stretched out towards the watergate, through which flowed explorers and pirates, prisoners, storm-survivors and news of great calamities or wonders – the first tell of a strange shore, an exotic root or spice-seed, a fragile colony in the vast new world.

The traces of Arwenack remain, half-hidden behind a hedge of ilex and viburnum and skimmia. The buildings were rescued from ruin some decades ago and are now private apartments. Stillness surrounds their black-painted lintels and squat pepper-pot tower. I ring the bell and wait, but no one comes to the door. Through the slats of a venetian blind, I glimpse a kitchen, an everyday kitchen with its worktops and eye-level cupboards, the swan's neck of the sink-tap rising against the opposite window, and the view of a garden beyond.

Turning to go, between the houses, I see something else: a high window and a section of ivy-covered wall. The window-panes are empty – you can look straight through them to the newer buildings beyond. The wall is just that, a two-dimensional relic of what was at one time Cornwall's grandest house. The Killigrews themselves have long since gone, vanishing almost as soon as Falmouth was established.

After Peter the Post died in 1667, he was succeeded by his son – also Peter – who came to Falmouth from London to take over the thriving new port. He had no knowledge of the sea, but brought with him the expansive ambitions of the Restoration capital, rebuilding itself after the Great Fire. It was this second Sir Peter (he inherited a baronetcy from an uncle) who put in place the fabric of the town, constructing waterworks and erecting the Town Quay.

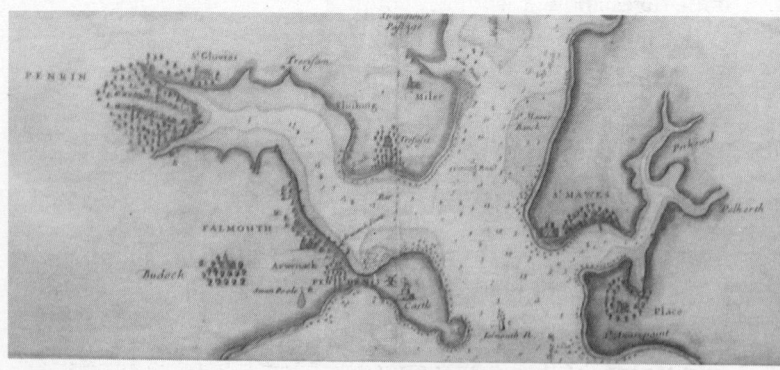

Detail from Greenville Collins' map of Falmouth.

In his name, the royal hydrographer conducted a meticulous survey of the Fal basin. A print of this chart hung outside my bedroom door as a child and I remember two things about it in particular: the very elaborate dedicatory illustration, and the shape of the Percuil river looking like a madman with long flailing arms.

Surrounded by images of classical plenty and power, the dedication involves swags of fruit hung from lances, ribbons and cannons, and the Killigrew double-headed eagle. The text itself reads:

FALMOUTH

To S^R PETER KILLIGREW
BARONET *this map is dedicated and
Presented by Capt* GREENVILLE COLLINS
Hydrographer to the King

In the print, Falmouth is still small beside Penryn, but here at last is Raleigh's wish fulfilled: the estuary's God-given advantages laid out, with the comfort of deep soundings and sheltering headlands. But as well as the military aspect – drums and gun barrels towards the bottom of the panel – the chart is offering access to Cornwall's own resources. The martial age is giving way to the commercial. Larger than anything else in the illustration are three miners with pick and shovel beside another who arranges a stupa of smelted tin; opposite them, a seiner and pilchard merchant stand over a barrel of fish and between them are a scallop shell and two exotic-looking sea creatures – part gurnard, part angler-fish – whose gleeful grinning expression always struck me as odd (given that they were dead).

The number of ships visiting Falmouth was growing by the month, as was the range of cargo: sugar and wine from Portugal, iron for anchor chain and barrel hoops, pipe staves and bricks for building, timber from Norway for ship-spars, pit-props and charcoal for the mines. Within twenty years of Sir Peter Killigrew coming to Falmouth, the amount of tin exported through its quays rose by nearly a hundredfold.

Each visiting ship looked to Falmouth for victuals – meat and butter, biscuit and bread – and the harbour spread its patronage deeper and deeper into Cornwall's fertile hinterland. One need overshadowed all others. Ships heading off into the Atlantic required thousands of gallons of fresh water. Sir Peter Killigrew addressed the problem with typical grandeur. He called in the great Dutch engineer Sir Cornelius Vermuyden who had worked at Dagenham breach and drained the Lincolnshire Fens. At Falmouth, Vermuyden created an extravagant series of pools and mills and leats and streams; and he designed a network of channels and canals between them.

The project cost Sir Peter Killigrew more than £700, but what was that beside the family's coming generations of prosperity? The more he spent, the more it convinced him of the great destiny of his port. It did not matter that despite the quantity of trade that was flowing through Falmouth, little tariff made its way to him.

There had been a fatal gap of a couple of years between the death of Peter the Post in 1667 and the arrival of his son. In that time the balance in Falmouth's new corporation had, imperceptibly, tipped away from the Killigrews and into the scheming hands of one Bryan Rogers.

Born in Bristol, Rogers had spent a childhood in various ports – his father was collector of customs in Plymouth and then Penzance. During the last years of the Commonwealth, he spotted the future in the settlement at Smithwick and, seeking to dominate it, vowed to make himself the region's principal merchant. He realised early on that his real struggle would be not in attracting ships to the port – that was now as inevitable as the tides – but in breaking Killigrew control.

'By cunning and sinister means,' explains the Killigrew chronicle, Rogers 'took possession of the Corporation, bringing his own little creatures into it as Aldermen and Burgesses.' Four times he was elected mayor. When Peter Killigrew tried to secure exclusive landing rights for his own Customs Quay, Rogers disputed it, won the case and transferred his own business to Penryn. Discovering that Vermuyden's new waterways crossed a short section of non-Killigrew land, Rogers persuaded its owner to open a case against Killigrew. Twenty shillings was the sum in dispute; the case cost Killigrew thousands.

'I will always be happy,' Rogers boasted, 'to spend £100 if it cost Killigrew £20.'

On another occasion, Killigrew lost £200 to a creditor because his writ was never presented to the plaintiff. The man charged with delivering the paper – a Mr Henderson – confessed he had lit his pipe with it. Rogers was so grateful to Henderson that he made him town-sergeant and mace-bearer for life.

Into the hands of the second Peter Killigrew had been delivered the prize sought by the Killigrews for more than a century. The sight of a mast-thick harbour and the Smithwick shoreline thronged with commerce would have gladdened and astonished Sir Peter's grandfather John, contemplating his own ruin from within the walls of Fleet Prison. Yet as soon as success was achieved, it began to ebb away.

By the 1680s the money left to Sir Peter by his father had gone. He had a little luck with his son George, a 'fine and hopeful young gent'. Sir Peter managed to marry him off to the daughter of his wealthy neighbour Sir John St Aubyn. Ann St Aubyn brought £5,000 with her, of which Sir Peter took £4,000. But his main commercial enterprise yielded little. He was the largest landlord in the area. The rector was his own appointment. The Market Strand and the Fish Strand and the Custom House were all on his property. Such hubs of activity would ensure wealth for any inland estate, but shoreside commerce had its own rules, its own licence – and its rewards did not reach Arwenack. Nor did the post that first elevated the Killigrews – governorship of Pendennis Castle – afford much to Sir Peter. The fort had sunk into disrepair, its hornworks were crumbling, its guns becoming less and less serviceable. The garrison, which during the Commonwealth had been so large that supplying it helped create the town, was reduced to a skeleton crew of invalided soldiers.

When Sir Peter wrote to the Crown begging for funds to repair it, none came. One night at ten o'clock, the desperate Killigrew led an armed gang to the Falmouth Custom House, kidnapped the collector and took more than £200. 'The King is my tenant,' he cried. 'I will use his money to repair his castle.'

Meanwhile, at Arwenack, his first grandchild was born to George and Ann: a girl, Amye, but nonetheless something of a hedge against the family's financial woes. Yet the marriage itself began to show signs of strain. In the eyes of the Killigrews, Ann was proving herself more and more ill-tempered, spreading disharmony through the high-ceilinged rooms of the manor. George began to roam, passing his evenings at the numerous shoreside inns. On 20 March 1687

Sir Peter Killigrew.

in a 'drunken humour' he became involved in a dispute with
a barrister named Vincent. Swords were drawn and as the
fight escalated, Vincent's rapier pierced George Killigrew's
forehead and killed him.

Such a meaningless end to the Killigrew dynasty sucked
into its void a number of explanations, of which the most
persistent was that the Killigrews had been cursed for all
their past ill-deeds. Vincent himself was acquitted, but died

suddenly two years later from a sudden apoplexy during a visit to the bishop's palace at Exeter.

George's widow Ann took her child and returned to her own people. According to the family chronicle, George's death finally broke Sir Peter's heart. 'Never again did he take delight in anything but his Lady and two daughters.' Sir Peter and his wife left Falmouth for good – first for London, then as far from the coast as they could go, to Ludlow in Shropshire where Sir Peter surrounded himself with books and pursued a lifelong passion for 'speculative learning'.

Sir Peter is one of the few Killigrews who has left a likeness, and he stands full-chested for the painter, gazing out from beneath Restoration curls, with oddly feminine eyes and a cupid's bow of a mouth. It is hard to imagine him as the rebel Protestant, the brutal privateer, driving south across the Channel by moonlight as the sons of Arwenack had a century before. Sir Peter died in 1704, last of the Killigrews, returning to Falmouth only in his coffin, to the church his father had built forty years earlier.

When he left Falmouth, Sir Peter placed his affairs in the hands of the incumbent, the Reverend Walter Quarme, with instructions to resist any ruse by Rogers and the Corporation. Quarme reassured the Killigrews: he would always remain 'firm in Sir Peter's interest in opposition to the encroachments of the said Rogers'.

But his flesh was weak and, with his masters absent and discredited, Quarme began to act against the Killigrews, letting out their property to his cronies for pitiful sums. From London, the Killigrews tried in desperation to wrest back a little power by appointing their own curate under Quarme. Having walked down from London, with little money, the young curate drank himself into a stupor in

Penryn, collapsed in a gutter and woke up without his trousers. The Killigrews told him there was only one way he could now win Quarme's favour. He must go straight to the inn above Falmouth's Market Strand and publicly abuse the Killigrew name.

It paid off. The curate began his surreptitious work against Quarme and soon, on the Killigrews' behalf, managed to remove Quarme as steward of Arwenack. In his place came Martin Lister, son-in-law to the second Sir Peter Killigrew.

It was as a young soldier that Martin Lister had first seen the waters of the Fal, serving as an officer at Pendennis Castle, with the great sweep of coast the daily backdrop to his work. Lister fell in with young George Killigrew, both being the same age, each as impetuous and high-spirited as the other. After George was killed, and after George's daughter was taken away from Arwenack by her mother, the mourning Sir Peter recognised the 'great intimacy' that had existed between his son and Martin Lister, and suggested he therefore marry Ann, George's younger sister.

Martin Lister became devoted to the Killigrews, to Sir Peter, to his mother-in-law – 'one of the finest women of her time' – to his own wife Ann, and to the constant memory of George. He added Killigrew to his name and now set about his stewardship of Arwenack with gusto. He stood up to the hostile Corporation – magnanimously giving them both the Town Hall and their maces. He ignored the threats and insults – 'I value not my head being loaded with curses.'

But after twenty years in Falmouth, in the summer of 1725, he was at last driven from town, not by the merchants – his military pride refused them that – but by the ill-health of his wife. Neither of them ever saw Falmouth again. Ann Lister Killigrew died soon after they left. Childless and alone, Martin had now survived every one of the male Killigrews, the entire family in fact, save for a couple of great-nieces.

He lived out his remaining days in London, maintaining a regular, soldierly life. He made sure that each day he travelled nine miles for exercise – six by coach, and three on foot. His letters from this time reveal a restless soul, prone to dark moods. 'At present,' he wrote to his agent at Arwenack, 'the thoughts of leaving this world are far from disagreeable to me.' He felt burdened by the weight of the Killigrew past, by the family's exile from Falmouth and by its imminent extinction.

In 1737, now in his early seventies, struggling against loneliness and torpor, he embarked on a project which aimed to set down 'something historically of the family, the memory of which is so dear to me'. He began to compile a family history, and wrote to ask his steward in Falmouth to do something for him. Take pen and paper, he said, go up to the church of St Budock above the town. Choose a Sunday afternoon, kneel down before the chancel steps and from beneath the armoured figure of John Killigrew and his wife, copy down the inscription. As well as the chronicle, Martin also commissioned a monument.

Opposite the remains of Arwenack Manor lies a small piece of municipal garden. I push open the gate. On this grey December afternoon, the rose bushes have been winter-pruned and the grass is well trimmed. Ringed by an iron fence, the garden encloses the 44-foot granite pyramid erected by Martin Lister Killigrew in the 1730s, in the name of the Killigrews. For years, I've walked past this strange edifice, hardly giving it a second glance. It's just one of those dusty corners in the towns of post-imperial Britain, commemorating something or other. But the Killigrew Monument never did very much to advertise itself. It was built deliberately without adornment, less the expression of a grateful populace than the discreet gesture of a fleeing outcast.

Far from Cornwall, Martin Lister Killigrew worked on his Killigrew Chronicle, taking long and brooding walks around Kensington Gardens, and applying himself to the question of a family memorial in Falmouth. He decided on a design that was something between an obelisk and a pyramid. Hawksmoor had just used an obelisk at Castle Howard, and the designs of Palladio were in vogue. Pyramids had been known to be funerary monuments since the Middle Ages and the structure was clearly linked for Lister Killigrew with the idea of posterity: 'It may remain a beautiful embellishment to the harbour,' he wrote, 'long, long after my desiring to be forgotten, as if I had never been.' But looking at its apex probing the December mist, it seemed to me that, in terms of form, it was a counter to all that brought down the Killigrews, the very opposite to the flat sea.

On gilt-edged paper, Martin sent copious instructions to his steward in Falmouth, a Mr Hall. From those that have survived you can sense the details of the project raising his spirits. It was to be constructed of granite hauled from quarries near Trevethan Beacon, whose seams he knew could produce ashlars two foot across. The details delighted him. The dressed stone, he explained, was to be joined in the following manner: the mason must fashion a thin board to the exact thickness of the lime and press it against the joint and these boards and the stones to fix them and the cramp-cavities must all be prepared in advance for each of the four sides ...

No aspect of construction was too small for his attention. He wrote to Hall about the foundations, from which beach to source coarse sand or fine, and with what dimension of tool to drive in the piles for the foundations. The sides should be smooth: 'true joints, close laid, with little lime, and well cramped is what I shall hope to hear from you'. When Hall wrote to him about the churning of mud by stone-bearing carts, he was told: 'You provide old shipe planke of the thickest; You lay a platform of it, of about Six foot wide, and square about the basses of the Pyramid, fastened to two sleepers, at each End of each Square side; The Said Sleepers in the ground so that the plank may rest flat upon the ground, the sleepers to bear no weight only to keep the planks together', and so on, for pages.

Martin Lister Killigrew was making up for decades of bad luck, for all the thwarted plans of the Killigrews. He poured into the project a vicarious enthusiasm which he did not otherwise feel. His own days were 'growing short' and he led a 'wretched life' in London – while in Falmouth the pyramid rose from its base. It is, he wrote, 'a darling thing I am never to see'.

For a century, the Killigrew pyramid stood in an elm grove, beside an avenue once laid out by Sir Peter Killigrew for the pleasure of his descendants. But by the time the trees were fully grown, the family had long since gone. The avenue was let out as a rope-walk. Donkeys trudged back and forth under the canopy of leaves, twisting halyards and sheets for the port's shipping. The pyramid never gained popularity in the town, being 'much ridiculed as a heavy lump of stone, neither ornamental nor useful'. As memories of the Killigrews blurred, and their old house slipped further and further into disrepair, the town pressed out towards the pyramid. The elm grove was cut down. In time, too, the site of the pyramid

The Killigrew Monument.

was required for building. In 1836 it was dismantled stone by stone and re-erected to the south, looking out over Falmouth Bay. There, after another thirty-five years, the spreading world again caught up with it: railway track was laid near its base and new buildings placed it in shadow. In turn a number of windows were blocked by its bulk and a certain retired naval officer, Captain Saulez, found it in his garden. Again it was dismantled, and this time taken down to the old manor, just yards from the sea.

Now the sea has been pushed back, the land reclaimed, the National Maritime Museum built and a large area paved before it, named 'Events Square'. Around the square is a skirt of bright-windowed shops and cafés, Rick Stein's Fish and Chips, Pizza Express, Musto. The pyramid stands between the road and the pay-and-display car park. Its sides rise above both, converging to a small finial, a copper arrowhead. The joints of the granite are beautifully cut. Nothing breaks the grey stone, no signature, no name-plate – except on its northern face, the tiny fronds of a hart's-tongue fern.

Inside the pyramid, buried pharaoh-like in the ashlar, is a bottle. Its top is sealed with wax and it contains several rolled sheets of parchment. The bottle was inserted during its last rebuilding in 1871. On the parchment, beneath a heading 'The Killigrew Monument', are the pyramid's dimensions (height 40 feet, base 14-foot-square), the cost of moving it (£455. 1s. 11½d.) and a lengthy account of the monument's story, its various resting places and its final moving here. A copy of the document was made and put in the Arwenack Manor office and in its detailed description of its odyssey, it reads almost like an apologia.

A couple of courses above this bottle, also deep inside the stone, lies another bottle, placed there by the masons who admitted to it only after the pyramid was complete. In this bottle they have placed a collection of coins, as if it was they who bore in some way the conscience of the town for shifting the monument, twice over. Now their gesture appears like a confession, a collective need in Falmouth for propitiation of the Killigrews' tormented ghosts, or even more than that, a wish to appease the spirits of the sea itself.

PART III

CHAPTER 13

In the parish register of St Gluvias Penryn, for the year 1648, is the baptism of one Peter Mundy. It was a late baptism – Mundy was then in his mid-fifties – and we do not know exactly what led him to the font, what weight of conscience or sudden press of joy. Mundy was the son of a pilchard merchant whose own father had been a cantor at Glasney College. He grew up shadowed by Glasney's ruins, in a wharfside world of fish and warps where the constant traffic of local craft, the cobles and gigs and coasters, was punctuated by oceanic visitors, Dutch and Breton traders and a growing number of privateers. He himself first watched land drop behind the horizon when he was 12, on a journey to Rouen with his father. He marvelled at the Seine's tidal bore, the rush of its course upstream and the 'great rolling feathering waves, overturning small vessels, boats, etc.' He recalled, too, the vast bell of *George d'Amboise* – eighteen feet in diameter (later melted down in the Revolution) – and the sight of impoverished couples, husband and wife, yoked like horses to tumbril-carts. He then spent two years in Gascony learning French. It is clear that his father saw the boy's future as an extension of his own, a respectable life in the Cornish pilchard trade.

But Peter Mundy was bound for the wider world. The early years spent beside the waters of the Fal were the longest he stayed anywhere in the six decades of his life. In thirty-six years of travelling, he covered 100,833⅝ miles. Even then, as he sat in Penryn around the time of his baptism to calculate that figure, he still had one great journey left. We would know nothing of him beyond the baptism roll had he not also chosen to set down on paper what he saw in the distant continents. His manuscript then lay buried for nearly 300 years before being published, in six meticulously footnoted volumes, by the Hakluyt Society.

Peter Mundy first went to sea just a few years after the death of Elizabeth I. Unlike most of the literate buccaneers of the time he did not fill his notebooks with jibes at the Spanish and risible tales of others' superstitions, nor whispered cities built of jewels. Peter Mundy represented a new breed of sea-shaped man, one that would become more common after the Enlightenment. Spreading out along the trade routes, these men travelled because they were able to, because in their childhood or in their working day they had watched ships come and go, and because they saw no good reason not to board them. Although involved mainly with commercial missions, Mundy's writings reveal that he was motivated less by wealth than by a yearning for the richness and diversity of the world. His life was a feast of marvels and horrors, both natural and cultural, about which he felt nothing more acquisitive than the urge to record them.

His early journeys took him to Spain and the Levant. For three years he lived in Constantinople before returning overland to England. He then sailed to India and while working for the East India Company wrote extensively of the splendours of Shah Jahan's court. He witnessed the construction of the Taj Mahal ('The building is begun and goes on with excessive labour and cost, gold and silver being used like common metal'). After seven years he was back in Cornwall, back at Penryn, but soon grew fidgety. Returning to London 'to look for a voyage', he was offered another post in the East India Company, as well as a less secure opportunity, on an expedition of 'unknown design'. Without hesitation, he chose the latter and a year later found himself in China. It is a measure of the particular age of his travels that he recorded, in August 1637: 'The people there gave us a certain Drinke called Chaa which is only water with a kind of herbe boyled in it.' For seven more years he sailed back and forth to the

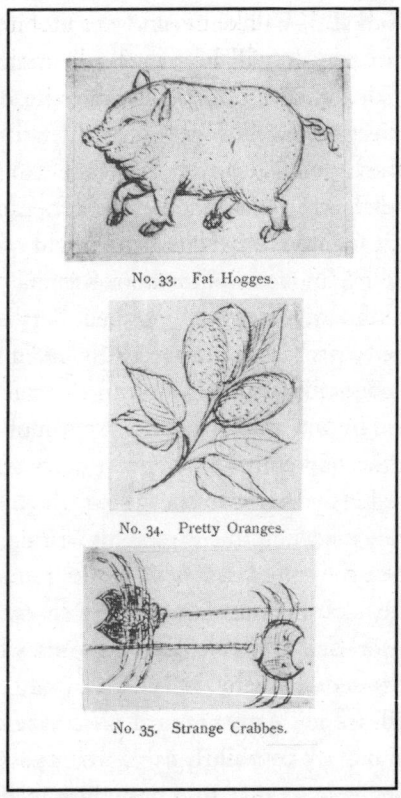

No. 33. Fat Hogges.

No. 34. Pretty Oranges.

No. 35. Strange Crabbes.

Drawings from The Travels of Peter Mundy.

Baltic, spending long periods in Prussia and Poland before reaching Archangel in the far north of Russia. He then retired to Penryn before leaving once more, at the age of almost 60, for a two-year journey to India and China.

And all the time he wrote and made drawings – 'fatte hogges, pretty oranges, strange crabs' reads one set of pictures. He described houses built of oyster shells near Canton, the organised spectacle of a fight between 'Madde Elephantts' in Ceylon, the manner of Ottoman torture, executions in Danzig and dress in Bremen. He described sucking-fish and sea-snails, skuas and weaver birds (comparing them to a Cornish 'gladdy' or yellowhammer), hunting leopards, buffalo sacrifices, dodos, hammer-head sharks and scallops four feet across. He recorded in detail the nautical practices of the harbours he visited and the strange rigs and hulls he saw. He learned a fair number of European languages, made a stab at Chinese characters and could converse in a fashion with the Samoyeds of northern Russia.

When not abroad, Mundy still roamed. Between voyages, he made a 'petty progresse' through England and Wales in order to 'follow my habituall disposition of travelling', and was in London in June 1658 to struggle through the crowds and draw a series of pictures of the great stranded whale that was also recorded by Pepys.

Peter Mundy made few mistakes in his writing. He did not exaggerate, nor rely on the tales of others to embellish his text. He rarely wrote about himself. He showed the same rapt humility for earthly wonders as for the stars which he lay back on a hundred different decks to examine through his own 'dear tellescope'. Astronomical observations filled his pages more and more frequently as the years passed, as if the sense of boundlessness that first drew him to sea could be reproduced in the heavens. 'As for the fixed stars, whether they be so many suns having worlds that goes about them, as this our earth wheeleth about our sun, it is beyond my poore capacity to determine … my reason tells me there is an immense unmeasurable endless space.' He was often able to approximate his position at sea by relating the times of the moon rising and the appearance of stars to times he knew for Falmouth (his travels predating the building of the Greenwich observatory).

Mundy had a keen eye for natural phenomena, but was also thrilled by the works of man. Wherever he went, he saw signs of progress, and witnessed several projects of a scale never seen before. First the Taj Mahal, then in the 1630s he was in Woolwich where Peter Pett showed him the half-model of Charles I's *Sovereign of the Seas*, as well as the ship itself, the keel already laid. Of all English ships, Mundy predicted, 'she will be the greatest and fairest ever built'. Days later he visited St Paul's Church and concluded that: 'These two wonderful structures, St Paul's for the land, and our great new ship for the seas, I believe, are not to be paralleled in the whole world.' Yet before the end of the century each would be destroyed by flames – St Paul's in the Great Fire and Pett's *Sovereign of the Seas* burned to the waterline at Chatham while waiting for a refit.

Peter Mundy's travels came at a pivotal time for the country's seaborne expansion. His career began when James I was building the *Prince Royal*. It continued, against the court-bound spirit of the early Stuarts, through the 1620s and thirties. By the time Mundy retired for good to the Fal, Charles II was on the throne and the distant seaways were growing familiar to British mariners. In *The Ocean in English History*, J. A. Williamson identified these years as the 'transition from one world to another': 'it would have seemed as out of character for Charles II to have allowed any step prejudicial to

English trade as it would for Charles I to have pursued any policy beneficial to it'.

Mundy was in London just after the Restoration, and saw Charles II's triumphal entry into the City of London. He describes in detail the efforts of his one-time employer, the East India Company, to impress on the new King the most rewarding direction for his royal energies: to send as many ships as possible to the East Indies. They had decorated their building in Leadenhall Street, adding special balconies and a tympanum of 'gallant ships sayling in the ocean'. In all his travels, Mundy wrote, he had never seen such a work so well done. Outside the building, beside the road, the company had built a model of a camel laden with spices. A boy was sitting on top of it, tossing bags of nutmeg, cloves and cinnamon into the crowd. The following year, Mundy wrote of a 'fleet of ships set sail for East India, including six frigates of the King's to take possession of Bombay'.

In London at that time, Mundy sensed the revived hunger for crossing oceans. He watched the construction of a dock at Blackwall, to hold as many as thirty large ships. In St James's Park he watched a pole erected with tackles and pulleys for a telescope. A thousand trees were imported to create an avenue along Pall Mall, a species he recognised from his time in Danzig as 'lindenbaum'. His entire lifetime of exotic sightings seemed to be reassembling itself by the day, in the middle of London. On his walks around the park and Pall Mall, he saw cranes and storks (whose springtime return he had once watched in Russia), spoonbills and pelicans on the newly dug lake. Nearby he saw a female bustard, peacocks, a cassowary, an elk, a cheetul, Indian antelopes and a 'small type of goat from Guinea'.

In September 1663, nearer 70 than 60, Peter Mundy declared his wandering days over: 'I resolved with my selfe at last to retire downe to my native country to end my sinfull weary daies.' He took a Falmouth ship, the *Goodwill*, for his final homebound journey. Coming round by Pendennis, he was amazed by the growth of the settlement he knew as Smithwick or Penny-come-quick. 'I can remember,' he wrote, 'when there was but one house there.' Now he found a town large enough to accommodate 400 French soldiers who had been waiting there a month for a ship.

On arrival at Penryn, he wrote: 'From thence I began my travels and here I hope to find my haven of rest.' Among his last entries are a great number of planetary observations and details of the comet of 1664. There remains no record of his death.

Twenty-seven years later, in 1691, a map of Falmouth was drawn by one of the town's publicans, George Withiel. It is lovingly done, each window and each shaded pitch-roof being picked out in a free black line. By now, two continuous facades run along the shoreside road, for over half a mile, from Greenbank right down to the new church of King Charles the Martyr and beyond, towards Arwenack. In its shape can be seen the future course of the High Street, Market Street and Arwenack Street. Half-built lanes run off in several directions, showing where the town would grow still further. From the same year comes an early estimate of the population, some 1,600. The previous estimate was 700, in 1664. In those twenty-seven years, Falmouth had grown by nearly two and a half times.

Withiel's map shows his own tavern, the Three Trumpets, standing across a small courtyard from the market-house, a grand two-storey building with a small steeple and three-storey tower – an impressive sight for all those climbing up the steps from the strand with their passage-weakened legs. Yet even here, amidst the solidity of the new port, it was not terra firma. Beneath the market-house was ground weakened by the deep incursions of the sea, and it was said that when a heavily laden cart passed along in front, the building perceptibly wobbled on its piles.

One afternoon in January, with a rare covering of snow outside the window of Truro's Cornwall Record Office, I am trawling the maritime catalogue when, by chance, I come across a manuscript entitled 'Avery the Pirate'. It turns out to be a single piece of paper. Carefully weighting its corners with lead snakes, I read:

Avery the Pirate
On his return from India either landed or shipwrecked near the Lizard where he buried three chests or boxes full of treasure in the sands of the seashore.

The particular site is described: 'About three miles east of the Lizard near three grey stones or rocks in a [blank]. WK says "these three rocks are covered with grass / now nearly overgrown with furze and grass".'

A couple of things make me think this is more than just some bar-room yarn jotted down at the end of an evening. It is partly in French and fairly specific (who was WK?). But perhaps more convincing are the elaborate details of what was buried:

1st chest – Haslar wood … in it were precious stones and bracelets large rubies sapphires emeralds topazes and diamonds.

*2nd chest … 120 ingots of gold 40 thick flat pieces of
gold as large as a round tobacco box, with various
characters on some of them. 25 bars of gold, some of
which were 4 or 5 inches long.*

*3rd chest has 3,000 pieces of 8 besides bullion
not weighed but crammed in with pieces
of brocades.*

I ask the archivists about the paper and they know nothing of
it, save that from its catalogue reference, it came with a
bundle of other documents from one of the larger houses in
Cornwall. I ask the family who lived there, but they know
nothing either.

The great expansion of oceanic trade that followed the
Restoration brought with it a corresponding rise in piracy.
Commercial enterprise raced ahead, outstripping the Navy's
capacity to defend it. Too many ships sailing too many miles,
with too much of value in their holds proved altogether too
tempting for the growing tribe of skilled and poorly paid
sailors. By the Victorian era, this period – the late seventeenth and early eighteenth centuries – was known, without
irony, as the Golden Age of Piracy. More than any others,
these years produced the popularised figure of the pirate.

One book in particular yielded details for a hundred
novels, films and prop boxes – the floppy shirts and
eyepatches, the cutlasses, the Jolly Roger. Published first in
May 1724, Charles Johnson's *A General History of the Robberies
and Murders of the Most Notorious Pirates* satisfied the ghoulish
appetite for violence, torture and sexual licence on the high
seas. J.M. Barrie, Walter Scott and Robert Louis Stevenson
all acknowledged the debt they owed to Johnson's book, and
first up in his rogues' gallery was 'Captain Avery', perpetrator

of what has been called 'one of the most successful crimes
ever committed'.

Avery was a West Country man. He was born probably at
Newton Ferrers, along the coast from Plymouth, in 1659.
Early acquaintance with the sea helped him climb the lower

J 2277

...es landed or was shipwrecked
three chests or boxes full of
...shore

du Lig. pres trois pierres grises
...d'ouest des trois pierres
now nearly overgrown with furz & grass.
...sont couvertes with grass,
high promontory juts out into
...tides now come over the place.
...feet long & 1 f wide. In it were precious
...in emeralds topazes & diamonds
...size & make as the first 120
...of gold as large as a round tobacco
...of them. 25 bars of gold, some of
...of 8. Besides Bullion not weighed but

rungs of the naval ladder. He was first mate on the privateer
Charles II when, en route to the Caribbean, he led a mutiny
at La Coruña. He and his men put their captain ashore,
renamed the ship the *Fancy* and sailed her round the Cape of
Good Hope. They cut away much of the ship's upperworks

to increase her speed and in September 1695 headed for the entrance to the Red Sea, to the straits of Bab el-Mandeb. There they joined forces with a couple of other smaller pirate vessels, lying in wait for pilgrims. The *hajj* was over and the faithful were returning home, thousands of wealthy Muslims from Mughal India. Soon the *Fancy* was giving chase to the *Ganj-i-Sawai*, the flagship of a pilgrim fleet on the passage back to Surat. Avery gained on them and, though the Indian ship was larger and more heavily gunned, a lucky shot from the *Fancy* toppled the mainmast and the pirates swarmed aboard.

The captain of the *Ganj-i-Sawai* was Ibrahim Khan and when he saw the Englishmen leaping on the deck of his ship he fled below, sending up to resist them a group of Arab girls he had bought for his harem. But they and the ship's company were soon overwhelmed. The Arab girls were shared out among Avery's men who, for the next three days, worked their way not only through all of these girls but through all the other women of the ship, servants and nobles, young and old. A number of the women killed themselves to escape the pirates, using knives or cutlasses or leaping over the rail and into the sea. The pirates tortured the other passengers to reveal the hiding-places of their jewels. Reports vary as to how much was looted – but the *Ganj-i-Sawai* carried a large number of the Mughal rich with their attendant wealth. Among the haul were thousands of specie, gold coins, silver, and an ornamental saddle decorated with rubies and intended for Emperor Aurangzeb himself.

When at last the wreck of the *Ganj-i-Sawai* limped into Surat, the Indians were horrified. A mob at once marched on the place which was guilty by association – the compound of the East India Company. An Indian force was despatched to guard the merchants and ended up effectively imprisoning them – for a full nine months. When the emperor heard of the outrages, he threatened to banish every one of the English merchants from his empire; his ministers, predicting economic collapse if the English left, talked him out of it.

The pirates themselves scattered. Each was allowed a share of the booty. Some used it to set themselves up as citi-

John Avery.

zens of the American colonies. Others settled in the West Indies; some were caught and hanged; one was eaten by a shark. Avery himself abandoned the *Fancy* in the Caribbean and disappeared. He was never caught.

Avery's mythology started to grow as soon as news of his crime leaked out. A book, purportedly by a Dutch prisoner of Avery's, tells how the *Ganj-i-Sawai* actually belonged to the Mughal emperor, and that his own daughter was on board. Avery at once fell for the princess and spared her from his men. They married and, with Avery as the noble brigand, set up a semi-utopian pirate state on an island off Madagascar. This fanciful account in turn spawned a notoriously bad play called *The Successful Pyrate* staged at Tom Killigrew's old theatre in Drury Lane in 1712. Daniel Defoe was the probable author of a much more competent novel about Avery, *The King of the Pirates*. Charles Johnson's *A General History of the Robberies and Murders of the Most Notorious Pirates*, presented as a factual account, also dipped into the soup that blended the true events of Avery's life with some spicy fictions.

From the same brew, just six years after the taking of the *Ganj-i-Sawai*, comes evidence of the first rumours of hidden treasure in Cornwall. An entry in the State Papers for February 1701 records a response to a letter from a Mr St Lo: 'The King has been acquainted with your letter of the 4th inst., concerning treasure said to be hid by some of the pirates of Avery's crew in Cornwall. You are to search for the treasure according to the information that is given you.' A reward was offered for its discovery, far less in all probability than the value of the finds. Perhaps that is why no further record exists.

I copy down the details of the manuscript and head down to the wreck coast south of Falmouth. The fishing village of

Cadgwith is 'about three miles east of the Lizard'. Striding the cliffs just to the north, and at Kennack Sands, I spot several possible-looking 'grass-covered rocks'. But out in the sun, with the vastness of the winter sea before me, and the years passed since Avery's deed, the idea of even looking for his loot seems absurd. Buried treasure! A pirate map!

Later, in a sudden shower of slanting rain, I accept a lift in a pick-up from a local man who for twenty years, it turns out, had been piecing together Avery's story. He is both coast-guard and driftwood artist, and becomes a little silent when I tell him of my interest in Avery. But I reassure him; I am not going to start digging. Giving him the reference to the manuscript in the Record Office, I wish him good luck and jump back down into the darkness.

CHAPTER 14

August, mid-late eighteenth century: no wind, the sea flat ...

On Harvey's Quay and Customs Quay, stevedores lie among the shoreside bundles of cordage and tarpaulins, the cloth-bales, fish maunds and timber stacks. From the open door of the King's Hotel comes the clicking of billiard balls. The wharfinger, tide surveyor, the excise men and the Packet agent sit in their offices. High above the town, in the fields around the windmill, harvesters are raking up the mowings in the afternoon heat.

The sound of boots on the dry road – *Packet!* Down from the Beacon – *Packet, Packet!* The boy is running into Market Strand, shouting to the mail station in Bell's Court, pocketing a coin from the women with husbands aboard, and on to the Middle Quay which is already abuzz: carters harness animals, porters grab barrows and officials call for punt crews. Cutch-brown sails go up, moorings are dropped.

Out at Pendennis Point, a small crowd is watching the Packet ship's approach, cheering as she strikes her bonnets and fires her signal-gun. They are scanning her sails and standing rigging for signs of battle. As she passes, they follow her, walking at first, then trotting as she rounds the head and into the harbour. Everyone is straining for the first sight of a familiar face, shouting questions, names; news of health and blessings mix with the cries of hawkers, and accounts of the journey – of encounters with privateers or Atlantic gales, of ships hailed and ships seen. Later, in the cool of the evening, the ship's company and their families will gather again on the decks and, to the sound of pipers and fiddlers, they will dance.

But for now there are passengers to be steered towards this inn or that lodging, to the barber, or the tailor. And cargo too: off come the crates of bullion, the surplus in the nation's trade converted into gold specie, dollars and moidores (speed and safety make the Falmouth Packet the ship of choice for bankers and merchants). The crates are rowed across the harbour. Heaved ashore, they are then hauled up to the specially built cave, dug into the town's hill and lined with sheet iron. They will await there the arrival of Russell & Co.'s coaches and a journey to London of almost a week, slow enough for the armed guards to walk beside them.

Less cumbersome and less visible are the bundles and cases brought up from below decks, the private ventures of master, officers and crew alike. There are bolts of fine cloth,

LEAVING THE OFFICES, KILLIGREW STREET EVERY MONDAY AT NOON, AND ARRIVING AT THE CASTLE AND FALCON INN, ALDERSGATE STREET, LONDON, ON THE FOLLOWING SATURDAY?

wine and fruit, and they are given no more than a 'fog-spectacled' glance by the revenue men, before being taken away by wholesalers who wait on the quays.

Yet none of these is the real purpose of the ships, none is Falmouth's lifeblood, nor the driver of its growth and its sustained prosperity. That rests in the leather case that comes ashore first. A couple of feet square, the pouch contains ministerial letters, governors' reports, accounts and military despatches.

For 150 years, from its selection in 1688, Falmouth was the nation's principal Packet port. The Post Office ran an official service first to La Coruña and Lisbon, then the West Indies, and New York, Halifax, the Mediterranean, Mexico, Rio de Janeiro and finally Buenos Aires. Falmouth's maritime success was based not on bales of wool loaded for export, nor on the products of the Cornish mines, nor sugar or tobacco or wine or slaves, nor on the presence of a naval fleet, but on an abstract commodity that would grow in importance over the coming centuries. Falmouth's trade was *information*.

The cases or portmanteaux were made of thick leather, oiled and re-oiled to withstand sea spray, Caribbean heat and the freezing nights of the North Atlantic. In Bell's Court, on warm summer days, they could be seen like hide-thick pillowcases hanging out to dry; in winter, the agent's assistant sat before the fire, restitching the bags' seams. At sea, they were often kept out on deck under a tarpaulin and inside them, alongside the documents, were carried two standard-issue lumps of Post Office pig-iron. If a sail was spotted, the bags could be swiftly suspended over the side, where, to avoid capture, a single cutlass-slash would send them plunging into the water.

Every few days, announced by a loud horn, the mails would arrive in Falmouth, brought down the turnpike from Exeter and London. Already, to gain time, the receiving Packet ship would have been warped out into the Carrick Roads, and even as the gig was crossing the harbour, coming alongside to hand the pouch up to outstretched hands, she was making sail.

Falmouth was chosen for its unrivalled nautical advantages: no need to beat down the Channel and risk the gauntlet of French privateers. In prevailing westerlies, the packets could comfortably fetch Ushant and the Bay of Biscay, La Coruña and Lisbon, or sail round into the Mediterranean, or pick up the trades to cross the Atlantic.

Official duty did nothing to rob Falmouth's commanders of their buccaneering instincts. Sometimes they returned with prizes, whole captured ships – infuriating the Postmaster General for risking the mail. But in the eighteenth century, most maritime activity still retained the unbounded spirit of the sixteenth, producing the same blend of impulsive heroism and greed, technological innovation and hubris. 'Among men of the sea,' wrote one nautical historian of the time, 'the ocean was regarded in the light of a lucky bag, into which you thrust your hand and pulled out the best thing you could find.'

The first Packet agent in Falmouth was Daniel Gwin, whose lucrative web of cuts and perks, when discovered, led to a £10,000 fine. For sixty years, the position of agent (perks still available) was passed down through a single family, the Bells. Eventually, in 1784, the Postmaster General in London grew tired of the abuses. His investigator uncovered some spectacular rackets. Agents and commanders were claiming for full crews and carrying fewer; sending a chit for illness if the commander did not wish to go to sea, assuring the PMG that such and such a Packet ship left Falmouth in good trim, when in fact the gunwales were low from private ventures. The Post Office contracted the Packet ships from the owners who added to their income by carrying passengers and by smuggling wares for Bristol merchants. The 1784 investigation revealed that Stephen Bell, the agent, owed a great deal of money to the service. Bell borrowed more to cover his debts, but in doing so the water around him merely rose higher. In July 1785 he took his own life.

In 1763, with the end of the Seven Years War, British supremacy of the oceans became more or less unchallenged. In his towering work *The Influence of Sea Power upon History*, Alfred Mahan suggested that there was just 'one nation that gained in this war'. Britain, he wrote, 'used the sea in peace to earn its wealth, and ruled it in war by the extent of its Navy, by the number of its subjects who lived on the sea, and by its numerous bases of operations scattered over the globe'.

It was at this time, too, that Falmouth entered its period of greatest activity, serving many of those numerous bases with its Packet ships. Deep in the storeroom of the Falmouth Art Gallery is an ink-drawn plan from this time: *AN ACCURATE MAP OF THE TOWN OF FALMOUTH As was found in the year of Our Lord 1773*. Moving a magnifying glass over its age-greyed surface feels like peering down from the clouds, inspecting a new type of global settlement, with little spillage inland and its gaze set firmly seaward.

The map still shows a shoreside strip, much longer than it is deep. From the main street, running along beside the sea, alleys and small pockets of residence now push up the hill. By combining the map with contemporary accounts and leases from the Record Office, it is possible to reconstruct something of the town.

Three granite quays push out to mid-tide and beyond, enclosing a number of larger vessels. Out in the harbour several ocean-going ships are anchored; numerous smaller craft busy themselves between them. On the new South Quay is the searcher's office; the Charles Quay has the tide surveyor, the watch house and weights house. On the Middle Quay stands the main Custom House. Beneath it, in the Lord's Cellar, are stored bales of contraband tobacco; and from time to time, to stop anyone else from trying to deny the Crown its duty on the trade, the stores are taken and batch-burned in the adjoining oven. The fat brick chimney which funnels the smoke upwards has become known to all as the King's Pipe.

The Market Strand is busier than ever. The Flushing ferry takes Packet commanders back and forth, and they jostle with the traders and seamen running to and fro with victuals and tackle. Just up the leat stand two grist mills and the brew-houses of Rogers and Webber. Pentecost Orchard has long been covered by gardens and stable yards and the dwelling known as Newman's house. Framed by hawthorn and bram-bles are the fresh quarry scars, the ferrous-streaked slate receding into the earth, blast by blast.

Southwards, along Market Street, run two rows of lodg-ings and trade-yards and shops and offices – tallow suppliers, Bluett the attorney, McLellan the upholsterer, Williams the barber and periwig-maker. Banfield's new Falmouth Bank stands among them. In open lofts, teams of seamsters stitch at sailcloth. There is a cotton warehouse, full of 'Manchester Goods', and beyond the church and the quays stretches a brand-new row of town houses into whose five-storey facades has been poured wealth from the furthest corners of the known world. Then quite suddenly, like a speaker inter-rupted, the buildings end and the town gives ways to trees

Arwenack in the eighteenth century.

and underwood. In their midst, unexplained and unvisited, stands a strange granite pyramid.

One afternoon, in March 1787, waiting for a Packet ship for Portugal, William Beckford wandered southwards through the town. When he reached the grove, he was struck by the silence. Coming through the trees, he stumbled across the ruins of Arwenack Manor and, though he made no mention of it, glimpsed something of the Killigrews' vanished presence: 'I spied the skeleton of a gothic mansion, so completely robed with thick ivy, as to appear like one of those castles of clipped box I have often seen in a Dutch garden.'

CHAPTER 15

The Packet service was not the Royal Navy and the records that have survived are scarce. By the end of the nineteenth century, long after messages were sent around the world by other means, little was remembered of the crews of the Falmouth Packets. But in a drawer in St Ives lay a memoir which gives a startling account not just of serving aboard the Packet ships but of a life shaped by the scattering force of the sea.

In the early 1920s the memoir was discovered in three tall notebooks, and handed to a Penzance bookseller, a Mr Bridger. He in turn showed them to a local writer, the mysterious Crosbie Garstin, who was then living near the artist's colony at Lamorna. Garstin was the author of a number of books himself including *China Seas* which drew on his years adventuring in the Far East and was eventually made into a film with Clark Gable. He had also written the Penhale trilogy of novels, and recognised at once the merits of the notebooks.

Garstin worked at them, cut them down and published what was left in 1925. One night a few years later, rowing aboard a yacht in Salcombe harbour, Garstin drowned. (Some say that he faked his death and returned to the Far East, and one credible report survives of an old man in London in the 1960s claiming to be Crosbie Garstin.)

The three notebooks are now held in an anonymous bottle-green folder at the Cornwall Record Office. On a morning in late February I take them over to a desk by the window. A piece of stiffening card lies inside the folder, and beneath it is the marbled cover of the first notebook. A hand-written label in the middle reads: *Life and Travels Volume I*. The pages themselves are covered in brandy-coloured ink, 200 years old, in a neat, well-ordered hand which opens on the title-page with the words: '*A short account of Samuel Kelly, whose days have been few and evil …*'

Samuel Kelly was an ordinary seaman of the age, in the sense that he fought no heroic battles, made no fortune and suffered no wrecks (though he was captured once, by an American privateer). Yet there is something mythic in the scale of his experiences, as well as in those of his roguish (and much-wrecked) father Michael. Samuel's account is told with such candour and colour that only the announcement that the Record Office is closing pulls me away; I return the next morning and finish that afternoon. After seventeen years at sea and 100,000 miles, Samuel Kelly stepped ashore in London and went to bed for two months, unable to move or eat. Neither apothecary nor physician could halt his decline. Within weeks, he had become 'no more than a skeleton'. Friends, he wrote, wept when they visited him, and as his condition worsened he himself became 'alarmed from fear of appearing soon at the Bar of Divine justice'. But no one could identify his illness. In the end he made his own diagnosis: 'I now discovered my whole life had been a scene of rebellion against the most High God.' Having been, until that moment, about as godly as any other seaman (in other words, more superstitious than faithful), he called for a preacher. Every day, the preacher called on Kelly and in time helped him impose some order

Samuel Kelly's Life & Voyages, Vol. III.

on his ship-tossed thoughts. His flesh reappeared and an equable balance returned to his soul – but he never went to sea again.

Samuel Kelly was drawn to the maritime life by an early childhood spent on Falmouth's wharves. He paddled in the shallows around Bar Pool and watched the harbour's endlessly changing cast of hull and sail. His father Michael, a trader captain working the route to South Carolina, was only an occasional presence. Long paternal absences, interspersed by sudden flurries of charm and gifts and stories, helped create in young Samuel a sense of yearning for his father's world and all that lay beyond Pendennis Point.

When he was 11, Samuel fought off a bout of scarlet fever. By that time his mother was dead, as well as several of his sisters. His anxious father, to aid Samuel's recovery, offered the only remedy he knew. He took the boy to sea, on a voyage across the Atlantic to Charleston. There, as he recalled many years later, Samuel saw exotic birds flitting among the trees of a tea garden. He saw the white-boarded mansions of the planters and squads of men training to resist the government. With some disappointment he watched as his father's ship was filled with rice for the return trip to Falmouth. Samuel was seasick for much of the time, but the thrill of the journey set the course of his life: 'During my voyage I was treated by my father with so much tenderness and indulged with so much fruit, nuts, etc., and brought home such a number of birds that caused me to wish to be placed at sea.'

Samuel's manuscript begins with his father. Michael Kelly emerges as a freewheeling, picaresque figure, rather the opposite of his sensitive son. But each in the end learned separate versions of the same mariner's lesson, that you submit to a capricious god when you go to sea.

Michael Kelly had been born in the early eighteenth century, in Ireland, on the banks of the River Shannon. He started out as an army officer, but soon found that his natural impulses could not be contained by the parade square and mess-life. He sold his commission and joined the Navy. He saw action aboard a naval frigate, but again broke free, for the looser regime on merchant ships. Soon he had his own command. Once, he woke to find his entire night watch missing – washed overboard or snatched by another ship – he never discovered which.

It is easy to picture this happy-go-lucky man yarning to his eldest son in Falmouth during his brief returns, speaking of the bounty and misadventures, confirming for the boy that any other life would not be worth living. Michael spoke of the years he had spent in the Caribbean smuggling goods between Jamaica and the Spanish Main.

'But unfortunately,' he explained, 'I was captured, and made to work like a slave in the silver mines – but I escaped! Escaped to the Indians until I tried to take my leave and discovered I was a captive there too.'

Trying to recall the words of his father years later, Samuel believed he said he'd killed his Indian guard as he slept in a hammock. Michael then fled to sea in a small boat, an ocean tramp again, with nothing to his name but sea-skills. In Kingston he found better luck with a wealthy woman, a Mary Thomas. He married her and, when she died a few years later, inherited a comfortable sum. He returned to trading, this time owning a share in the merchantman he commanded, the *General Wolfe*.

Like many masters before and many since, Michael Kelly discovered the perils of a Cornish landfall. Driven into St Ives Bay he battled to beat away from the shore, dropped his bower anchor but couldn't prevent the *General Wolfe* foundering. Breathless and dripping, Michael and his crew stumbled ashore at St Ives with little more than a few bottles of

Kingston rum. Soon Michael was wooing a young woman in the town named Mary Wheelwright. Before long they were engaged. But first, he told her, with a phrase familiar to a thousand women of the time, he had to go back to sea. In Jamaica he collected his belongings and his money. On the way back, he suffered another shipwreck and lost everything. So it was as a pauper again that he reached St Ives and married his second Mary.

Michael and Mary Kelly waited for children for four years before Samuel was born. After that the births came at the rate of more than one a year. By the time they had six, they were living in Falmouth with Michael sailing the *Admiral Spry* on regular trips to South Carolina.

Falmouth in the 1760s was approaching its prime, with a constant flow of crews and passengers, zealots, misfits and exotic goods. In 1762, when three ships arrived from China and sold their silks and tea, not only Falmouth but the entire region was said to have been emptied of ready cash (and the Customs received not a penny).

Michael was at sea when Mary died giving birth to their seventh child. Over the coming years, four of the daughters died too. Samuel and his brother, just thirteen months younger than him, were sent to school in Helston until, after three years, Michael Kelly deemed his eldest son ready for sea. He found him a place on the *Thynne*, a Packet ship of 200 tons, fourteen three-pounders and eight swivel guns, chartered to the Post Office. His father sponsored his place in the mess, telling the captain there was no need to pay the boy just so long as he was well looked after, and properly introduced to the arts of the ship.

But it didn't happen that way. From the moment he boarded the *Thynne*, Samuel's view of the world began to change: 'I may date the beginnings of the troubles of my life from this period.' With the Manacles slipping astern, he sensed the first waves of nausea. Unable to eat, he lacked the strength to assert his position, lost his bunk, had his chest thrown down below and crawled around the deck, unwashed and sleeping in corners. When it was time for his watch, he was doused with chilling water to stop from him from sleeping. Often he would wake to find his face had been tarred.

For seven years, he suffered from seasickness. But such was his conviction that ships were his destiny that he remained afloat. In time the sickness eased, making way for all the other perils of sailing on an eighteenth-century Packet ship. On one crossing, verdigris on the copper cooking pans left the crew half-poisoned, while the lead flashing of the fire-place melted and the fire was only just contained. One night in port, returning from an evening ashore, the cook fell between two moored ships and was drowned.

Samuel liked to climb high up into the maintop, where he slept 'for hundreds of hours' with a box of gunpowder as a pillow. Tropical storms would wake him, booming and flashing around his head. From the mainmast, the topmast rose another thirty feet, flexing in a swell 'like a coachman's whip'. He would have to haul himself up to set the skysail. Sometimes the ship's baboon – a vast and vicious creature named 'the Evil' – escaped, and with bared teeth scrambled up the mast to chase him to the very tip of the topgallant yard.

In March 1782 he began an eventful trip on another Falmouth Packet, the *Grenville*. A few days out of Madeira, heading west, they were closed by a ship that turned out to be an American privateer. The Packet captain ordered the portmanteau to be sunk. He surrendered the ship. Samuel hid on board the *Grenville* while the others were taken as prisoners to Boston. He emerged, blinking, from his hiding place and at once began to help the small prize-crew. When the Americans discovered the pipes of sweet Madeira, the able hands were reduced further. The wind freshened to a gale. They took hours to reduce sail, the guns broke loose; water soaked their food. They were too hungry and short-handed to escape when a few days later, another ship gave chase. This time it was an English ship whose crew captured Samuel's captors (before helping themselves to whatever they wanted on board). They then sailed the *Grenville* into the small pocket of King's territory that had survived at Charleston.

The town had been transformed since Samuel's first visit as a wide-eyed and convalescent boy. The planters' mansions were half-ruined, the statue of Lord Chatham spattered with shot. A mere two years after the siege and with the American lines just inland, the town was a place of nightmares. One day in the reeds he gazed at a dead alligator; on another he witnessed a slave, who had stolen a goat, being tarred and rolled in white feathers and paraded through the town. Samuel wandered Charleston's streets as if in a dream; the experience at last punctured his innocence.

'All appeared void and waste,' he reflected on this period years later, 'like the soul of a natural man unrenewed by grace.'

One of the most striking features of Samuel Kelly's manu-script is the sense it gives of an Atlantic village, a closely connected network of stops, with Falmouth at its north-eastern corner. A mariner might sail thousands of miles of open sea, landing on any one of dozens of islands, up and down vast stretches of seaboard, then tie up alongside a ship whose decks he had once worked on. It was rare to meet another seaman who did not have news of some acquaintance or other, of the fate of a former ship or friend. In Charleston another Packet lay in the harbour and it was no surprise to find that the captain's father was the Falmouth neighbour of Samuel's own father. When the captain's brother was placed in charge of the crewless *Grenville* for her return journey to Falmouth, Samuel found him to be none other than his old friend, his 'boon companion' from boyhood.

Over the coming years, Samuel encountered more of destiny's sea-borne trickery: in Philadelphia he met a man whose mother was the landlady of two of his own sisters. In Rotherhithe he was delighted to come across the crew of his first Packet ship the *Thynne*. The carpenter took him to have tea in Fleet Prison where he found, in a cell, his old friend the boatswain from another former ship, the *King George* (the boatswain had been convicted of some ill-advised speculation). Some time later he heard with horror that the *Grenville*, her name changed to *Earl of Shelburn*, had been lost with all hands returning to Falmouth from New York. Once, in London, he was pulled up short by a shop window in the Strand. There he spotted a book about the *Antelope* – a ship that he had been invited to join once when she lay in the Carrick Roads. She had disappeared on the same voyage.

Sometimes, on a busy dockside, Samuel would catch news of his father. He was married again, to a woman from Penzance. What she and Michael had had in common was the delusion that the other had money. She died giving birth to their only child. Samuel heard of his father's death sometime in the mid-1780s, while working on a transport as a 'drudge' for a female captain. Samuel's once-large family was reduced now to one sister in Cornwall and his beloved brother John. In the autumn of 1785 Samuel tracked down John to lodgings in Deptford. Since leaving Helston, they had both been at sea and had not laid eyes on each other.

Now the great ocean-orbits of their lives spun them together again. Those few weeks he recorded in fond detail, a respite from the toil and isolation of deck-life.

Samuel found John to be 'possessed of all that spirit and generosity incident to the character of British seamen' – much more akin to their father Michael than the prudent Samuel. Crossing Tower Hill, he was amazed to see beggars crawling towards him, calling 'John! John!' in order to receive the ha'pennies that he always handed out. Under John's influence, Samuel bought town clothes, a blue coat and ruffled shirt, and had his hair powdered. The two brothers spent their Sundays not in worship but in paying visits to friends and sauntering through St James's Park. They went to the theatre together – to Tom Killigrew's Drury Lane Theatre – but only, claimed Samuel, to look upon the King and Queen and their family. They said goodbye on the docks, as Samuel boarded a ship for Falmouth. John had a place on a ship bound for Canton. He hoped to qualify as a fourth mate. Samuel never saw him again. In China, John fell out with his shipmates and went ashore, and that was the last anyone heard of John Kelly.

Samuel himself took a few weeks to sail back to Falmouth. Some years had passed since he last had leave in Cornwall and it was something of a homecoming. He met up with old friends in Falmouth, then travelled to his mother's town of St Ives. Everyone wanted to see him, from the town crier to the sexton. One man invited him to his house where he opened a bottle of Jamaica rum rescued by Samuel's father from the wreck of the *General Wolfe*. He saw his only surviving sister. His uncle unwrapped a cloth and showed Samuel what his father had bequeathed him, the paltry scrapings from a life at sea – a silver watch, some buckles, a razor and brush, a few charts, a quadrant and a hat.

Ten years later Samuel himself crossed the Atlantic for the last time, returning from Kingston with a cargo of coffee. It was a terrible voyage. He was now a commander and his crew mutinied before weighing anchor, demanding money. The mate spent the journey dipping into the rum puncheons, sleeping on watch; the hull leaked, the sails were rotten and the halyards parted in any sort of a blow. In London, the ship's apron was found to be rotten at the stem. She was put up for sale at Lloyd's Coffee House but, failing to find a buyer, was scrapped. At the same time Samuel developed his mystery illness which turned out, he wrote later, to be 'principally soul trouble'. When he recovered enough to leave London it was by coach. He never returned to sea.

Samuel Kelly went to live in St Ives, setting up in trade. He married and raised a family. Martha, his only surviving sibling, married a Customs man on the Thames, but died with the birth of her first child. Another seventeen years passed before Samuel began the account of his seafaring days. His motive in doing so was, he claimed, 'amusement'. Yet although there is no shortage of wonder on his voyages, the tenor is one of worldly toil and suffering – 'my past pilgrimage through this Wilderness'. His father had ended up lying on a bed in lodgings in Falmouth, with only money enough left to pay for his own funeral. Samuel himself had nothing to show for his years at sea. As he wrote his account, of a time of ceaseless movement, from Colombia to Ireland, Malaga to New York, he too was afflicted by 'a great debility of body and mind' and for more than twenty months was unable to walk further than the end of his garden in St Ives.

CHAPTER 16

Winter drags on. After weeks of gales and cold easterlies, there comes a morning in late February when the skies clear and the air warms with such suddenness that it is like waking up in another country. The tides are making, so I drive *Liberty* into the beach and let her drop gently on the ebb. I lie on the shingle and reach in under the hull to scrub off the winter's gathering of marine life. Along the keel-band is an aquarium of sea squirts and mussels and tiny shoots of channelled wrack. Fronds of algae hang from the garboards. Each of the clinker-seams is thick with growth. These places never really dry out; the water itself swells the boards to seal them. To give them as much time as possible to drain, I wait until the last moment – until the tide is coming in again and tiny waves are nudging at the rudder – to mask up the boot-line and put on the paint. I lie down again to roller on the first line of burgundy antifoul paint. The sun bounces off the rising water, and makes flickering reflections on the under-hull.

Below-waterline fouling is one of those marine questions whose solution invariably creates more trouble, a reminder of the essential hubris of being on the water. It happens so often with boats – you deal with some minor dilemma, make an improvement, then find that it causes some other problem: in no other context is the law of unforeseen consequences so diligently enforced than at sea.

Breaming was the method once used – burning off the weed. The sheltered beaches of Falmouth harbour were used for centuries to rid hulls of weed in this way. But with increasing demands on shipping, such a method proved less and less convenient (it also happened that many craft burst into flames). Until recently, TBTs (*Tributyltin compounds*) were used in antifoul paint, and their gradual leaching created a very effective cordon around the boat. But it was also highly poisonous. Chipped and sandblasted from a thousand hulls, tons of TBTs now rest on the seabed around Falmouth and other ports, a layer of sediment paper-thin in geological terms but one that will remain toxic for years.

Lying on the beach in waterproofs and applying the antifoul (now TBT-free), I recall an extraordinary description of Samuel Kelly's. From his Packet ship he witnessed the aftermath of one of the worst marine disasters of the eighteenth century – and one which owed a good deal to a misguided antifouling treatment.

In August 1782 Kelly left Falmouth on the *Thynne* to sail up the Channel to London. Off the Isle of Wight, they discovered that a length of anchor cable was damaged, so bore away and made for Portsmouth. Passing the Mother Bank, they spotted the top masts of a wreck, and were astonished to hear it was the *Royal George*, one of the greatest of the Navy's ships. As the tide fell, Kelly watched more of the spars emerge. Hanging from them, caught in the stays and lifts and yards, suspended by their feet and arms, were dozens of bodies.

When ships began to sail to the tropics, not only were journeys made dangerously long by weed-dragging hulls, but a new creature found its way into the fertile habitat of ocean vessels: the shipworm, *Teredo navalis*. Stirred into feeding by warmer water, these tiny creatures regarded a wooden hull as

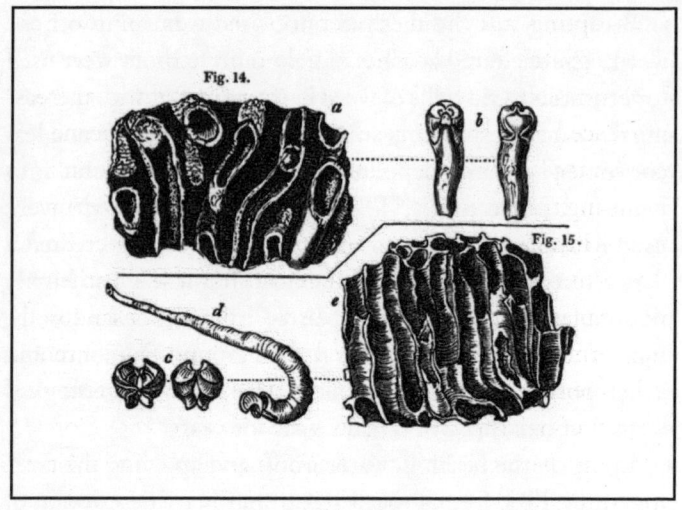

Ship-worm (teredo navalis).

one big feast, as they happily drilled their shell up and down the strakes, into oak knees and stringers, until inch by inch the vessel fell apart. Shipowners took to covering the hull in an outer skin, a sacrificial layer of planking, but the worms soon bored through this. At the same time, to prevent weed, various compounds were smeared on the boards – made from such things as tar, pitch, train oil and sulphur, and known by the workers who had to apply them variously as 'white stuff', 'black stuff' and 'brown stuff'.

From the late seventeenth century, with British power more and more dependent on its merchant fleet and its Navy, a new protection was developed that kept out both worm and weed – metal sheathing. Lead was used at first until it was found to wear. Also there was a strange corrosion of iron fittings (now understood to be electrolysis). By the mid-eighteenth century, experiments were being made with copper and it was found that if the rudder-irons were made with cuprous alloy and copper trenails used for the hull fastenings, the ship was safe. But to replace every iron nail was impossible on such a scale, so an ingenious safeguard was introduced to keep the metals separate: a layer of lacquered paper was placed between the copper sheath and the hull.

During the Seven Years War, a vast programme of coppering was instigated. By the end of 1781 every ship of the Royal Navy – more than 300 – had been sealed and sheathed in copper plates. At last, British ships were free from the risk of shipworm. Devoid of weed, naval craft outsailed their French and American counterparts. Commodore Byron kept the *Dolphin* cruising for two years without careening. Copper sheathing, he declared, is the 'finest Invention in the World'.

The following year, in August, a fleet assembled and anchored off Spithead. Under Lord Howe, the ships prepared to sail for Gibraltar to relieve the besieged garrison. Among them rode the *Royal George*. Over 2,000 tons, with 100 guns, the *Royal George* had taken ten years to build; her timbers required the clearing of 110 acres of broad-leaved woodland. When completed in 1756 the *Royal George* was the world's largest ship. She had served in the Western Squadron and as Hawke's flagship at the Battle of Quiberon Bay – the Trafalgar of the Seven Years War. Now, in 1782, with her bottom sheathed in copper, she had just returned from a cruise to fit out and revictual in a very short time.

On the afternoon of 29 August the task was almost complete. A lighter lay alongside loading the last caskets of rum. Admiral Kempenfelt – whose system of signals was to revolutionise naval communication – was in his cabin; his barber had just left. For fear of desertion, shore-leave had been cancelled and the *Royal George*'s company of 800 was swollen by families and friends, sweethearts, bumboat women, prostitutes, money-lenders and itinerant hawkers. A

febrile atmosphere pervaded the ship, combining the celebration of a last day out with the anxiety of sailing to war.
One final repair was being made – the intake for the deck-
wash required work. To bring the small hole up above sea-
level, the officer of the watch called for the ship to be heeled
over by three or four inches. Down below, the starboard guns
were brought in amidships while on the other side they were
run out. What happened next is disputed. Some say it was a
breeze that caught the hull, others that it was the weight of
the rum detail and the sloop, or perhaps the shifted guns, but
water began to flood the gunports, the heel increased and a
great noise was heard far below. The added stress of the heel
and the guns brought to a head what had been going on
unnoticed for months: the copper sheathing had been slowly
corroding her frame. The *Royal George* went down so fast
that none of the neighbouring ships had a chance to do
anything. Nearly 900 died, including Admiral Kempenfelt
and more than 200 women.

Her loss confirmed an alarming trend: many of the ships
that had been so carefully copper-plated sank within three
years. The lacquer paper was found to work loose with the
natural flexing of the ship. In another spectacular feat of
logistics, the Navy Board recalled the entire fleet and replaced
the iron fastenings with copper.

From his Packet ship, Samuel Kelly spent several days
assisting with the clearing up of the *Royal George*, and his
description blends a sense of fascination and horror. He
himself manned a capstan which dropped and hoisted a
diving bell, in which a Bengali man went down inside a great
lead-lipped bowl and walked on the sunken decks.

But he felt, too, profound compassion for the victims.
Writing from his Cornish retirement, his particular concern
was that they had spent their last hours in 'debauchery and

drunkenness' and, as the ship went down, had no time to rinse their souls of sin.

With her new coating of antifoul, I take *Liberty* across to Falmouth. It's a fresh March morning, the wind cool from the north. Clouds are congregating over the land like cattle at a trough, while out to sea the sky is clear. I come in around the docks and see the town spread out: a low sweep of shore-side walls and windows following the land-rise to the left, up from Arwenack to the shoulder of Porhan Hill, then a sharp dip down to the Moor, and down to Smithwick. I pick up a friend's mooring, drop the loop over the samson post and row ashore.

Taking the old road to the north-west, I walk out of town towards Penryn. The road runs parallel to the river and is flanked by a series of buildings, each an imprint of the people who make up Falmouth's sea-gazing past. Near the site of 'Cock's great house' stand the pricey new developments named Admiral's Quays and Packet Quays, and then the real Packet houses, set back from a raised pavement, a row of Georgian facades, stucco-fronted, slate-clad or brick, each as different from the next as the commanders who built them. Beyond them are the more leisurely villas of the Victorian age, leading on out to low-topped terraces and then the 1920s bungalows with names like 'Barquentine', 'Port of Call' and 'Idle Moorings' and swinging signs offering 'B&B – Ensuite – TV'.

Reaching the ringroad, I try to match my photocopied map to what I can see – two roundabouts, a stretch of waste ground and, beyond it, the rippling flags of Vospers Ford New Car Sales. In the sales hall of Vospers, a man is buffing an already over-buffed Focus. He swivels hopefully at the ding-dong of the mat sensor.

'Sorry,' I say. 'I'm not buying a car. I'm looking for the Jewish cemetery.'

His shoulders sag. 'Steve?'

Steve comes over and burrows in the desk before going to another desk and, reaching far down into its lower drawer, produces a plastic bag. In the bag is a key. He points through the floor-to-ceiling glass, across the waste ground with its buddleia and brambles to a small clutch of trees.

An old door leads to a high-walled enclosure. The ground inside rises steeply. Amidst the fresh grass, the primroses and ramsons, limps a platoon of root-skewed headstones. In the distance I can hear the swish of traffic, and the clang of halyards against masts from Ponsharden yard, but the cemetery is silent. I crouch before one of the slate faces at random: *To the memory of Betsy, third daughter of J & K Jacob, Falmouth, who departed this life 29th March 5598, Aged 16 years …* The Hebrew is more poetic: *Here lies the unmarried woman, Beila the daughter of Jacob from Falmouth. She died on the eve of Sabbath, 4th Nisan and was buried on Sunday 7th Nisan 5598. May her soul be bound up in the bond of eternal life.*

I run my palm over the stone. It leaves a musty vegetable smell on the skin. The inscriptions are highlighted with lichen and I feel a sudden awe at the Hebrew letters and all the miles, the years, the fleeings and searchings that brought them to this Cornish shore.

Falmouth was always a town of outsiders. Rising from bare fields, it had no native population. From the outset, it attracted freebooters and buccaneers, entrepreneurs, pietists and wanderers, who found no long-established community to resent their settling. By the mid-eighteenth century the town's population was little more than a few thousand people, but each night an ever-changing cast of visitors was added to it – those just landed at the quays, or waiting to take ship, or bunked-down below decks in the brigs and Packets, naval frigates and returning merchantmen. As Britain and its

Jewish Cemetery, Falmouth.

European rivals spread their fights, their avarice and their curiosity across the world's seaways, Falmouth became more and more diverse.

Men like Michael Kelly arrived via Ireland, America, the silver mines of Venezuela, Jamaica and St Ives. The Dillons were also Packet commanders, also from Ireland; the Carnes came from Wales. The Daubez brothers, among the greatest of Falmouth's eighteenth-century merchants, were Huguenots who had received Louis XIV's personal endorsement to flee France and its persecutions. The Falcks were from Denmark. In 1756, 250 so-called 'Acadian Indians' arrived from Canada (mainly French settlers driven out by the British). Foreign powers found it expedient to appoint consuls in Falmouth – Danish, Dutch and American – in part to deal with the problems of their own nationals, but also to keep abreast of the news for which the town was a conduit.

Sephardic Jews had been landing at Falmouth since the seventeenth century. One is recorded being caught up in a scam with Sir Peter Killigrew, landing Dutch goods there to escape duties. Numbers grew with the eighteenth century, Marranos from the south, merchants from the West Indies. But they did not settle. The founding member of the Falmouth Jewish community was an Ashkenazi from Germany who arrived in 1740. His name was Alexander Moses, but such was his association with the town that he soon became known on the swelling circuit of English Jewry as Zender Falmouth.

For nearly 400 years, since Edward I expelled the Jews in 1290, England had been off-limits for Jewish immigrants. But the shock of the Ukrainian massacres in the mid-seventeeth century led many Ashkenazim to begin to look westwards. In 1650 Menasseh ben Israel published in

Amsterdam a visionary book named *Spes Israelis* ('The Hope of Israel') in which he identified England as the missing piece in the Jewish diaspora. Readmission to England would fulfil the prophecy of a worldwide scattering before the coming of the Messiah. Such ideas chimed with the millenarian thinking of Cromwell's Commonwealth and, due in part to Rabbi Menasseh, Jews began to settle again in England. To begin with they were Sephardis, merchants and bankers who were confined to the financial centre of London.

The 1740s brought a new wave of immigration, from Alsace and the Rhineland. Finding many employers in the capital unwilling to accept the strict limitations of their working week, they became small-time pedlars and hawkers, drifting out to market towns such as Canterbury and Norwich, or spas like Bath and Cheltenham. But the biggest draw was to naval ports, Chatham, Portsmouth and Plymouth, where Jews exchanged foreign currency, bought slops and slush-piles, sold optics to officers, trinkets to sailors and in the years before uniforms, fitted out crews with suitable seagoing clothes. Among the victims of the *Royal George*, said one survivor, was a group of Jewish traders who had brought aboard a stock of heavy winter clothing.

Falmouth was not a naval port but its ceaseless traffic of ships offered the same opportunities. Zender Falmouth set up as a silversmith. He brought his wife Phoebe to the town and they started a family. It is probable that other Jews passed through, from land and sea, but rarely enough to hold a *minyan*. Zender worked hard to attract settlers. The first prayers were held in his house, then in a synagogue in St Dunstan's and eventually in a larger one on Porhan Hill. Not only did Falmouth develop one of the earliest Jewish communities in Britain but, in proportion to its size, one of the largest.

Like Alexander Moses, Barnet Levy was a German Jew who reached Britain in the 1740s. He made his way to the Jewish districts to the east of the City of London. He had been given the name of a man from his hometown, on a street favoured by Jews – but no house number. He knocked on a door at random and a young girl opened it. Seeing he, too, was Jewish, she asked kindly: 'What do you want?'

As his grandson recounted in a private memoir written 150 years later, the course of Barnet Levy's life was set that day – not by the fellow townsman he finally reached, but by the girl in the doorway. In the footloose years to come, he carried the conviction with him that she would one day be his wife.

Surviving accounts of Barnet suggest a gentle man, diligent in his work and armed with that particular firmness of belief that is both protective and isolating. He was a soap-boiler by trade and in London he did the rounds of small plants and factories. All insisted he work on *shabat*, and that he refused to do. So he left London for the open road, seeking employment where he could find it, buying and selling whatever he could afford. After some time he heard of a Jew in Falmouth who was drawing rovers like himself to the port.

A great deal of money was now passing through the town, fresh in the pockets of sailors on shore-leave, stale in the pockets of wealthy travellers who sometimes waited days for the Packets to sail. Prosperity was beginning to rise, too, in inland Cornwall, in the mining districts and, with growing rents and land prices, among the gentry.

Zender Falmouth laid down the conditions to pedlars like Barnet Levy: he would provide them with a hawker's licence; he would let them have on credit a stock of goods; they would tour the towns of Cornwall with their *marsh*, a wooden ware-box whose name comes from 'buckle' in German patois. But on Friday they must return to Falmouth to help make up the quorum for prayers. They would spend *shabat* together and on Sunday settle up with Zender and take another *marsh*-load of goods back on the road.

They had a network of inns with special agreement from the landlords. When they arrived, the Jews would ask him for the key to a cupboard. Inside they would find a kosher frying pan chalked with the name of the last user, the date and a text from the current *Sedrah*. When the pedlar had finished with the pan he would wash it up and leave it in the cupboard with another text. Zender Falmouth also insisted his pedlars had Jewish names (Barnet Levy was Bernard Beer before he came to Falmouth) and, to encourage them to settle in Falmouth, found nice Jewish girls for them to marry.

In the case of Barnet Levy, finding a suitable bride was not necessary. When he was ready, he made the journey back to London. He had knocked on a thousand English doors but had never forgotten this one, the first one, in the East End. The house belonged to a tailor nicknamed Fine Schneider, and Barnet told him at once why he was there. Fine Schneider was a respected tailor and a well-known man in London. He employed a good number of people and his clothes were worn by some very important men. And now here was this roaming pack-man from some far-flung province wanting to marry his beloved Esther. But when Barnet mentioned Falmouth and Zender, Schneider suddenly took notice: Zender Falmouth was the uncle of his wife. So Schneider wrote to Zender, received the right commendations and gave Barnet his blessing.

Barnet returned to Falmouth alone. He took out a lease on a shop with quarters above and filled it with furniture and new linen, before travelling up to London for the wedding. He and Esther came back by Russell's bullion wagon – he bouncing with the bundles on the straw, watching her through the flap, elegantly side-saddled on a packhorse. Militia marched beside the wagon. In Falmouth they settled into the shop and within a decade had helped fulfil a little of Menasseh's mystical vision and Zender Falmouth's more modest hopes by producing eight children.

The Jewish community in Falmouth prospered for a century or more. At its height, in the 1840s, it boasted more than fifty members. They were pawnbrokers and money brokers, druggists and herbalists, purveyors of fancy repositories, clothiers to the nobility, milliners, watchmakers and turners. But the community's strength, like the town as a whole, derived from the traffic that passed between St Anthony's Head and Pendennis Point. They acted as agents and ships' suppliers, as chandlers and outfitters, and the boats that they sent out to meet approaching ships became known as 'Tailor's cutters'; one was even called the *Synagogue*. As a protection against drowning, the Jews provided sailors with an *afikoman* biscuit wrapped in a prayer shawl. Many of the community were multilingual, and in 1776 one of them placed an advertisement in the regional newspaper offering translation services to 'those Mercantile Gentlemen who have connections in France, Germany, Holland etc.' with assurances that as well as propriety and accuracy 'SECRECY will be the principal object attached to'.

But just as it reached its height, the community began to decline. The great currents of oceanic traffic shifted and by the mid-nineteenth century, Falmouth was not attracting so many ships as other ports. Young Jews left Falmouth for towns closer to the industrial heart of the country. A number joined the California Gold Rush of 1859.

In 1879 Samuel Jacob, jeweller and minister to the now-vanished congregation, surveyed the empty Gylling Street synagogue and commissioned a series of repairs. He had it redecorated. Then he locked it up and left Falmouth for good, taking his family to London. A few Jewish shops remained in the High Street – among them the ships' chandlers of Nathan Ross. He continued for a while before retiring. He was the last to be buried in the graveyard.

A few weeks after my first visit, I go again to the cemetery. A mini-digger stands before the door. They are installing a gas governor and through the open doors of its brand-new shed I glimpse the yellow machine squatting like a pasha among its pipes and valves. The graveyard is now thick with calf-high spears of green; the ramsons and bluebells are in flower.

It takes me some time to find Nathan's tomb. The headstone has toppled and lies half-buried in the sprays of new growth. Brushing it aside, I make out the words of a broken sentence: ... *but not forgotten.*

At the top of the cemetery are the oldest tombs, the round-topped slate memorials of the early patriarchs. Here stands the headstone of Barnet Levy. His wife Esther is buried with him; he outlived her by eleven years: beside them lies Barnet's mentor and the founder of the community, Zender Falmouth: *Here dwells and takes delight a faithful man, a leader ... His house was open and his table laid for all.*

CHAPTER 17

In the eighteenth century it was said that of all the towns in Britain, Falmouth had 'a greater proportion of persons adhering to different religious sects'. In the steep-sloping alleys and terraces, Baptists, Congregationalists and Independents had all built houses for prayer. Another group came and, having erected their own chapel, had the cheek also to call themselves the Independents. The next group, who put up another chapel, at least announced that they were the New Independents. In time, all of them were joined by the Irvingites, Rechabites and Unitarians. The Freemasons added a Lodge of 'Love and Honour', while on the quays hot-gospellers would swiftly explain their own route to salvation before boarding ship to the New World.

Yet in case the suggestion of indiscriminate tolerance should sully the good name of Falmouth, a gang of men in the summer of 1744 put paid to the efforts of yet another visiting preacher. The men were mariners and privateers, good stout men who went about their task with vigour: 'Avast, lads, avast!' they cried as they shouldered the preacher's door. The poor man took flight in a boat, up the river to the safety of Penryn. The mob followed him along the bank, jeering and threatening.

Many years later, the same preacher returned. This time people 'lined the streets from one end of the town to the other, out of stark love and kindness, gaping and staring as if the King was going by'. That evening, with the sea behind him, the preacher addressed a huge crowd. 'God moved wonderfully in the hearts of the people,' he wrote of that occasion, 'who all seem to know the day of their visitation.' This man was John Wesley. His Methodists – proving themselves no slouches in their duty of dissent by fracturing into Primitive, United Reformed and Bryanites – would eventually outstrip all other denominations in Falmouth.

But it was George Fox and his Society of Friends, or Quakers, who probably left the greatest mark on the town. During the years of the Commonwealth, when the land was shadowed by regicide and millenarianism, Fox toured the West Country with his charismatic teaching. By the time he reached Falmouth – still called Smithwick – he was a prisoner, on his way to appear before the governor of Pendennis Castle. But in that burgeoning harbour settlement, open to the sea, there was great curiosity in what he had to say:

'There came to our inn the chief constable of the place, and many sober people, some of whom began to inquire concerning us. We told them we were prisoners for Truth's sake; and much discourse we had with them concerning the things of God. They were very sober and loving to us.'

George Fox's Cornish ministry ended in Launceston gaol where he and his followers were put in a murderer's dungeon known popularly as Doomsdale. Ankle-deep in uncleared excrement, they stood while through the floorboards the gaoler above poured the slops of other prisoners, shouting: 'You hatchet-face dogs!'

Religious dissent in Cornwall has a formidable history and one of the most treasured books in the Quakers' Library in Euston is a large folio with the handwriting of Fox's own son-in-law on its tooled leather binding: *The Record of Sufferings of Friends in Cornwall*. Their sufferings were very great. For many Quakers, the countless punishments, fines and distresses of those who refused to pay tithes, attend church or doff their hats, or who opened their shops on Christmas Day, were proof itself of the rightness of their ways: for did not the Lord Himself suffer similar persecution?

George Fox's teachings had found fertile ground in Falmouth and its Quakers feature prominently in the book. In April 1670, just outside Falmouth, several constables burst in on a Quaker meeting. They found some sixteen or so people, men and women, in the customary position of Quaker meetings. No one was praying, no one was preaching. They were sitting in silence, 'waiting upon the Lorde'. But the authorities of Falmouth and Penryn recognised subversion when they saw it. They authorised the constables to seize goods from the Quakers – petticoats and bed-curtains, pewter and working tools.

Some years later, after the Act of Toleration of 1689, the corpse of a Quaker body was brought into a Falmouth meeting. Samuel Tregelles had drowned in the harbour after a fishing expedition, and the Friends looked upon his body and quietly considered the fleeting nature of their earthly lives. Into the collective silence one man dropped his words:

'We have before us an example of the brevity and uncertainty of human life.'

The same thought was in the hearts of all, but this man found more within him, driven by the presence of poor Samuel. He spoke of the risks always attendant on us in our mortal endeavours and was given to warn his fellow Friends, urging them 'to consider for what end God gave you life, whether only to get money and to amasse abundance'.

His speech may have been stirred by the fate of poor Samuel Tregelles, who filled his boat too full of fish and overturned it. But perhaps, too, the man was moved by the memory of his own father, Daniel Gwin, first agent of Falmouth's Packet service, whose spectacular corruptions led to a crippling fine. The meeting dwelt on the fate of these men and of all their kin in Falmouth and the temptations of the sea and its boundless fruits, which each year now became harder to resist.

In the early 1760s, with Britain becoming convinced of its maritime dominance, a man arrived in Falmouth whose family would shape the town more than anyone before or since. George Croker Fox was a Quaker. He had been born further up the Cornish coast in Par, to a family with a long tradition of good works. In 1601 Carew wrote of a branch of Fox's forebears that they showed a 'continual large and inquisitive liberality to the poor ... beyond any apprehensive imitation of any in the shire'.

Like many Quaker families, the Foxes managed to combine selfless principles with commercial acumen. While other Quakers established banks and confectionery brands, offering the allure of compound interest and chocolate, the Foxes operated in the even more corrupting environment of shipping. From a single house, George Croker's father built a trading enterprise, eventually owning two ships that sailed almost continually between Par and Bilbao. Of his sons, one went to the port of Wadebridge in north Cornwall, another to Plymouth while two more – George Croker II and Joseph – moved to Cornwall's busiest port at Falmouth.

G.C. Fox & Co. continued for more than 200 years as the hub of Falmouth harbour – trading and acting as ship-broker and agent. With each generation, the range of Fox interests grew. They dominated the local pilchard trade, building cellars around the coastline to press and cure the fish, and constructing hogsheads to export them to the Mediterranean for the Lenten fast. They imported coal from Wales and timber balks for Cornwall's mines from the Baltic, hemp and flax from Russia. They set up an iron foundry and became involved inland in the mining of tin and copper. They had a hand in the development of the north-coast harbour of Portreath. For a hundred years, one or other member of the Fox family was US consul in Falmouth. It was the Foxes who installed a telegraph line to the Lizard so that orders to and from shipping could be conveyed.

Yet diligent and successful as they were, the Foxes' real passions appeared always to lie elsewhere, away from commerce for its own sake, in matters closer to their Quaker beliefs. Their letters and journals are full of a love for the

Letter from George Croker Fox.

world and its wonders, and for their friends, and a zeal for science, schemes of improvement and philanthropy.

Some were scientists and inventors, some artists. One of George Croker Fox's grandchildren, Robert Were Fox, pioneered a dipping needle that improved navigation; another, Anna Maria Fox, was one of the first to use the word 'Polytechnic' in establishing an institution in Falmouth dedicated to the promotion of science and the arts. The members of the original committee, in 1833, indicate the local prevalence of the family – Dr Fox, Mr & Mrs R.W. Fox, Mr & Mrs G.C. Fox, Mr T.W. Fox, Mr G.P. Fox, Mr & Mrs A. Fox, Mr J. Fox, Mr & Mrs C. Fox of Perran, Miss Fox and Misses A.M. and C. Fox and Mr R.B. Fox of Bank.

Some were doctors. Joseph Fox, who with his brother George was the first to settle in Falmouth in about 1762, married the daughter of a Penryn 'surgeon-apothecary'. He became a Falmouth surgeon and produced several generations of medics. From Edinburgh to Bristol, Leiden to Melbourne, the Foxes pushed the bounds both of access to medicine and its techniques.

The Foxes also displayed a remarkable affinity with the natural world. Joshua Fox would stand in his garden at Tregedna while birds flocked to him, perching on his shoulder and eating from his hand; Howard Fox had the same rapport with birds. Others were botanists and plant collectors, whose exotic plants were brought in as seeds by obliging Packet captains or sometimes, as with the tree fern, *Dicksonia antarctica*, as ballast.

There was a time when Falmouth was ringed by Fox properties. They built houses and laid out grounds on land bordering Arwenack, and on round to the north, and several more down towards the Helford river. In these properties, there was always more emphasis on the gardens than the house. On one occasion, Charles Fox, an Orientalist, returned to find his home in flames. Realising there was nothing he could do, he pulled out his sketch book and sat down calmly to draw the fire.

One afternoon, with an easterly flicking up a lively sea astern, I cross the Carrick Roads, moor up at Custom House Quay and climb up to Arwenack Street. Facing the quay, standing above the short approach road, is a red-brick building with a double bay. It was from here that for 200 years G.C. Fox & Co. operated as ship agent and where at various times the Dutch, Greek, Danish and American consular shields hung on the wall. But recently the company has been split up and the office sold.

In a low-ceilinged attic-room not far from the old office, I find my friend Charles Fox. Equipped with the humility of his Quaker provenance, Charles is a polymath, a qualified landscape designer, a plantsman, a painter and poet. Today he is deep in the task of arranging the papers of the firm and the family. The attic is filled with stacks of age-stained notebooks, sheaves of typescript letters, memos, newspaper cuttings and photographs. They stand on boxes, cover the partner's desk and the burgundy serge of the sofa. In one corner is a block of low shelves where Charles has begun to arrange yards and yards of company records.

I sit on the floor to scan them. The miscellany of the family's activities is spelt out in their tooled spines. Here are Cash Books and Ledgers, Minute Books and Letter Books, an English–Latin Dictionary, a vast Holy Bible, the Steamers Day Book, the Fish Account Current Book. One

Books from the old G.C. Fox & Co. offices.

gold-stamped panel reads *Consulate of the United States*; inside, the pages begin with copperplate transcriptions of letters to and from the Secretary of State in Washington; the spare pages are filled with the pilchard-catch of the Portscatho seines (hundreds of thousands in the months of August and September by *Rufus* and *Providence*).

I take down the earliest of the Letter Books. It opens in 1759 when George Croker Fox was still based in Fowey but beginning to spend more time in Falmouth. The letters are filled with the hazards of sea-based commerce. One tells of two Fox ships, carrying cargoes of salted pilchards for Naples, which were captured by French frigates; the letters record Fox's efforts to release the officers and men from Brest prison. Another letter expresses his anger at receiving a consignment of reeking fish.

The Falmouth Foxes did not go to sea themselves, but the sea came to them and they ministered to the needs of those upon it. In a longer-established town, with more traditional pursuits, Nonconformists might never have achieved such a central position. One Fox was quarantine doctor for years in the early nineteenth century and a letter survives that he wrote to a member of the family, a boy of 9 or 10, preparing him for a shoreside career: 'Greetings in the Lord. Tomorrow morning, if the weather is fine, I propose to show you a ship-wreck. All the sailors died in the water ...'

Another early incident reveals a rather different shipping problem. One of the original two brothers to settle in Falmouth was Joseph the doctor. Being a surgeon in Falmouth did not provide a living, so he bought shares in a couple of cargo cutters. When war broke out with the French in 1778, his partners did what a great many shipowners did at the time: they fitted out their vessels as privateers. Joseph Fox was appalled, citing the Quaker conviction that 'no human laws can authorise men to kill each other, nor take away property by force'. He told them he would sell his share – but they refused to buy it. In due course, one of his ships managed to capture a French ship – unarmed and ignorant of the outbreak of war. Fox's partners now did offer to buy him out, in exchange for a handsome fee, but this time Fox refused *them*; he took the prize money and said nothing of it, not even to his wife. At the time, his son Edward was study-ing medicine in Edinburgh and Joseph wrote to him, urging him to suspend his studies. He must go to Paris. There, with discretion and tact ('be steadfast to thy principles'), Edward must seek out those who had been robbed and return the money. But despite all his efforts, including an advertisement in the *Gazette de France*, Edward failed to produce a claimant. Then Joseph died from pleurisy and the search was swamped in the years of revolution and war. Several decades later, in 1817, Edward was able to return to France with the money, which had since grown into many thousands of pounds. Unable to trace the rightful owners, Edward used it to estab-lish a fund for aged and distressed seamen in French ports.

Not since the Killigrews had a single family so dominated life in Falmouth. But it would be hard to think of a neater opposite to them than the Quaker Foxes, with their piracy in reverse.

CHAPTER 18

In the early 1790s, just to the south-west of Falmouth, there lived one of those maritime figures who seem to come not just from a different age but from a different species. Edward Pellew had already spent twenty hard and heroic years at sea, but lacking enemies to chase and vessels to command, he had come ashore and moved with his wife and children to the family farm at Treverry. Edward Pellew was a consummate seaman, and thus a hopeless farmer. The planting rotas were baffling, the cattle dull, and the great stillness of the land troubled the ocean-seared soul within him. Watching crops grow, he moaned, 'makes my eyes ache'.

One dead day in January 1793 Edward's brother Samuel galloped up to Treverry. Samuel Pellew was collector of customs at Falmouth and news had just reached the quays that France had declared war. Edward had been expecting it for some months. He saddled his horse, rode back with his brother to Falmouth, and continued on up to Portsmouth where he took command of a 36-gun frigate, the *Nymphe*. A few months later came the sighting of a French ship in the Channel, and Edward and the *Nymphe* were on their way to the first decisive naval engagement of the coming decades of war with France, and the most famous frigate-clash of the age. To the battle-conscious public, it was no surprise that it was Edward Pellew who was behind it.

Two centuries earlier, the Pellew family had been yeomen, trudging the fields around the village of Breage in west Cornwall. At the beginning of the age of sail, one or two drifted off to sea. From then on their attachment to the land grew more tenuous and their circumstances, like all those drawn to such a life, fluctuated wildly. At different times, Pellews took up temporary residence in ports of the south coast – Penzance, Fowey, Plymouth, Dover. If they had a land base it was the shoreside around Falmouth and the Penryn river.

In the early eighteenth century, Humphrey Pellew made a small fortune as a merchant seaman and bought a 2,000-acre tobacco plantation in Maryland. He used the profits from this, and from his various ships, to build a sizeable chunk of the town of Flushing, just across the Penryn river from Falmouth. Humphrey Pellew himself lived in its manor, but within a short time after his death, a series of calamities washed away his wealth. By the time of Edward and Samuel, all that remained was the small farm at Treverry.

No one better illustrates the ups and downs of the Pellew family – and indeed of anyone who took to sea in those years – than Humphrey's cousin, Thomas Pellow. At the age of 11, Thomas had grown tired of getting up so early for Latin lessons in Penryn. He did what any high-spirited boy would if they had the chance – he hopped aboard his uncle's ship. It was Lent. Salted pilchards were in high demand in the Catholic south. Thomas left the quay at Falmouth in the spring of 1715; by the time he reached Genoa he was so bowed down by the rigours of ship life that he began to pine for his early-morning Latin lessons. Returning north, up the Galician coast, two sails were spotted bearing towards them. They turned out to be Sallee pirates and within weeks young Thomas Pellow found himself a slave in Meknes.

Twenty-three years later, after conversion to Islam and service as a cavalry commander in the oceanic sands of the Sahara (thus contributing in a small way to re-establishing Muslim rule in Morocco), and after leading caravans to Timbuktu and outliving a wife and daughter, he finally engineered a perilous escape. Face bearded and desert-pocked, Thomas Pellow once again stepped ashore at Falmouth in 1738. His family didn't recognise him, nor he them.

At the same time, the once-wealthy Flushing Pellews were represented by Samuel, a Packet commander driven by that particular brand of patriotism which helped justify so many seaborne adventures. When he was at home on a Sunday, Captain Pellew would make his four boys kneel on the floor and drink the King's health. Captain Pellew died young, leaving four sons and two daughters. His widow married again, but unhappily, and the children were banished, spread out among distant relations in loveless and impoverished households.

The Pellew brothers – a second Samuel (later collector of customs at Falmouth for fifty years), Edward the naval hero, Israel and John – remained close as long as they lived, bound by the shared adversity of their childhood, by their Cornish blood, by the sea and by a zeal for the great struggles of their amphibious nation. Israel commanded the *Conqueror* at Trafalgar and became an admiral. Barely out of his teens, John was killed on the Hudson river, fighting alongside Edward for the town of Saratoga.

But more than any of them, it was Edward who displayed that particular blend of talent, energy and luck that make martial genius. He was impulsive and fearless, a combination that served him well once he was master, but almost did for him in early life. He first ran away to sea to escape a flogging at school and from then on was rarely off the water – and often *in* it. Once, sailing single-handed up to Plymouth from Falmouth he leapt overboard to recover his hat – and nearly drowned before he managed to swim back to the still-moving boat. He was thrown off his first ship as a troublemaker and had to make his own way back home from the Mediterranean, reaching Falmouth again on a Packet. But he had already found the sea fitted him too well ever to leave it, and learned as second nature the techniques of sail.

Many years later, shortly after Edward Pellew's death, Sir Edward Codrington was assessing Pellew's achievement against that of Nelson, ever the benchmark of naval prowess. Nelson, explained Codrington, surpassed Pellew in his flair for command, in the unthinking devotion his men showed for him. But Pellew was the greater seaman. He always felt that victory at sea depended on good sailing. One midshipman who served under him recalled that he never allowed them 'an idle hour' and that he himself was willing to perform the most perilous duties 'with such cheerfulness of manner … that we were all happy to imitate his example'. Sailing out to Newfoundland, they once had to shorten sail in a severe gale. It was close to midnight and they were trying to reef the main-topsail yard. With Pellew shouting orders from the deck below, each of the crew hesitated to edge out along the yard. The sail was thrashing itself to pieces, and needed making fast. The crew was amazed to see Pellew appear – shimmying *down* from the topmast-head, having 'clambered like a cat' up the rigging, over the backs of the sailors to reach the end of the yard from above, by its single-rope lift.

Edward Pellew had an innate feeling for ships, that animal sense for balancing rig and trim and hull that allowed a vessel to excel. His eye for design and construction was developed during an extraordinary campaign in the American War of Independence. He was part of a force trying to wrest control

Edward Pellew.

of Lake Champlain from the rebels. During the autumn of
1776 some 700 men hauled a flotilla of thirty or so fighting
ships up to the lake, past the rapids. Once there, they felled
trees to build numerous gigs and punts. One ship, the
Inflexible, some 180 tons, was already on the stocks at Quebec,
half built. They carefully took her to pieces, carried her up,

then reassembled her at the lake. The 700-man carrying corps was overseen by Lieutenant Schank, a brilliant marine engineer who was assisted by the 19-year-old Pellew.

Decades later, blind and frail, Schank recalled to Pellew's children their late father's ceaseless activity during those months. When installing the masts of the *Inflexible*, he was standing on top of the high scaffolding when part of it collapsed, pitching Pellew far into the lake below. The aged naval officer recalled the moment. 'Poor Pellew, I thought – he is gone and lost!' But then he had watched the young man bob up to the surface, dash out of the water, and back up the scaffolding.

'My dears,' Schank wiped the tears from his sightless eyes, 'he was like a squirrel.'

In the latter half of 1792, sensing that war with France was imminent, Edward Pellew had been urging his patron Lord Falmouth to find a command for him. In January 1793, when his brother brought him news of the war's outbreak, he said farewell to his wife and children and hurried up to Portsmouth. There he took over the *Nymphe*, captured from the French during the previous war when her wheel was shot out. (Dr Joshua Fox remembered the prize being brought in to Falmouth, 'exceedingly shattered'.)

Now that Pellew had his ship, he needed to address the problem faced by every would-be commander of the age – manpower. One of the failures of the Admiralty in the eighteenth century was not to sustain a corps of proficient seamen. Pellew found the quays at Portsmouth already stripped of anyone competent. The *Nymphe* was useless without hands to sail her.

Pellew tried an unusual tack. He wrote to his brother Samuel back in Falmouth. Go inland, he asked him, put out the word in the mining areas, among the hungry tinners, tell them there is work aboard the *Nymphe*. They will be fed, given the king's shilling. Their tasks will not be unfamiliar, going aloft in a blow is not so different as going down a shaft. Knowledge of explosives will help with gunnery – and assure them, Edward added, that the ship is commanded by a stout Cornishman like themselves.

Eighty miners travelled up to Spithead and stepped aboard the *Nymphe*. The first leg of their service was to sail back down the Channel to Falmouth. The ship's normal comple-ment was 220 – on board now were no more than thirty proficient seamen. Pellew himself took the wheel for long periods and pulled himself onto the yards to bring in sail. Most of the miners lay retching in the scuppers. Going ashore in Falmouth, they then managed to turn over the ship's punt. Pellew's experiment had failed. He offered leave to those who wanted it, and told them to return on 17 March. He then sailed on the 15th. A number of the miners remained, overcame their fear of the sea and their seasickness, and in time became an invaluable part of Pellew's crew.

For several months, Pellew performed his duties in the Channel, taking every opportunity to add to his skeleton crew. Returning convoys, their journeys begun before the outbreak of war, now needed protection. From Falmouth Pellew escorted up the Channel a fleet of merchantmen and helped himself to some of their crew. He then joined a squad-ron at anchor, cleverly taking up position where he could be the first to board homecoming traders to press their men. Sometimes he would spend all night in an open boat, waiting for passing ships and the chance of snatching even one half-decent mariner.

By mid-June Pellew was back in Falmouth. A ship just returned from the South Seas filled the last gaps in the *Nymphe*'s company. They were also joined by Edward's brother Israel who had failed to secure a command of his own and joined Edward as a volunteer. On 18 June Edward Pellew received news of a sighting of two French frigates in the Channel, and he and Israel went ashore to find Samuel. The three brothers sat around Samuel's table at the Falmouth Custom House, discussing the best way to track them down. The *Nymphe* sailed that day and by dusk had reached Start Point without seeing anything. Edward laid a course: *let's see what there might be mid-Channel.*

Dawn came within hours, smearing the sky to windward with a sickly grey; against it, some four or five miles to the south-east, was a sail. The ship was the *Cléopâtre*, one of the most powerful of the French Navy. She and the *Nymphe* were fairly evenly matched in terms of gunnery, though the *Cléopâtre* was bigger and carried a hundred more men. Her commander was Captain Jean Mullon, a survivor of the *ancien régime* whose skill with a ship had until then trumped any Jacobin inclination to purge him. As the *Nymphe* drew closer, Edward Pellew watched every sail-trim and helm-change of the French ship, and ascertained two things: that she was not trying to run away, and that she was being sailed by very competent seamen.

Edward summoned his brother from below.

'Israel,' he said, 'you have no business here, and I am very sorry I brought you from your home.'

Still buttoning his coat, Israel was only half-listening, looking with wide eyes over his brother's shoulder at the French ship. 'That's the very frigate I have been dreaming of all night! I dreamt we shot away her wheel! We shall have her in a quarter of an hour!'

Edward shook his head. 'See how she is handled.'

The two ships edged towards each other in the Channel swell; the heavy splash of their bows grew louder as they closed. Approaching the *Cléopâtre*'s quarter, Pellew ordered his men up to the leeward rail and into the shrouds. Raising his hat, he cried: 'Long live King George!' Across the short stretch of water, the French heard three booming cheers.

'*Vive la nation!*' responded Captain Mullon.

A sailor then took the cap of liberty up the rigging and fixed it to the masthead. Pellew replaced his own hat, signalling to his gunners to open fire – and the first cannonade ripped through the morning. The French guns fired a moment later and for forty minutes or more the two ships sailed in parallel, their topgallants maintaining way, while their guns fired with such intensity that, from the first broadside, smoke reduced visibility to a few yards. Still they fired. Shortly after seven, Pellew saw a shadow in the mist – and the bowsprit of the *Cléopâtre* came thrusting out of it, driving in over his decks until her whiskers were locked against the mainmast. The firing ceased. In the silence, the ships' timbers creaked against each other. Pellew called his men to prepare for boarders. All eyes were on the bows of the French ship – but not a single man approached. So Pellew issued his own command: *board!*

His men scrambled up over the head, in through the for'ard gunports. They found the *Cléopâtre*'s decks scattered with bodies. Those still uninjured fled below while on the quarterdeck, with his hip shot away, lay the dying Captain Mullon. Hurriedly, he was stuffing his mouth with the signal codes. In his panic, though, he had inadvertently grabbed his commission papers. The signal codes were removed from his pocket and taken by Edward Pellew back to the Admiralty.

The *Cléopâtre*'s bowsprit was still working against Pellew's mainmast. The *Nymphe*'s stays had parted and the toppling of the mast threatened at any moment to cripple the *Nymphe*.

When it came – the timber-crack – it was the French sprit that broke and not the *Nymphe*'s mast. The *Cléopâtre*'s hull swung round, Pellew dropped his bower and the two ships broke free of their deadly embrace. Pellew gybed, put the prize in tow and headed for Portsmouth.

In the feverish afterglow, the officers discussed the course of the battle, reassembling its decisive moments with half-glimpsed clues and theories: it was, they concluded, the *Cléopâtre*'s loss of control that led to her defeat. With her wheel gone and the torn sails hanging overboard, nothing could prevent the bows from slewing round into the wind. The two ships were so close, her bows were at once over the *Nymphe*'s rail. The *Cléopâtre*'s guns were then useless.

Israel Pellew spoke up. He had followed the portent of his dream. From the very start of the battle, he had taken control of a gun on the quarterdeck and concentrated fire on the *Cléopâtre*'s helm. The first shot missed, striking the mizzen and sending out a shower of splinters that killed the man at the wheel. Three more helmsmen died before Israel managed to knock out the wheel itself.

Having seen to the casualties and assessed the damage to the *Nymphe*, Edward's first impulse in victory was to complete the triangle of Pellew brothers by writing to Samuel in Falmouth: 'Dear Sam – Here we are – thank God! Safe – after a glorious action with *la Cléopâtre* … We dished her up in fifty minutes, boarded, and struck her colours.'

As soon as he reached shore he sent the letter off, along with the captured cap of liberty.

Edward also wrote to the widow of Captain Mullon offering his condolences. He wrote again before a reply was received.

'Sir,' replied Mme Mullon, 'I have received the two letters which you have had the complaisance to write to me. The afflicting news of the death of my dear husband, which they brought me, is to me a thunder-stroke. Nothing can console me for so great a loss, as he was the only resource of myself, and my five children; and with him our only hope is lost …'

Edward Pellew sent her what money he could afford.

Within days of their victory, Edward and Israel were presented to the King, and Edward was knighted. Their victory helped define the popular perception of the war. In the archive of the National Maritime Museum in Greenwich is a sixpenny propaganda sheet which celebrates the victory of Pellew's *Nymphe*. It expresses the hope that the loss of the *Cléopâtre* might make the French people see sense, and

> convince our old inveterate enemies of the insufficiency of the efforts of Republican Frenchmen and desperadoes, fighting under the banner of FALSE LIBERTY, held forth to the misguided multitude, by hundreds of TYRANTS, calling themselves National Legislators, against the heredi- tary loyalty, the undaunted bravery, and the true courage of the BRITISH TARS.

CHAPTER 19

During the 1790s, while they burned effigies around the Fal
estuary of Jacobins and Robespierre and Tom Paine (not
being quite sure whether he was French or not), the port of
Falmouth grew busier than ever before. The inner harbour
and the Carrick Roads filled with ships of every kind. For the
first time, Falmouth had a permanent naval deployment – the
frigates of the two Western Squadrons, one under Sir John
Borlase Warren, the other under Sir Edward Pellew. When
French prizes were brought in, the harbour rang with the
sound of applause and cheering; on land two prisons were
established for the captured. Ships-of-the-line edged their
stately hulls into port, dwarfing the frigates. Their topmasts
and upper yards towered above the Roseland shore opposite:
two-deckers, second-raters and their ninety guns and 700
men, and from time to time a first-rater like the *Victory* slowly
escorted to her anchorage.

It was at this time that a certain Mr Guillibard stood on
the hill at Pendennis and looked out with admiration over
the harbour. Mr Guillibard had spent a lifetime working in
London and now in retirement was touring the country (his
handwritten notes I stumbled on in the Cornwall Record
Office while looking for something else). He gazed down on
the waters of the Carrick Roads, on the yawls and bum-boats
hurrying between the cliff-like sides of the 'gunships', with

their grids of open ports. All around were scattered the sloops of war, cutters, barges and bomb ketches. Pennants flowed like so many streams from the mastheads. Falmouth, wrote Guillibard, with the anxious eye for defence that war had sharpened in the country's citizens, 'is the finest entrance from the Channel of any seaport in England'. That evening, as he dined in his hotel, some of the anxiety was lifted from

French Prizes arriving in Falmouth.

View of Falmouth & Sir J. Borla

Mr Guillibard: '*Ate a large turbot and a fine pig. Supper 1/6 per head. No beds charged.*'

Wartime also swelled Falmouth's Packet station. Thirty or forty ships were now employed to convey urgent despatches to the outposts of British territory. While the merchant seamen remained furtive in port, vulnerable as they were to the press gangs, the Packet crews were exempt. At the Market Strand, they swaggered up the steps, eager and full of appetites. They joined the crews and officers of the coveted naval

...'s Prizes entering the Harbour.

frigates, with their proud epaulettes and prize-heavy pockets.

Wealth poured ashore. Captured vessels were so abundant that the prize commissioners set up representation in Falmouth. War added value to the clandestine cargoes of the Packet ships; it is estimated that during these years some £4 million of smuggled goods and money were landed at Falmouth.

At the centre of it all were the Pellews. In Falmouth, Edward's elder brother Samuel was, according to one source, 'the ruler of the town'. As prize-agent and collector of customs, he was the arbiter of dozens of avaricious hopes and dubious ventures. He remained scrupulous about his own rules, deciding the boundaries on what was contraband and what was not. He pursued transgressions with the same furious energy as his younger brother did French frigates. For his first thirteen years in the post, he spent not a single night away from the port. He drove the two armed cutters at his disposal so severely that one of the skippers issued a formal complaint of 'excessive duty' and resigned. It was a measure of his power – and Falmouth's perennial brigandry – that one morning a rash of posters appeared on the walls of the town promising a generous reward for anyone who killed Samuel Pellew.

At the same time, a couple of hundred yards across the water in Flushing, Edward Pellew's fame placed him at the centre of the harbour's social life. Dances took place most evenings while each morning at ten, Pellew's barge would come ashore from the *Indefatigable* to take him aboard. When not at sea, he lived with his family in a house next door to one of his best friends, Captain Kempthorne. The two men had a door cut into the party wall so that they could visit each other more easily.

So passed Edward Pellew's happiest years. Falmouth provided the perfect base for him – far from the nannying of Navy Board or Admiralty. Its position provided swift and tack-free access to the Western Approaches, or Ushant, or the French fleet's base at Brest. His frigates, pouncing on any enemy sail they spotted, earned prize money for all. Pellew's name echoed far beyond the wharves of England's sea-ports and the salons of Bath and London, to France, where it was mentioned with both fear and admiration.

He worked tirelessly to blockade the French fleet in Brest. During the winter surveillance of the port he was remembered by his midshipmen for the spells he spent with them at the masthead. Often they became so numb with cold that after their watch others had to help them down the rigging. Pellew remained up there all day, without food or water, watching the approaches to the harbour until he knew not only every ship that was there but every pattern of wind and tide that might affect their offing.

When it came, in December 1796, the great French naval expedition to invade Ireland, the fleet emerged at night. They ran large before a brisk easterly, scattering lights and signals to confuse the blockade. Pellew brazenly sailed in among the French, letting off his own decoy of false signals, lights, gunshots and rockets. But with only three frigates, he was unable to stop most of the French pressing north. The French still reached Ireland, and were prevented from invasion only by errors of seamanship and adverse winds.

Pellew was relentless. Just months earlier he had lain secretly off the French coast, for days, landing stores for the Chouan rebels and destroying passing ships. On the way back to Cornwall, he spotted an enemy sail and after fifteen hours and 168 miles of chase, he and his two accompanying frigates

The Indefatigible *engaging and capturing* La Virginie.

captured the *Virginie*, a French ship of forty-four guns. Honour in this case – that curious relic of fighting convention – was awarded to the French master, Captain Bergeret, for resisting for so long a superior force. Witnesses said that Captain Bergeret wept as he was brought to the *Indefatigable* from his captured ship. But his spirits were lifted when he was told who it was that had defeated him.

'Oh!' he cried. 'That is the most fortunate man that ever lived. He takes everything and now he has taken the finest frigate in France.' Captain Bergeret was entertained by Pellew's family and became a lifelong friend of Edward's. The fates of seaborne warfare brought the two men together again, ten years later, off Madras. Again Bergeret was a prisoner; again his ship, for hours, had fought off a stronger British force. After the battle, he was brought before Pellew on the quarterdeck of his flagship. Pellew's secretary watched him approach the admiral: 'The two men embraced with lively feelings of sympathy; and the manly tears then shed found an honest welcome in every heart which witnessed the interview.'

Even Pellew, however, was not infallible. Off Ushant he made what would now be deemed a gross error. He drove the *Indefatigable*, doing some nine or ten knots, onto a submerged rock, where she hung, her garboards stoved-in and the water rising in her bilges. Pellew at once ordered the upper-deck guns to be shifted. With a slow creak and a flop to leeward, she fell into deep water. Pumps going day and night, Pellew made sail for Lisbon where to inspect the damage – and thereby save weeks of repair work and inactivity – he leapt into the Tagus and ran his hands along the keel.

Jumping into the water was Pellew's forte, a habit that summed up the way he treated the world, disdaining its thresholds and borders, never hesitating in battle, nor in quitting the deck for a splash. At Spithead he went in to save a drowning cox, just months after injuring his nose on the ship's rudder as he grappled in a swell to save two other men. The following winter, with the *Indefatigable* in Plymouth, he was in again.

It was late January. Pellew was with his wife, on his way to dine with Dr Hawker, an old friend of the Pellew brothers. A southerly gale was blowing and when he saw a crowd hurrying down to the Hoe, Pellew told the driver to follow them. A transport ship, the *Dutton*, was in trouble. Bound for India, she carried a total of 500 or 600 souls, made up of troops and civilians. The gale had forced her to seek shelter in Plymouth and she had been short tacking in towards the harbour, following the channel. But a buoy was missing and she soon struck the bottom, bumping and lurching along the seabed. Her rudder broke, the helm fell slack and within minutes, she was stuck in the sand, lying broadside to a vicious surf.

Wreck of the Dutton.

Pellew rushed down to the beach, chastising the officers who had abandoned the ship with a *sauve qui peut*. Finding no one else willing, he plunged into the white water himself, diving beneath the seas as they broke, then swimming out through the break-line to the stricken ship, injuring himself beneath the fallen mainmast, but managing to haul himself up over the gunwales. On board he discovered chaos and terror. The soldiers had already raided the spirit store. He drew his sword and assured them, his voice clear above the gale, that if anyone disobeyed him, he would run them through with his blade. He then directed the rescue of every one of those on board, making cradles for the transfer. Two boats managed to drop back, nudging in from deeper water towards the wreck. In his journal Pellew played down the event: 'Sent two boats to the assistance of a ship on shore in the Sound.'

Then he was back to Brest, manning the masthead to keep up the blockade, capturing two frigates as he was relieved.

While the English fleet was stuck further up the Channel, he and the Western Squadrons were left to deal with the French expeditionary fleet to Ireland; a few days later, accompanied by the *Amazon*, he took on the eighty-gun *Droits de l'Homme*. The three of them, manoeuvring, were caught in Audierne Bay. Pellew just managed to get out, the *Amazon* was driven ashore and the crew escaped, while the French ship, crippled by Pellew's guns, lay breaking up on a sandbank for three days, unreachable from land, while one by one the thousand men aboard drowned. The following year Pellew and his frigates took fifteen cruisers.

In February 1799 he slit open a letter from the First Lord of the Admiralty, Lord Spencer, and read that he was being promoted. He was being given command of the *Impétueux* – 'the most active and desirable Line of Battle Ship'. Taken by the British at the Glorious First of June, she was an example of French shipbuilding at its finest.

Pellew read the letter with its silky tones ('I have no doubt but that you will in the new Line of Service continue to gain as much as credit as you have already …') and felt mounting fury. He did not want to leave his razée frigate. He did not want to forfeit the free-roaming flying squadrons, the bold frigates, for a ship-of-the-line. A ship-of-the-line! Every move pre-signalled, synchronised, not a feint or bear or sudden luff allowed. Parade-ground seamanship. He did not want to serve under the craven Lord Bridport, a man Pellew considered 'scarcely worth drowning'. He did not want to leave Falmouth which gave him the freedom to sail as he wished, where he and Samuel held sway and where Israel had just joined them. Most of all he did not want to leave his loyal and highly trained crew for the *Impétueux* among whose men, it was well known throughout the Navy, had spread the fever of mutiny.

But Pellew was not a man to shirk his orders. He joined the *Impétueux*. He moved his family east, away from Falmouth and Cornwall. He found himself the object of Lord Bridport's jealousy, and was placed at the back of the lee line. Later he entered politics for a while, was given command in the Far East, then in the Mediterranean. He received a string of titles and honours. But nothing ever matched the easy motion of his early years, his cat-climbing in the rigging, the impulsive swimming, nor the freewheeling seasons at Falmouth and Flushing in command of the *Indefatigable*.

Mid-summer 1832. Edward Pellew, Viscount and Baron Exmouth, Vice-Admiral of the United Kingdom, Admiral of the Red, 75 years old, his battles all fought, his great frame heavy and slow, left his house at Teignmouth for the last time. He travelled to Plymouth to visit his brother Israel. Samuel came up from Falmouth and the three of them were together again as they had been through the orphans' odyssey of their childhood, in the glorious years of Edward's Western Squadron, and on that midsummer afternoon four decades earlier, around the table in Falmouth's new Custom House at the very outset of the Napoleonic Wars, when they discussed the first sighting of the *Cléopâtre*.

Israel was dying. He had been suffering for some time from a crippling illness and was now bed-bound. He lay between his seated brothers, and the scene made an impressive tableau. Each of these men had followed a life shaped as much by the random action of the waves and maritime service as by their own will.

Years earlier, Samuel had qualified as a doctor and taken up a post here, in Plymouth, as assistant-surgeon to the dockyard. He had then moved on into Cornwall and a successful practice in Truro. But something made him abandon Truro and medicine to become Collector of Customs at Falmouth – better money perhaps, or duty, or the wisdom of generations of Pellews before him: that anywhere inland was somehow unsettling. Samuel had remained for half a century in Falmouth, a provincial official while his brothers had risen through the Navy. Unlike them, however, he was still serving, still active.

Israel himself had once spent so long at sea – from the moment he joined Edward on the *Nymphe* in the first weeks of the war – that for a decade he did not see his family. His only child was 10 years old when he met his father knowingly for the first time. Now Israel had no descendants. His son had been killed in a duel in Paris in 1819.

Israel had never had Edward's luck. The youngest of the three, it was he who now lay dying. He had played his part in the taking of the *Cléopâtre*, a decisive part, and was appointed post-captain as a result. But he would have remained ashore in Larne with his wife and infant – another officer waiting for a posting – had Edward not plucked him up and taken him aboard the *Nymphe* to face the French frigate. Israel was then defeated in Cuba and ran his ship aground in the Bahamas. During the naval unrest of the late 1790s Israel's men mutinied and put him ashore. (When the *Impétueux*'s crew had turned on Edward, in Bantry Bay, 200 to 300 brooding faces pressing aft towards him on the quarterdeck, he had stood firm before his officers, his sword drawn, and the mutiny's leaders were soon swinging from the yards.)

Israel had had his successes – in the North Sea, in the Caribbean. At Trafalgar, his ship was the fourth of the van and he took the surrender and sword of Villeneuve – but somehow the French sword, which should have been his, went to Collingwood. In the summer of 1796, en route to Falmouth to join in the bonanza of the Western Squadrons and his brother's little fief, his ship blew up. He had put into Plymouth when the magazine ignited; he had time only to throw himself through a poop-window, and land on the deck of the neighbouring hulk. Three hundred of his men died and the scars from the explosion still pocked his face.

Edward had always tried to help his brother. The charge of nepotism was one levelled at him in his later years – winning for his sons choice commands in the Indian fleet, favouring cousins and kinsmen and the Cornish. He appointed Israel as his chief of staff during his final posting in the Mediterranean. But Edward was never a good politician. He was born for the confines of a ship, at his best in dealing not with human intrigues, but the brute forces of wind and tide and cold, with the mysteries and art of sailing. In later years – burdened by high command – he harked back to the time when his whole life had clarity of purpose, contained as it was within a single hull, with his guns, sails and crews, afloat in a hostile world.

Age came harshly to a man for whom physical action was the very reason for existence. In 1804 Edward wrote to a friend: 'I can't get to the Mast Head as well as I could.' In 1809, having driven the French cruisers from the seas around India, he complained in another letter: 'I begin to wear … My floor timbers are very shaky.' Sixteen years of continuous war, and four decades at sea, had left their mark. Yet casting an eye around his naval contemporaries, most looked even older – those who were still alive.

Edward Pellew himself had one more action. It came after the end of the French wars. In August 1816, to punish the Dey of Algiers for the massacre of Christian slaves, he assembled a fleet to pound the city. It was one of his greatest victories, achieved through meticulous preparation and ruthless gunnery. One witness was amazed to see Pellew prepare for the battle, and then to watch his conduct during those furious, hellish hours of bombardment: 'my astonishment was increased to see his Lordship, who is about sixty-five years old [in fact 59], and of a stout body, during the battle, with a round hat on his head, a telescope in his hand, and a white handkerchief round his body, running from one place to another, directing all the people, as actively as any young man on board.'

Pellew's later years, though, were tinged with melancholy and suspicion. 'How is it, dear,' his wife wrote to him, 'that you always think you have Enemies projecting evil for you and yours?' As decorations spread across his dress-coat, and the list of his titles grew – not only accolades from his own country but from all over Europe – so his genius for sail became ever more redundant. The post-war generation had a new set of priorities, pursuing change and reform with all the vigour and ingenuity that used to be required simply to stay alive.

'The fact is,' he wrote later to one of his brothers, 'the people are mad, and the world is mad; and where it will end the Lord alone knows.'

His last posting in the Napoleonic Wars was Admiral of the Mediterranean. Many wrote of the splendours of Pellew's fleet. Under the eye of 'one of the best practical seamen that ever adorned the navy-list,' wrote Chamier of the blockade of Toulon, 'it was a glorious sight standing so close to the enemy's harbour'. Another witness, who saw his ships at Port Mahon, Minorca, has left a wonderfully vivid image of this moment and the heyday of the sailing ship. Like big cats of the savannah, the naval vessels had the slow confidence of those at the top of the food chain:

The British Mediterranean fleet, under Sir Edward Pellew, now Lord Exmouth, was anchored not far from us; and it was impossible to witness a more splendid naval armament. Together with several seventy-fours and frigates, there were five immense three-deckers. [Such a sight was accompanied by sounds, not only of the great guns to mark morning and evening bells, but music.] ... There was a military symphony every evening after sun-set: this, performed in reciprocal responses by the different ships, and associated with a serene sky, and the stillness of the sea, really seemed to partake of magical illusion.

Yet something moribund already hovers over this twilight scene. During all those years, and to Pellew's frustration, the French fleet avoided any engagement. There were those who believed that the Battle of Trafalgar had dealt the French such a blow that their policy became one of simply avoiding battle at sea. Others pointed to Trafalgar as the start of complacency in the British Navy and a softening in discipline and readiness. Whatever the reason, never again did such ships sail towards each other in such numbers, nor fight on such a scale, nor were skills like Pellew's ever again to have such a decisive role in the course of history.

PART IV

PART IV

CHAPTER 20

On the shelves of Truro's Courtney Library, too large to be stored in any way but flat on its back, is the only surviving set of Cornwall's first newspaper, *The Cornwall Gazette and Falmouth Packet.* The paper was published by T. Flindell, a zealous and enterprising native of the Helford river who had already blackened his fingers with printer's ink far afield, in Edinburgh and Doncaster. The paper lasted just two years, from 1801 to 1803. But its pages, soft as cotton now and frayed at the edges like an old shirt, provide for the first time an intimate view of Falmouth: its briny opportunities, its yearnings, its hopes and anxieties.

Here, offered for sale by Geo. Fox & Sons, is the Good Brigantine *Aurora* (90 tons measurement 'well calculated for the Mediterranean coasting trade'); in Flushing the prize *Sally*, late wrested from the French, 77 feet 6 inches in length, $130^{24}/_{95}$ tons, and now open to bids; also one half of the pilchard seine *Diligence.* The Port of Falmouth announces a Public Sale and Auction for 4,500 barrels of American flour, 6,324 gallons of brandy, 2,476 gallons of gin, and 18,998 pounds of leaf tobacco. Anxious souls can find comfort in a sermon entitled *Christian Confidence in the DAY OF TROUBLE*, while herd-owners can purchase a treatise on the Inoculation for the Cow Pox. Others might find useful a set of Tax Tables, Kearsley's efficacious tincture, Welch's Female

Pills (for removing Obstructions and other Disorders more especially incidental to the younger part of the female sex) and Essence of Anchovies for fish sauce (Genuine and Superior).

Each issue carries the Ship News, a record of the harbour's comings and goings. The extraordinary scale of Falmouth's maritime traffic during these years leaks out of reports of anchorings in the Carrick Roads: 'outward bound Lisbon and Oporto fleet of 130 sail … 200 sail of the West Indian fleet'. Each entry is preceded by a weather report, a brush with a day

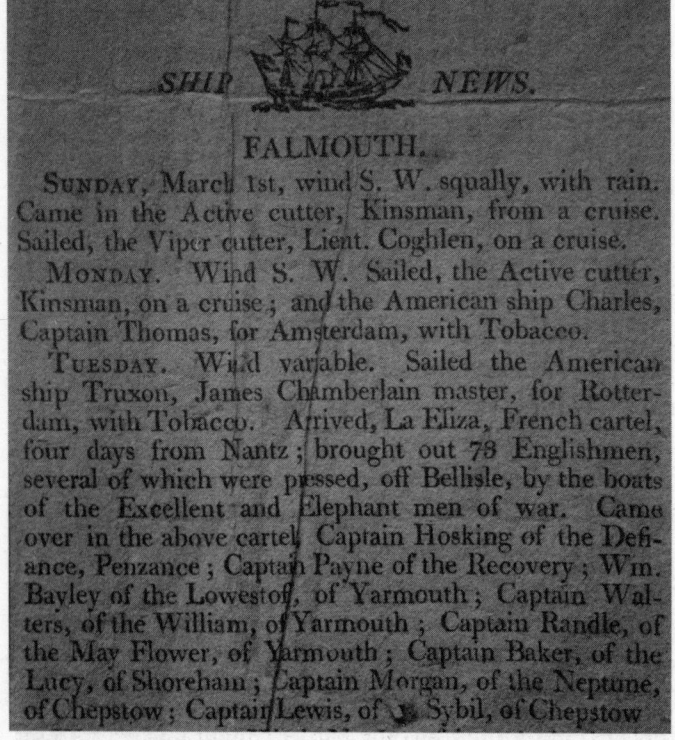

SHIP NEWS.

FALMOUTH.

SUNDAY, March 1st, wind S. W. squally, with rain. Came in the Active cutter, Kinsman, from a cruise. Sailed, the Viper cutter, Lient. Coghlen, on a cruise.

MONDAY. Wind S. W. Sailed, the Active cutter, Kinsman, on a cruise; and the American ship Charles, Captain Thomas, for Amsterdam, with Tobacco.

TUESDAY. Wind variable. Sailed the American ship Truxon, James Chamberlain master, for Rotterdam, with Tobacco. Arrived, La Eliza, French cartel, four days from Nantz; brought out 78 Englishmen, several of which were pressed, off Bellisle, by the boats of the Excellent and Elephant men of war. Came over in the above cartel Captain Hosking of the Defiance, Penzance; Captain Payne of the Recovery; Wm. Bayley of the Lowestof, of Yarmouth; Captain Walters, of the William, of Yarmouth; Captain Randle, of the May Flower, of Yarmouth; Captain Baker, of the Lucy, of Shoreham; Captain Morgan, of the Neptune, of Chepstow; Captain Lewis, of Sybil, of Chepstow

From The Cornwall Gazette and Falmouth Packet.

two centuries past – *Wind SSW fresh … Wind ESE foggy morning, fair and mild at noon … Wind SW squally, with rain …*

In early November 1801 a gale came up out of the southwest, swung nor'nor'west and increased to a violent storm. The paper reminded its readers that in such conditions there was no better place to be than Falmouth: 'The excellent anchorage and capacious size of this noble harbour which allows shipping to veer out the full extent of their cable, while the land locks it on all sides, enable the shipping of all description to ride out the storm.' All those with commercial ventures based on the harbour and its marine traffic (the greater part of Falmouth and Flushing) felt reassured by such a thought. But it was not entirely true. During the same gale a seventy-four-gun ship-of-the-line dragged its bower anchor, and wound up on the mud. No damage was done, and the master – Edward Pellew, visiting the port of his carefree frigate days – was able to save his dignity and quietly warp off on the tide.

Lest any sense of provincialism trouble the *Gazette*'s readers they could read of London's markets and the price of grain and flour, hops, leather and tallow. Bulletins on the King's health were published, as was the casualty list from naval battles.

In the summer of 1802 the *Gazette* was able to celebrate its own success. It was now being widely circulated throughout Cornwall and Devon and into most of Britain's towns. Through the Packet ships, it was delivered to the coffee houses of Lisbon and the West Indies. The paper's information was even quoted, wrote Flindell with pride, in the newspapers of America. Yet, as any merchant of the time could have testified, oceanic reach brought its dangers as well as its chances. Within months the paper had closed and Flindell was crouching in a debtor's cell in Bodmin gaol.

Immediately beside the self-congratulatory column in the issue of 31 July 1802 is an advertisement. At 7 p.m. on 19 August 'A Grand Miscellaneous Concert' will take place at Wynn's Hotel (tickets 3/6). Nine years of war had produced Falmouth's most prosperous and vibrant period to date. Plays and concerts were growing in popularity; the range and number of visitors meant a flowering of the performing arts.

The Grand Miscellaneous Concert was led by a single musician, only a couple of years resident in Falmouth, and one of the most remarkable men ever to step ashore at its quays. Joseph Emidy would be playing pieces by Stamitz, Eichner and Martini, as well as his own compositions: a violin concerto and pieces for guitar and mandolin (which instruments he also 'teaches in a most easy and elegant stile'). An account of a similar concert reveals the eclectic nature of Falmouth musicians. Violin was Major Wall from the garrison at Pendennis, first flute was the young social reformer James Silk Buckingham, second flute Mr Lott of the Post Office, and the tenor was the Deputy Collector of Customs – all under the leadership of the same Joseph Emidy.

Word of Emidy's musical skills spread far over the coming years. His playing of the violin, wrote one admirer, reached 'a degree of perfection never before heard in Cornwall'. Another reckoned him to be 'the most finished musician [he had] ever heard of'. This was an impressive transformation for a man who had just spent four years playing hornpipes on the decks of a naval frigate, still more for one whose first music was more likely to have been Mande *jeliya* than Bach, played on *kora* and *ngoni* rather than on a church organ. As a boy, some fifteen years earlier, Joseph Emidy had been taken from his home in West Africa, and led in chains onto a Portuguese slave ship bound for Brazil.

Joseph Emidy was not the first freed slave to arrive in Falmouth. In 1757 the 12-year-old Olaudah Equiano, born on the banks of the Niger, witnessed snow in Falmouth harbour and thought it was salt falling on the deck. Writing of days waiting for fair winds in Falmouth, William Beckford remembered games of billiards 'in the company of Barbados Creoles'.

Throughout the eighteenth century, ships had been criss-crossing the oceans in ever greater numbers, picking up goods, people and ideas, dumping them on far-off shores, swapping them for others, before once again setting their sails for the blue distance. What they carried might end up anywhere. Each moment at sea, vessels risked being diverted by weather, driven into some half-known port, shipwrecked or requisitioned by a rogue privateer. Never before had there been such fluidity. Falmouth thrived in this fast-spreading and fateful world, and blow-ins like Joseph Emidy enriched it.

Little is known about Emidy's early days except that they were spent somewhere in Guinea, a loose name for the inte-rior of West Africa. Where he was taken in Brazil and how he came to Lisbon is not recorded, any more than when he began to play music. But in Portugal his talents were already obvious. His master provided him with a teacher, and within a few years he was playing second violin in the orchestra of the city's opera.

It was there, one evening in the summer of 1795, that a group of English naval officers strutted in. The men were from the frigate *Indefatigable* and among them was Sir Edward Pellew, the ship's celebrated captain. All that summer they had been languishing in Lisbon – ever since the *Indefatigable* limped up the Tagus, pumps awhirr, having struck that loath-some pinnacle off the Breton coast. After extensive repairs, with the boards scarfed and the seams caulked, the ship's company was again turning its land-bound thoughts seaward – to open waters, French ships and the pre-clash whiff of the slow-match. As he sat with his officers listening to the orchestra, Pellew had his eyes on the second violinist, struck not just by his colour but by the unusual vigour of his playing. It occurred to him that the *Indefatigable* would benefit from the addition of such a fiddler. 'Be so good,' he whispered to the officer beside him, 'as to send some men round the back.'

When he left by the stage door later that evening, violin case tucked under his arm, Joseph Emidy found himself suddenly surrounded. The English sailors dragged him to the quays and rowed him aboard the frigate. Within a week the *Indefatigable* was sailing out past Belem for the open sea, and Emidy was again a captured man. In the Muster Books, he appears as 'landsman', the lowest grade of seaman. Afraid he would escape if allowed ashore, Pellew confined him on board. For the next four years, while he fiddled, Emidy's feet never touched dry land.

In 1799 Pellew received his posting to a ship-of-the-line and left the *Indefatigable* and Falmouth. Emidy too was allowed to leave, and stepped ashore free for the third time in his life, and with only his violin case under his arm.

Within a year or two, he was leading Falmouth's Harmonic Society. He earned money from teaching and by staging concerts. In Falmouth's open-sided, multi-faith society he found a degree of acceptance. A couple of weeks after his 'Grand and Miscellaneous Concert' of 1802, he married the daughter of a 'respectable tradesman'. Before long he and his wife and his growing family moved to Truro, and his reputation spread further.

Some years ago one of the curators of the Royal Truro Museum spotted a striking image in a local flea-market. He realised its significance at once and although the trader could not recall its provenance in any way, he bought it for the museum. The picture – a pen-line and wash – is entitled *A Musical Club* and dated 1808. It shows a relaxed and jovial gathering of frock-coated men. They are grouped around a long table, playing four violins, two cellos, two flutes and a pair of horns. Candles flicker among them. The men all have the wine-flushed faces of Georgian worthies – except the lead violin, Joseph Emidy. Alone of the string players, he is standing. The entire ensemble is delicately turned towards him. Hunched over his instrument, his bow-arm a perfect right-angle, Emidy has an animation that the others lack. Looking at the image in the museum's store, I could almost hear the notes he was playing.

'I have had the privilege,' wrote one William Tuck about Emidy, 'of listening to most of the stars who have appeared on the London stage during the past fifty years, but not one has equalled him.'

As his playing became better known, Emidy's supporters began to think of advancing his career. Not just his playing but his own compositions destined him, they felt, to greater things than their own Cornish salons. The pieces he had written for quartets and his symphonies had been performed in Cornwall and were 'much admired'. In 1807 the young James Silk Buckingham took some of his manuscripts to London. Buckingham had had flute lessons with Emidy and now began to track down members of the capital's musical establishment. Being resourceful and tenacious, Buckingham secured an interview with Johann Peter Salomon who had brought Haydn to London, suggested the idea of *The Creation* to him and who was a friend of Beethoven. Buckingham laid Emidy's scores before Salomon and explained the strange story of their composer.

A few weeks later, Buckingham was summoned to the shop of the violin-maker John Betts near the Royal Exchange. A group of professional musicians was there, as was a select and distinguished audience, gathered by Salomon and Betts. The musicians performed a quartet, a quintet and a symphony 'with full accompaniments' – all by Joseph Emidy. Buckingham waited nervously for a reaction.

It was Salomon the impresario who spoke first. He said that the composer of such music should be brought at once to London. But John Betts shook his head. However stirring his music, however accomplished his playing, a man like Emidy would flounder in London. Audiences, he predicted, would not accept a black musician. The others agreed, and although they began a subscription fund for Emidy, one which grew over the coming weeks and convinced Buckingham that at least in the world of professional musicians there existed an appreciation of merit without prejudice, he headed west again with a sense both of disappointment and indignation.

Joseph Emidy taught and played and continued to enthral his audiences. He carried on composing, more for his own satisfaction than from hope of wider performance. In the *Royal Cornwall Gazette* there were occasional approving references to evenings of his music, and a couple of memoirists recall hearing him play his own pieces – but he never left Cornwall. Of all the notes that he played or put to paper, not one survives. We will never know what characterised his concertos or rondeaux, whether they bore any trace of his own native traditions, or subtly shifted the motifs of a familiar form. Perhaps he shared something of that affinity for sound and meaning with Pushkin (whose great-grandfather was probably also from the southern fringe of the Sahara). Perhaps the more sombre moments of his scores suggested the horrors he had experienced, always at sea, in the slave ship as a boy, or the cramped and deadly conditions of the *Indefatigable*, her decks hidden in smoke and thudding with musket balls, or the days of the terrible engagement with the *Droits de l'Homme* in the trap of Audierne Bay.

'With the same advantages as were enjoyed by most of the great composers of Europe, this man,' wrote James Silk Buckingham, 'might have been a Mendelssohn or Beethoven.' As it was, Emidy left nothing but glimpses of his own work, recalled through the words of others.

Late one afternoon, I trot down the steps of the Royal Cornwall Museum and walk out of Truro, past the cathedral, under the viaduct and up to the hillside suburb of Kenwyn. A track leads along the bottom of the churchyard, tunnel-like beneath a thick canopy of beech. Pools of sunlight fall through still leafless branches. Emidy's grave lies some way from the church, beneath a large yew. The letters of his head-stone have been recently picked out; in the shadowy light they glow with a strange intensity. A few lines of verse are written in epitaph:

> Devoted to thy soul-inspiring strains
> Sweet music! Thee who hail'd his chief delight
> And with fond zeal that shunn'd not toil nor pain
> His talent soar'd and genius marked his flight.

The grave looks well kept. Beneath the stone are two plastic urns of fresh roses and marigolds. In the grass beside them crouches a tiny glittering figurine, something like a leopard, fashioned out of tinfoil.

The yew boughs creak in the wind. Looking at the bold new black lettering and the recently laid flowers, it occurs to me that although the churchyard contains the great and the good of nineteenth-century Truro – the sturdy professionals, the naval officers, the merchants and mineral men, the scions of ancient families rooted for centuries in the sea-surrounded duchy – it is the grave of one of Falmouth's countless ocean waifs that now receives more visitors.

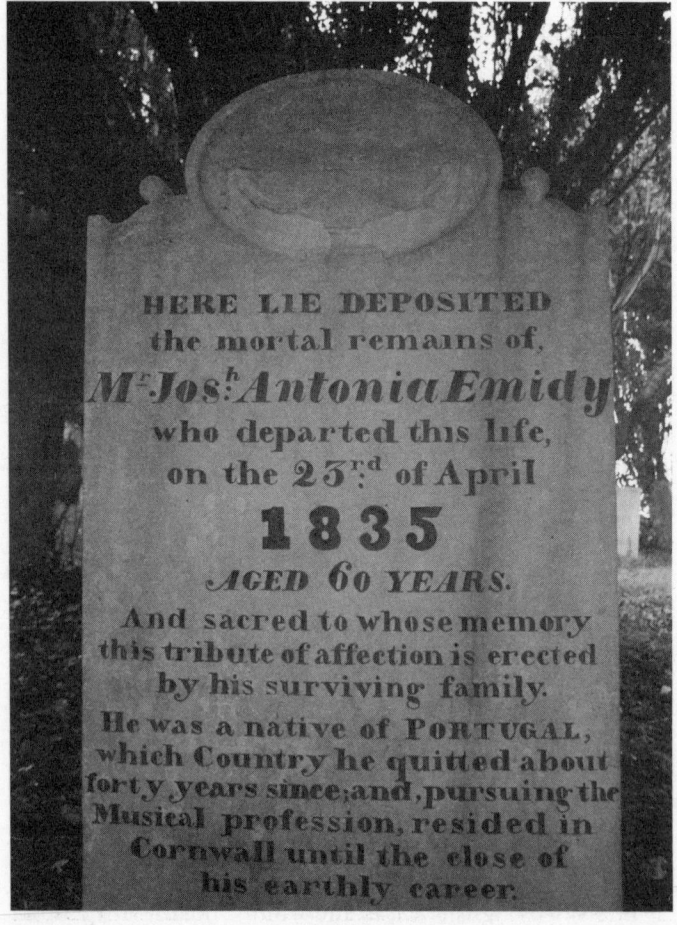

HERE LIE DEPOSITED
the mortal remains of,
Mr. Josh. Antonia Emidy
who departed this life,
on the 23rd of April
1835
AGED 60 YEARS.
And sacred to whose memory
this tribute of affection is erected
by his surviving family.
He was a native of PORTUGAL,
which Country he quitted about
forty years since; and, pursuing the
Musical profession, resided in
Cornwall until the close of
his earthly career.

Grave of Joseph Emidy.

CHAPTER 21

As Britain's position on the world's oceans rose ever higher, the growth of Falmouth, in a modest way, reflected it. By 1801 its population had doubled in fifty years (it had trebled in the previous hundred and grown by more than seven times since 1664, the year of its charter). The total number of people was still no more than 5,000, divided into tight circles of family and faction, merchant guild and religious sect.

If you wanted to invent a single character to represent the type of individual created by Britain's oceanic power, then you might choose Falmouth harbour as his proving ground. You might create a boy whose sea-skills were learned early, whose curiosity about the world outside was first excited by the port's colour and diversity. You might place him alongside the well-known figures of the community, before propelling him on a life of seaborne adventure. And because the early nineteenth century was an age of growing moral purpose, you might choose to temper his wanderings with a little social improvement, the urge to raise the lot of his fellow man. But even if you did conjure up such a man he would still pale beside the real figure of James Silk Buckingham.

Delivered into the world by Dr Joseph Fox the Quaker, Buckingham was befriended by Edward Pellew, ran around the decks of the *Indefatigable*, and learned music with Joseph Emidy. In later life he never experienced feelings more 'exquisitely delicious than the ecstatic elevation' of the religious meetings around the quays of Falmouth and Flushing. When 400 starving tinners arrived at the coast, armed with sticks and clubs, to storm a grain-stocked warehouse, young Buckingham was there. In desperation, Pellew's friend, the famous Packet commander Captain Kempthorne, lifted the boy on a sack of grain before the mob and hissed: 'Sing a hymn!'

'Which hymn?'

'Any will do, but be quick.'

'*Salvation! Oh! The joyful sound*' – Buckingham knew all of Watts's hymns – '*'tis music to our ears …*'

The miners came to a halt before him and, one by one, took off their hats.

'*A sovereign balm for every wound, a cordial for our fears …*'

The hymn over and their temper eased, the tinners took their sticks and cudgels and went home.

Although Buckingham witnessed much of the shore-based turbulence of those years, it was the harbour that made him. His family's house rose straight from the water, and looked out on Falmouth's seafront – the Market Strand, the Fish Strand and beyond them the Custom House Quay. He became a keen and proficient sailor. For several hours each day (except Sunday), he sailed in and out of the moored ships, dodging the traffic of punts and skiffs and gigs. He showed off his skills to the tars, idly leaning at the rails of naval ships above him – until the afternoon when his yawl turned turtle and trapped him underneath. Hauled up on board a Packet, declared dead, he was saved by a naval surgeon who forced an emetic through his grey lips. Such an incident might have put him off the sea; it did the opposite.

Buckingham's father died young and as the youngest child he was constantly surrounded by his older sisters. At the age of 8, he fell in love with a girl of his own age and was mocked for his comic imitation of adult passion. But it was, he wrote later, 'an ardent and sincere attachment'. When the girl died suddenly from an illness, he was crushed by grief. In a daze, he followed her cortège to the church at Mylor, resting ground of the Packet captains. He was transfixed by the sight of her coffin and its pall-bearers, six young girls dressed in white. He was found that evening lying on the crumbly soil of her shoreside grave 'in a state of torpor amounting almost to insensibility'.

Women and the sea became entwined for him in a lifelong association of beauty and hardship, comfort and discomfort, painful yearning and painful parting. In his autobiography he dwells on one particular incident. He was 4 or 5 years old, walking with his mother's maid on the bowling green. It was a fine day. They stopped and stood hand-in-hand on the soft grass. They looked out over Pendennis and St Anthony's Head to the silvery-blue beyond. A Packet ship was leaving harbour, pressing south in a shrinking display of white sail. As they watched her go, slipping out of view towards the

Falmouth from above Flushing.

Manacles, Buckingham looked up and was amazed to see tears in the young woman's eyes. He had never seen an adult cry, nor did he understand the strange look on her face. She explained that her fiancé was on board that Packet ship.

'What is beyond the Manacles?' he asked.

'Nothing but sea and sky for many long and weary weeks! Till the ship should reach the West Indies!'

Buckingham identified this moment as the beginning of his sea-longing, a moment that in various forms was repeated a thousand times a day around the coasts of Europe. Entire lives were changed in the instant of ships leaving, or returning. In Caspar David Friedrich's *Moonrise Over the Sea* three figures are watching the approach of two ghostly ships. It is not clear why the figures are so rapt, whether by anxiety or curiosity. But the tension of sea and shore and people reminds us that the real maritime drama, the countless individual experiences of the coming and going of ships, escapes the sweep of the historian.

Buckingham's reminiscence does the same. When the maid spoke of the Atlantic's vastness, he glimpsed its equivalent in the scale of her feeling. The picture of emptiness was haunting: 'I remember, as distinctly as if it happened yesterday, that this vague uncertainty kindled in my infant breast an intense desire to go and see for myself whether this assertion, which seemed to me so strange, were true or not.'

When he learned to read and write, Buckingham found himself called on by young women from the neighbourhood to interpret letters from their 'sailor-lovers'. Sitting close to them, immersed in their breathy presence, he read aloud of Atlantic gales, reefs shaken out, prizes captured – 'French West-Indiamen in the chops of the Channel'. It was this frequently repeated exercise – as well as his daily boating in the harbour – that 'helped feed my passion for the sea'.

He went to study at Duckham's marine academy in Falmouth. The building was set high above the town. He could peer out of his dormitory window at the open sea below. It was, he realised later, like the blank map of his future. So reverently did he take the study of sea-skills that he calls *Hamilton Moore's Navigator* 'the greatest treasure that I ever possessed'. He slept with his sharpened pencils and dividers under his pillow and reflected later that he 'never entered on any task before or since with greater zest and alacrity'.

Buckingham was just 9 when he first went to sea. He stood on the wharf waiting to board the Falmouth Packet *Lady Harriett*. His sisters and mother surrounded him with passionate 'adieus and tender maternal tears'. For a moment, standing there, he regretted his decision. In fact his sisters were hoping the journey would put him off the sea. The husband of one was the *Lady Harriett*'s sailing-master and he had been urged to put James through such a vigorous round of spar-clinging, tops-tinkering and night-watches that he would never want to see a ship again.

But the voyage, at least through the filter of retrospection, proved ecstatic, a series of intense and surprising revelations. The first hours were filled with a wonder so intense that the memory of each moment never left him. As they passed the Manacles, cleared the Lizard and left the land far astern, Buckingham was struck with 'feelings of awe and solemnity difficult to be described'. It grew dark. At midnight he was dragged from his hammock, but remembered 'the night being lovely, beyond all that I have ever witnessed'. The deep colour of the sea, the canopy of stars above and the phosphorescence below astonished him, and 'there was an exhilaration in the breeze, the bounding motion, the following of the white-crested waves'. Even his trips up the mast – which seemed rather more frequent than was necessary – thrilled him.

The third journey on the *Lady Harriett* did not end so well. Heading for Lisbon on the same Packet, the crew watched the approach of a French corvette off Cap Finisterre.

'*D'où vous venez?*' a voice called to the English ship.

'Anyone speak French?'asked the captain.

One of the gunners had spent three years in a French prison. 'He says "Haul down your colours, or I'll sink ye, by God!"'

The Packet captain thought it odd that so much could be loaded into four syllables, and asked for a second opinion. Buckingham, who knew a little French, explained what had really been said.

'Falmouth,' the captain shouted back.

The corvette attacked – outgunning the *Lady Harriett*. She had no option but to surrender. From then on, Buckingham's account reads like something from *One Thousand and One Nights*. The crew was thrown below the French decks to join other prisoners. The only water they had was in a single padlocked cask tied to the foot of the mast, with the key kept at the mast-head. Only those with the strength to climb the mast were allowed to drink, by sucking the muddy water out through a musket barrel. After a week or two they were landed at La Coruña and kept in an old abandoned house. The governor's young daughter took a shine to Buckingham and began to bring him food. Her name, Dona Isabella Dolores, rolled off his pen after sixty years with pleasurable ease. Her visits became more frequent and whenever she managed to get him on his own, would wrap him in 'a warm and fond embrace, by which she pressed [him] to her bosom as if never intending to relax her grasp, and kisses and tears rained in equal abundance'. She insisted they elope and although Buckingham was equally keen on Dona Isabella Dolores, he was terrified of what would happen when they were caught. His dilemma was solved by the order for their release, and the march south to the Portuguese border.

After many days they reached Santiago de Compostela. The opulence of the buildings and the flamboyance of the pilgrims added to Buckingham's growing sense that life in Cornwall was a parlour game compared to what lay beyond the sea. One night in Compostela, in the early hours, he was woken by singing. He looked outside to see a group of men serenading a woman in the moonlight. Appearing at an upper window, she threw up her mantilla while below, surrounded by musicians, stood her lover, dressed in 'the ancient Spanish custom': white satin hose slashed to crimson beneath, a slouch hat whose diamond clip glinted in the moonlight. When the woman let down a rope-ladder, he put aside his guitar and began to climb.

Several weeks later, the party stumbled into Lisbon – just as Sir John Jervis's victorious Cape Vincent fleet sailed up the Tagus. From its decks, impressment gangs fanned out through the city to make up for the battle-dead. Many of the weary crew of the *Lady Harriett* were bundled back to sea. Buckingham escaped by hiding in an attic for three days. When he spotted the masts of the *Prince of Wales* Packet, and his near-neighbour Captain Todd, he knew he was as good as home. In Falmouth he was reunited with his older sisters and his mother. Never again, they implored him, 'must you trust the fickle element of the sea'.

The next stage of Buckingham's boyhood odyssey was land-based. For a couple of years he worked behind the counter of a shop in Devonport, full of nautical books and instruments. When not in the shop he walked constantly around the Plymouth area, onto the Hoe, across the Tamar, through the grounds of Mount Edgcumbe and the crowded dockyard of Hamoaze and out along the cliffs above Cawsand Bay. And wherever he went he saw ships – the tempting tangle of rigging and masts; and he saw seamen brimming with the relief of reaching home again.

Buckingham was a wide-eyed 15-year-old, standing on the threshold of the world, while those returning from it jostled and sauntered past him. 'I was thrown constantly into the company of naval officers and seamen of every class; and their very recklessness had for me something irresistibly attractive.' One night at Plymouth's Fountain Hotel he joined a big party, which included Nelson, Pellew and the 'fire-eater' Captain Jeremiah Coghlan. The entire town was filled by the spirit of those coming ashore, while its traders and restaurateurs, its singers and actresses found it easy to part a seaman from his prize money. 'The idea of hoarding or laying by for a future day was never entertained by either officers or men.' Buckingham watched such a group hire a line of expensive coaches, wondering where they might go. They went nowhere: they climbed up and danced hornpipes on the roofs.

A cook on a ship-of-the-line, a freed slave, had been at sea for seven years and stepped ashore with slush-money and assorted bounty of more than £3,000. He took a large suite of rooms in one of the better hotels, and summoned a tailor to make him several satin-lined suits from broadcloth, kerseymere and gold, and each morning had his hair dressed and powdered before taking off in a carriage and four. At night he would throw large dinner parties for anyone who was around, take the stage box at the theatre, and escort up to six women 'of compliant character' back to his rooms. What finally finished his funds and swung him round into debt was the chartering of a Packet sloop which he filled with hangers-on and women, then sailed to Portsmouth and back. Three weeks later, according to Buckingham, he was found shivering in a shop doorway, and was dead within days.

For some time, Buckingham fell in with this life, throwing himself into the parties of libertied seamen, frequenting their ribald gatherings in the hotels, theatres and green rooms. While he never actually left the harbour, he tasted the fruits of its returning ships and was 'daily fed by all the bustle of and excitement of a great naval port' – until one morning in St Aubyn Street. There he stumbled into a church and was brought up short by a sermon on the Prodigal Son. The parable spoke directly to him. 'I thought of my dear indulgent mother and felt that I had disregarded her wishes and injunctions in feeding rather than repressing my inclination for a sea-life.' Seen from the gaiety of Plymouth's shore, a 'sea-life' was synonymous with dissipation. For the coming months, he did nothing but read – the Old and New Testament, endless commentaries, the tracts of Bunyan and Jeremy Taylor and particularly the American Jonathan Edwards – one of the driving forces of the colonies' 'Great Awakening'.

From then on, and for the rest of his life, his adventurous spirit was bound by principle. Around Plymouth, he sought out preachers who found the words for the sense of truth that was growing within him. He recalled his own budding faculty for speaking (a boast that is confirmed, to a degree, in the fluency of his writing). One day his favourite preacher was taken ill and called on Buckingham to take his place. He found that he 'ascended the pulpit with the firmness of an apostle'. He had not the faintest idea what he would say but, taking as his text the tenth chapter of Paul's Epistle to the Romans, spoke easily. He found that he was often called on again. With the unwavering views of a neophyte, and in keeping with his belief in predestination, he considered it 'sinful to make any preparation for any discourse'. He spent more and more of his time with the core of Plymouth's dissenting ministers, and most of all with the Reverend Dr Hawker, the same man whom in 1796 Edward Pellew had been about to visit when he was diverted by the foundering of the *Dutton*.

CHAPTER 22

Like an incurable gambler, even the newly principled Buckingham found himself unable to resist his attraction to the sea. Far from the influence of his mother, he went down to the quay at Hamoaze and volunteered for service on a corvette. The ship turned out to be the *Mars*, the very same ship – now in British hands – that had captured him off the Galician coast several years before.

But the reality of naval life shocked Buckingham: 'the tyranny and cruelty exercised on the greater part of the crew was really revolting'. Impressment made most of those who served something between slaves and hostages, and he felt nothing but sympathy for those who rebelled or deserted. Within a week he had witnessed countless whippings on the gangway and had watched one man hanged from the yard for mutiny. When another ran away, back to his family, he was captured and sentenced to 'flogging around the fleet'.

On this occasion, Buckingham was forced to follow the punishment launch as it was rowed from ship to ship. He saw the man stripped to the waist and tied to a frame. He saw an officer, together with two boatswain's mates, climb down into the launch and give the order to start. He saw the two mates raise their cat-o'-nine-tails and begin lashing his back, the blood spreading across the skin from the very first blow. He saw the agonised restraint that kept back the man's cries until, after six or seven, 'the pent-up agony had vent in a shriek, enough to rend a heart of stone'. Buckingham fainted, and was brought back to consciousness by the whip of his own commanding officer. Beside each ship, the man was flogged again. He had been rowed around a dozen or so before the surgeon came forward, examined him and declared him dead.

Decades later, Buckingham described it as 'the most horrible scene it has ever been my lot to witness'. Although he risked the same fate, he too fled the *Mars*, weaving in terror up through the crowds at Hamoaze, reaching the open road and hurrying like a fugitive back to Falmouth on foot.

Within two years there he had met and married Elizabeth Jennings and, on the promise of the capital from his inheritance, began a business. He opened a shop for marine charts from around the world, with a printing press in the back. The Navy never caught up with him and for a while in Falmouth, surrounded by the paraphernalia of the sea and the constant traffic of the harbour, with his loving wife and a baby daughter, and with the money waiting from his mother's trust, he had everything he wanted. Had he then understood, he wrote later, the pattern of Greek drama, he would have known that that was precisely the moment to start worrying.

One of the trustees fell foul of Falmouth's perennial traps. He had sunk Buckingham's mother's money into a cargo of smuggled goods and lost the lot when Samuel Pellew's men discovered it. Buckingham's only option was to go to sea. Leaving his wife and baby daughter in Falmouth, and now with hardly a penny to his name, he worked his passage up to Dover and walked to London docks. From there he set out 'to begin the world entirely anew'.

A portrait of James Silk Buckingham provides some idea of what happened to him in the next twenty years. Painted in

1825 by William Pickersgill, it shows a man dressed in the flowing silks of an Ottoman merchant. Around his head is wrapped a turban half a yard wide; thrust into his *kamarband* is a rhino-horn dagger. A black beard fans out from his chin; it is hard to think that this is the same man who spent his boyhood among the harbour scamps of the Carrick Roads.

His path to the Middle East was via the Atlantic, where he began as crew and was noted for his unseaman-like habit of reading books (usually high in the rigging). Promoted to captain, he used his first command to exercise his own ideals: no drinking, no swearing, strict cleanliness and on Saturday night, dedicated to remembering those at home, a dance and stories in the fo'c's'le. Those most obedient to the rules, as well as most efficient in their nautical duties, would be given prizes for their 'wives and sweethearts'. Winners would be selected not by the officers but by fellow seamen.

Soon he was leading a busy, rootless life as a Mediterranean trading-captain, hopping from port to port, fighting off pirates, amazed to see places he knew by name from his reading of the classics. It didn't take long before he had amassed a small fortune. At the insistence of his wife, however, he gave up the sea and with his languages (Arabic, Greek, Italian and French) sailed to Malta to set up as a merchant. Plague crept onto the island and spread so rapidly that all stores of foreign goods had to be destroyed. Buckingham lost almost everything.

Instead of returning home he went to Egypt, and explored Cairo and the Pharaonic sites of the Nile. He pushed south into Nubia, where he was robbed, stripped of his clothes and left to die. Struggling back to Cairo he fell in with the pasha, Mohammad Ali. Being opportunistic, Buckingham put a plan to the ambitious pasha: to build a canal from Suez through to the Red Sea. The pasha scoffed, saying with some prescience

Buckingham encounters robbers in Persia.

that such a canal would simply give the British an excuse to occupy his country, but agreed that if Buckingham could reach India, he would be happy for him to act as his trade envoy.

With the pasha's harem and a party of pilgrims, Buckingham travelled down the Red Sea to Mecca. The ship though was badly damaged in a storm, and Buckingham became so ill that he had to be carried ashore at Jeddah. Once he had recovered, he found an English ship and finally reached Bombay. There he was given the command of a vessel in the China trade but, the victim of jealous sea-captains, he found himself expelled from India.

Back in Egypt he spent another year wandering – this time through the Levant and down into Mesopotamia, avoiding hostility by dressing in silk robes and pretending to be a Muslim. His later records of these journeys, five volumes of travels, are distinctive for their plain speaking, impartial observation and, for many of these places, as the first ever account in English.

It was during this period in his life, as the wanderer in antiquity, the constant stranger, the *giaour* on the dangerous fringes of the Ottoman Empire, that Buckingham was painted by William Pickersgill in 1825. The picture now hangs in the Royal Geographic Society, above the fireplace in the fellows' tea-room, and there I went to see it. Buckingham is looking away from Pickersgill, giving the impression of mild distraction – but for one thing. In his hand he delicately holds the fingers of a woman. She is seated next to him on the divan, her head-dress more modest than his turban; black plaits hang to her shoulders and she wears robes of apricot silk; her gaze is directed at the painter. She is Elizabeth, his wife.

Despite Buckingham's roving life, which took him back and forth to America, across the Mediterranean and through the Ottoman Empire to India, he remained loyal to the Falmouth girl he had married at 19. After fifty years of marriage, he declared: 'our mutual attachment has never for a single moment been even clouded with doubt or indifference, but we have loved on until the end, with the same fervour as we began.'

Another portrait of Buckingham is published in his *Autobiography*. Described simply as 'James Silk Buckingham in Later Life', the transformation is again remarkable. Gone is the flamboyant Ottoman disguise, the dagger and the imam's beard. In its place is a frock coat and a black silk waistcoat. He is toying with a fob watch, his eyes are sparkling and his mouth is open – as if he's been caught mid-sentence. Snowy curls and sideburns frame his still boyish face.

Buckingham spent the second half of his life campaigning. His years at large had convinced him that he was put on this

James Silk Buckingham in later life.

earth to address its glaring injustices. He admitted that he was incapable of looking at anything without wanting to improve it. From the Middle East, he reached India for the second time in 1817. Offering his services as sea-captain, he was given a slave ship to Zanzibar. He refused it, renouncing his profession and setting up the *Calcutta Journal* to rail against the iniquities he saw around him. He used his columns to chronicle the tyrannies of the East India Company and those of the Bengal government, urging readers to call, at the very least, for a free press and its levelling influence. In response, the governor-general closed down the *Calcutta Journal* and for the second time Buckingham was expelled from India.

Back in London in the 1820s he carried on exposing the moral hypocrisies both in the British Empire and in the wider world. He called for self-rule in the colonial territories and, to provide a platform, began first the *Oriental Herald and Colonial Review*, then the *Athenaeum*. He fought a long battle with the East India Company, and won from them hefty compensation. Influenced by his experiences in Muslim countries, and by the devastation he saw in London, he became a strong advocate of temperance, declaring himself a teetotaller. He was elected an MP in the first reformed parliament in 1832 and stuck at his causes like a terrier – repeal of the corn laws, restrictions on alcohol, more public parks and open spaces, more libraries, more museums.

Not satisfied with Westminster as a platform for his message, Buckingham conceived a plan which would combine the twin callings of his life: he would sail around the world in a ship of 'Temperance, Education, Benevolence and Peace'. Although the idea came to nothing, he found a new arena for his fierce and boundless hopes: America. Three years of touring and campaigning followed, in all but two of the union's

states, and he was by turns thrilled by the energy and free-
doms he saw, by the republican freshness, by the women
('almost uniformly good-looking'), and horrified by the sight
of slavery. He published eight volumes of travels and
reflections.

In 1849, in the last stages of his life and after another
grand tour of America, he wrote *National Evils and Practical
Remedies*. It stands as the culmination of all his idealism. 'God
is love,' he quotes at the beginning of the opening chapter,
before urging us all to adopt the wisdom of the spheres. He
died in 1855.

At first light, I row out to *Liberty*, drop the mooring and head
across the harbour. Dawn is a distant blush in the southern
sky; the surface of the Carrick Roads lies thick as oil, unruf-
fled by even the slightest breeze. As the sun rises, I watch the
bow-wave send tiny bubbles skidding across the water.
Coming into the Penryn river, I anchor off the New Quay at
Flushing.

The waterside lanes are empty and I follow them to the
foot of St Peter's Road, once known as the New Road. The
houses here rise in a line of impressive Georgian facades. In
these few buildings lived, at the harbour's height, a good
number of its seafaring giants. In numbers 5–6 was the Packet
commander Captain Yescombe, until he was killed in action
on the *King George*. Edward Pellew then took it over with his
family, presiding over the ships of the Western Squadron,
before some successful prize-taking earned him enough to
rent Trefusis House. Another naval family, the Sulivans,
moved in and Rear Admiral Sulivan was still there when his
son sailed with Darwin on the *Beagle*. Nelson stayed in the
house on at least one occasion. Immediately below, number
4, was the house of Captain Kempthorne, with the connect-

ing door to Pellew's house so that he could talk with his friend, despite having lost half of his mouth to a French musket.

In number 7 lived the greatest of all the Packet captains, John Bull, who had suffered a similar injury. In 1804 his Packet was attacked by a French privateer. Having sunk the mails, he felt a ball pierce his cheek, fly out of his mouth and lodge in the mast. When the battle was over, Bull had time to prise the ball from the splintered timber and pop it in his pocket.

This modest terrace now consists of quiet town houses, wisteria-wound, children's bicycles against the wall, 4x4s against the kerb. I wander back through the town. At the main quay a large trawler, the *Golden Fleece*, is preparing for sea. Its high bow and gantry dwarf the cottages beyond it. A man kneels on top of the wheelhouse, repairing the navigation lights, while another heaves aboard a clutch of Tesco bags.

I carry on back towards the New Quay and my dinghy. Along the front, the houses back onto the water; a number of them have punts at the water's edge, raised on davits. It was in this row that James Silk Buckingham spent his childhood. The threat of invasion hovered over the Channel ports during the 1790s, yet these were the years, the decade or so leading up to Trafalgar, when Britain assembled the final pieces necessary for its naval domination of the globe.

Buckingham was looking back on the same period when he wrote of his sea-gilded boyhood here: 'there was probably no spot in England, in which, on so limited a surface and among so small a number in the aggregate, were to be seen so much of the gaiety and elegance of life ... Dinners, balls and evening parties were held at some one or other of the captains' houses every night.'

His house was close to the quay on which the sailing club now stands, near the old bath-houses. When the tide came in, the waves tapped at his walls. He would look down at them from the first-floor window, and as the mood took him, leap some ten or twelve feet, straight down into the water below.

As with Edward Pellew, the sight of the sea brought out in young Buckingham the reckless urge to leap into it. For Buckingham, as for Peter Mundy nearly 200 years earlier, it was a leap that took him far beyond Cornwall, beyond the bounds of the Navy, beyond the familiar ports of the Packet service, on a lone odyssey that pushed at the limits of the known world. Both men produced many volumes of plain-spoken wonders, but in Buckingham's case his witness bred convictions that then set the course of his adult life. Such convictions were now being added to the cargo of ocean-going craft and carried to far-off peoples in order to brighten their dark and impoverished lives. That ships – and particularly British ships – now moved so far and so fast somehow added to the confidence with which these principles were held.

CHAPTER 23

One day in high summer, towards the end of the Napoleonic Wars, a busy ruddy-faced man jumped down from the mail-coach in Falmouth. He carried a vellum-bound sketchbook and a copy of Cotman's *British Itinerary – Exhibiting the Direct Route to every Borough and Commercial Town in the Kingdom*. J.M.W. Turner was on his first, feverish tour of the West Country. In just two months, he covered 600 miles of coast, from Bridport to Somerset, an average of ten miles a day if he had travelled consistently. But he hadn't. He stopped in places for several nights to scurry along the shoreline, stride up inlets and creeks, onto hills and bluffs. During those heady weeks he made hundreds of drawings in the leaves of his sketchbook, before buying another in Penzance. Sometimes he continued a sketch on the next page to hang like a dream-image in the sky of a subsequent view; and when the sketchbooks weren't to hand, he used the blank pages of Cotman's *Itinerary*, interspersing the printed details of coach-routes and turnpikes with his own pencil-lines, which with a few strokes performed the miracle sought by every artist, that of creating a living world from base materials.

The sketchbooks and Turner's travelling copy of Cotman's *Itinerary* are now in the Clore Gallery at Tate Britain. By studying their sequence, it is possible to piece together his brief stay in Falmouth. He took a trip up the river to Penryn, meandered back, stopping three or four times to make drawings, looking down the estuary towards Pendennis Castle; he sketched the last above the Moor, near Erisey Terrace. He walked out westwards to Swanpool and drew Pendennis Point from there, adding (possibly back in his London studio) an incomplete wash to the image. At some point, he took a boat across the Carrick Roads to St Mawes, making a sketch in his copy of Cotman's *Itinerary* of ships at the granite quay, and the bustle surrounding a seine-haul on the beach below. It was the time of pilchards, the annual migration when shoals the size of small towns would sweep along the Cornish coast, and teams of seiners would row out and encircle sections with nets, before drawing the mass to shore. The drawing became the subject for the first large oil painting of his journey, *St Mawes at the Pilchard Season*.

As well as sketching during those weeks, Turner filled the empty pages of Cotman's *Itinerary* with the draft of an epic poem. He had been an occasional poet for some years but the 900-line poem he wrote during that two-month journey is by far the longest. It is also, even considered as a work in progress, largely unreadable – turgid, eccentric and often making no sense (the Cooke brothers, who had commissioned Turner's illustrations of the journey, instructed the printer 'not to insert a single syllable'). But alongside the drawings, the lines offer a glimpse of Turner's thinking as he dashed around the coast. He speaks of the 'Nelsonion star' falling at 'gory Trafalgar'. He dwells on the power of waves – 'all smooth and polished harshly sounding roll / and clamourous till the oceans great controull', and on Cornish havens, which 'To those who dare to cross the Atlantic sea … still offer safety to them to [?house] / From the winds the winds that rage upon our isle.'

Turner's couplets, scribbled down in the pause between coaches, in lodging-houses, on cliff-tops and shores, are also evidence of the creative energies that swept over him that July and August. Writing many years later, John Ruskin was convinced of the formative effect of that 1811 journey. 'I believe it was in the watch over the Cornish and Dorsetshire coasts ... that [Turner] received all his noblest ideas about ships and the sea.'

Turner had always been a sea-painter. Of his earliest surviving drawings, from his teens, a large number were of boats. His first exhibited picture was maritime, as was his last. In later decades, the sea became the context for his misty abstractions and allegories, effects that become more mannered when fogging the fixed lines of the land. His whaling series, *Dawn after the Wreck (the baying hound)*, *Europa and the Bull* and dozens of others allowed Turner to convey the wonders and horrors of the sea. Ruskin considered Turner's greatest painting to be the harrowing *Slave Ship (Slavers Throwing Overboard the Dead and Dying, Typhoon Coming On)*.

'The whole picture,' wrote Ruskin, is 'dedicated to the most sublime of subjects and impressions ... the power, majesty and deathfulness of the open, deep, illimitable sea.'

Turner's achievement as a maritime painter was not so much in his renditions of the sea itself (which though atmospheric are often formally unconvincing), but of man's career upon it. He remained fascinated by the drama of sailing vessels, and later by the new steamers. He owned a display box with several ships' models in it, chief among them being a sixteen-gun three-master with a striking resemblance to a Falmouth Packet. He had boats of his own, and in 1806 may well have commissioned a sailing boat. He sought to *experience* what he painted (although the story of him being lashed to the mast for *The Snow Storm* is probably untrue), and his understanding of the precariousness of seagoing craft informs all his maritime pictures: Ruskin was in no doubt about the supremacy of Turner's vessels: 'No other painter ever floated a boat quite rightly; all other boats stand on the water, or are fastened in it; only his *float* in it.'

It was Ruskin who in 1856 wrote the text for *The Harbours of England*, an edition of Turner's mezzotints from the West Country tour of 1811. The one of Falmouth he singles out as being 'one of the most beautiful and best-finished of the series', but many years had passed between the West Country trip and Turner's preparations of the plates, and Ruskin rightly concludes that he was unable to reproduce in them the 'innocence of delight' of his original journey. The Tudor castles are wildly distorted, and the scene is filled with melodrama.

The unexpected interest of the book lies in the introductory essay, one of the most remarkable pieces of maritime writing in the English language. Ruskin – the high aesthete,

Falmouth *by J.M.W. Turner.*

the self-confessed landsman – begins with a startling admission: 'Of all things, living or lifeless, upon this strange earth, there is but one which, having reached the mid-term of appointed human endurance on it, I still regard with unmitigated amazement … and that is the bow of a boat.'

Like Turner, Ruskin considers the craft of boat-building to be a mystical art, but he raises it still higher: 'I know nothing else that man does, which is perfect, but that. All his other doings have some sort of weakness, affectation, or ignorance in them. They are overfinished or underfinished; they do not quite answer their end, or they show a mean vanity in answering it too well.' The 'miracle' of a boat's bow lies in its simplicity and Ruskin believes it is at its most obvious in the plain, undecked version: 'You may magnify it or decorate it as you will, you do not add to the wonder of it.'

Trying to describe the shape of a boat's bow, Ruskin struggles, reverting to an analogy. 'Those mysterious, ever-changing curves,' he writes, put him in mind 'of the image of a sea-shell.' Like Matthew Baker and his cod, Ruskin finds no equivalent for ship shape in the man-made world, nor even on land, but only in the sea itself, and the adaptations of its creatures. Success in withstanding the seas requires imitation; the fluidity of a ship's bow mirrors 'the flowing of the great tides and streams of ocean'.

Ruskin's prose is always exhilarating and having read the essay I row straight out to *Liberty* and inspect her bows. The clinker makes the effect more obvious: each stepped board arcing in towards its opposite, each fusing into the raised column of the stem, itself steel-banded to cleave the water. Until now, I thought I knew it from that intimacy that comes with a dozen arduous scrapings and sandings and paintings. But Ruskin's appraisal makes me look at it afresh: 'the bow of the boat is the gift of another world'.

Liberty's *bow*.

Ruskin is speaking not just of form. He uses the bow to represent the ship as artefact, one that has immense historical significance: 'No other work of human hands ever gained so much.' In terms of the nation, as he sees it, ships liberated Britons from their island and the 'prison wall' of 'unconquerable waves'. Like a zealous preacher, he uses the tiniest detail as an emblem of universal good: 'the nails that fasten together the planks of the boat's bow are the rivets of the fellowship of the world'; each vessel, he suggests, 'leads love round the earth'.

In the light of his analysis, Ruskin goes on to propose a new division of historical periods. The Middle Ages and the Ancient World should be known as the 'Age of the Chariot', while the hundred years before his own era, 1750–1850, might be termed 'the Age of Boats'. The intervening period, from Elizabeth I onwards, he suggests should become the 'Age of Starch'. It was during this period that manners, clothing and hair were all gradually refined and stiffened: 'a change of steel armour into cambric, of natural hair into peruke … and plain language into quips and embroideries'. At the same time, far from the whispering halls of state power, a divergent force was at work: in ports and rivers, hull upon hull was being hammered into life, to sail to ever more distant shores. 'It was not possible to starch the sea; and precisely as the stiffness fastened upon men, it vanished from ships.' To be successful, vessels must serve first the laws of the ocean; in doing so, they reveal for Ruskin the natural genius that land-bound man was losing: 'there is not, except the very loveliest of creatures of the living world, anything in nature so absolutely notable, bewitching, and, according to its means and measure, heart-occupying, as a well-handled ship on a stormy day'.

Ruskin was exaggerating when he said of Turner's later maritime paintings that, after 1818, 'he never painted a ship quite in fair order'. But it *is* true that Turner's ships became more and more vulnerable, wrecked or under stress. As Shakespeare found, a ship in peril is an endlessly supple representation of man's frailty in nature. Yet it is no natural force that haunts Turner's most popular painting, *The Fighting Temeraire Tugged to Her Last Berth to Be Broken Up*, but the flood-tide of human progress.

One of the heroic ships of Trafalgar, second in the line behind the *Victory*, the *Temeraire* is being towed down the

Thames to the breaker's yard at Rotherhithe. The last of the day is spread in a fiery glow across the horizon. Ahead of the *Temeraire*'s high bows, dwarfed by her bulk, is the sprightly little coal-fired tug towing her to her grave. The historical symbolism is obvious, the age of sail giving way to steam. But the picture's impact at the time was more immediate. The significance of the Battle of Trafalgar seemed to grow with each passing year, and the relief from fear of invasion remained palpable.

The *Temeraire*'s end was witnessed by many 'naval officers and seamen who fought and bled for their country'; one Trafalgar veteran who watched said he could not 'believe they would treat her so' – though as consolation the breakers did give him some of her timbers for the leg he lost in the battle.

Turner himself also watched the *Temeraire*'s funereal progress that day. Now in his sixties, he was facing his own mortality. Ruskin believes *The Fighting Temeraire* was 'the last picture he ever executed with his perfect power'. Although several of Turner's best-loved paintings were still ahead of him, they lack the precision of his earlier works. It is this technical precision – the sureness of the line of the *Temeraire*'s cut-down mast, the strange convexity in the curve of her topsides, the way she sits in the water – that, when set beside the hazier water and sky all around her, gives the painting its power. Throughout his working life, Turner had been using the same contrast, of a ship's orderly lines in the formless, ever-shifting sea – the small, sharp works of man in an omnipotent and infinite universe.

All of the pictures that Turner worked up from his Falmouth sketches feature one or other of the Tudor castles of Pendennis or St Mawes (several show both). He knew that the public liked a castle, and his journey was, primarily, a commercial enterprise. Yet there are a couple of images which he did not develop, that feature neither castle that, with the sense the sketches give of the storm of creative energy that summer, reveal Turner's private passions. Taking time off from his commission, he lingered at the two places near Falmouth where ships were built. One was at Richard Symons's yard at Little Falmouth. The other was at Bar Pool where he drew a leafy area with the faintest hint of a roofline – the remains of Arwenack Manor. But the boldest lines, and the picture's focus, are the ribs of a vessel rising from the keel. Whether it is a ship in the process of being built, or one being taken apart, is not clear.

The images of two men frame these maritime centuries. At one end stands Matthew Baker, from Pepys's *Fragments of Ancient English Shipwrightry*, prancing about beside his plan-table, dividers in hand, calculating the proportions for his race-built hull and helping to set the course of ship design for the next quarter of a millennium. At the other is J.M.W. Turner, hunched over his sketchbook on the Falmouth shore, transcribing the bones of a ship to the page, conscious perhaps even in 1811 that the sailing ship had already performed its greatest deeds.

CHAPTER 24

To coincide with the end of the Napoleonic Wars, Falmouth's first guidebook was published. *Falmouth Guide 1815* is the earliest book of its kind in the West Country – a companion volume not to a whole region but to a single town. Only one public copy of the book exists in Cornwall. At Redruth's Cornwall Centre, I watch the librarian carry it towards me in both hands, a pair of white gloves lying on top like the service-cap on a military coffin.

With some excitement, I raise the cover and explore the now thriving port – its nine inns and taverns, its nineteen recognised lodging houses, its two physicians, six attorneys-at-law, two banks and various consulates (Messrs Fox & Co. alone representing France, Spain, Portugal, Russia, Prussia, Austria, America, the Ottoman Empire and others). Falmouth was now the most populous town in Cornwall; three-fifths of its citizens were women; the paved roads of the town were unusually bumpy because of the raised quartz veins in the rock ('unpleasant to those accustomed to the flag-pavements of a great town, or the decks of a ship'). Wynn's Hotel was being refurbished but would soon be 'the most elegant in the West of England'. Visitors might notice the 'extremely moist air' and the frequent heavy showers, but could be reassured that 'pluviometers' show the rainfall to be lower than the Midlands.

Lake's took the risk of publishing such a specialist guide because of one observed fact – the large number of bored and well-heeled visitors knocking around the town's streets. Every year several thousand passengers were carried by the Falmouth Packets – diplomats and their parties, clandestine emissaries, scions of the nobility, flop-haired adventurers. The weather often meant waiting several days in Falmouth.

Lake's *Guide* makes no great claim to Falmouth being a destination in itself: the book would be bought by people who were waiting to be somewhere else. But, during their ambling, it did encourage visitors to take note of two ways in which it claimed the town was unrivalled in the country: the proportion of religious sectarians (and the recent addition of a Unitarian chapel), and the number of charitable institutions. Among the not very numerous buildings were schools, hospitals, Bible Societies, a Public Dispensary and a Widows' Retreat. Its residents had organised a Lying-in charity (linen for poor women in childbirth), and two Societies of Ladies (who stitched clothes for the needy while a gentleman read edifying texts to them). With some civic pride, Lake's *Guide* apologised that competition for 'moral excellence' meant that, apart from Mr Fisher's theatre and the billiard tables in the taverns, the town was sadly lacking in amusements. It did not point out the irony that a port founded on the seamier side of maritime enterprise should now exhibit such piety. Nor did it list the sort of diversions presented to Sessions of the Truro court in 1813 when Falmouth residents Caroline Mitchell and Elizabeth Roberts were convicted of running brothels.

* * *

The end of the war in 1815 meant that the growing urge to roam overseas, to trade, to explore or improve, could again be indulged. The Packet service was now busier than ever, its ships speeding passengers and messages out across the oceans as part of the renewed frenzy of global commerce. Briefly their hulls would lie at anchor in Falmouth harbour, sleek brigantines whose arrival prodded those in shoreside stores and lofts to hurry out to them with sail-cloth, cordage and victuals. Officers and crews would swap the rigging and

THE PUBLISHER OF THIS WORK,

J. LAKE,

Printer, Bookseller, Stationer, and Bookbinder,

Opposite WYNN'S ROYAL HOTEL,

HAS CONSTANTLY ON SALE

Upwards of Five Thousand Volumes in the English and Foreign Literature;

CONSISTING OF

The most valuable Works in History, Divinity, Lexicography, the Sciences, Biography, Topography, Travels, Voyages, &c.

The favourite Productions of the best English Poets, including those of LORD BYRON, WALTER SCOTT, &c.

Walker's, Suttaby's, & Sharpe's Miniature Editions of the Classics.

The newest and best Novels and Romances.

Works on Ship-building and Navigation, the Mathematics, &c.

BESIDES THE FOLLOWING,

the French, Spanish, Portuguese, Italian, German & Latin languages.

And the best Works in Medicine, Chemistry, and Surgery.

From Falmouth Guide 1815.

below-deck crowding for fleeting roles as family men. Waiting passengers would prepare for the perils of the voyage with a final visit to the store also run by Lake & Co. for the latest volumes of English or European literature, salt of lemons, blacking-balls and cakes, silk kerchiefs, walking sticks and hair caps.

The commanders of the Packet ships were doing well, adding to their Post Office commissions with passenger fees and even better returns on their below-board ventures. Captain Lovell had bought Rosemerryn in Budock, Captain Boulderson lived in the spacious Bereppa. A number of others had left the terrace on Flushing's New Road for a leafier, grander life.

Most successful of all was Captain John Bull who had begun his career on the New Road, in number 4, but ended up erecting one of Falmouth's finest buildings. Marlborough House was named after his own Packet ship, the *Duke of Marlborough*. A marble plaque of the ship, its courses furled but topsails full, can still be seen set into the pediment. Inside, Bull is said to have laid out the rooms in capacious imitation of a ship, with the dining room as the captain's cabin and the study as the forecastle. The drawing room was hung with fine painted wallpapers from the Mediterranean, depicting scenes of the Olympic Games and *Don Quixote*, papers which Bull had smuggled back in sealed tubes hidden in barrels of tar. He bought up the land around the house, ordered thousands of trees to be planted, and placed the capital he had accumulated – largely from smuggling – in ship-shares and stocks from Brazil and Mexico. Like Arwenack and many other houses across Britain built on maritime trade, the tasteful Georgian rooms of Marlborough House belied some of the darker dealings of its owner.

John Bull himself was the exemplary sea-captain, terse, unbending and immensely skilful with his ship. Obedience to the laws of the sea made him, like many such mariners, a little cavalier with the law of the land. The likenesses of him that have survived show a blunt gaze and a fighting chin. He was wounded several times, saw off many French privateers and rescued a number of distressed ships. The appearance in the harbour of the *Duke of Marlborough* usually fed the quayside conversations with tales of some far-off scrape, while the Customs men wondered if they dared send their rummage-crews aboard his Packet.

Such was the stature of John Bull in Falmouth that he was known simply as the Commodore. In October 1810 the *Duke of Marlborough* was returning from Lisbon when, within sight of Pendennis Castle, a French privateer closed with her, flying the 'bloody flag' of no surrender. Bull sank the mails. The privateer was larger, with more guns – but pointing at the castle, he reminded his crew how close they were to home. For nearly an hour they fought, with no wind to separate them or drive away the smoke. A crowd gathered at Pendennis, unable to see what was happening until the French suddenly emerged, paddling away from the battle. The *Duke of Marlborough* limped into harbour.

John Bull was as much a hero on the quays as he was a curse to the revenue men. He once wandered into a Customs auction, hoping to pick up cheap some of the seized goods that they sold off. Among the lots that day, the casks of rum and brandy, the deals and canvas, the calico (as well as forty-five kaleidoscopes), was an item familiar to Bull, a favourite piece of the *Duke of Marlborough*'s on-board tableware: a silver pig, bought in Portugal, which Bull had used to keep toothpicks in. The Customs had scooped it up in a recent raid on his ship.

Bull's voice boomed across the hall: 'Damn 'ee!' he cried. 'That's my pig!'

No one bid against him, and Bull and his Portuguese pig were reunited through a threepenny ransom.

For a century and a half, Falmouth and its Packet ships survived as an outpost of the old freebooting spirit of the sea. From time to time the authorities made a stand against the smuggling that sustained the Packet crews and captains. But the practice always crept back. In October 1810 one of Samuel Pellew's revenue crews rowed out to Bull's *Duke of Marlborough*, boarding her in the moments before she was due to sail and seizing the crew's countless little ventures. When they heard of the move, the other Packet ships refused to sail. A mob of men converged on the Packet office in Bell's Court. Their response was declared a mutiny and the Riot Act was read.

As punishment, the Post Office abolished the crews' immunity from the press gang. Many of the rebels found themselves pulled from the 'easy' life of the Packets and forced into the Navy. The Post Office also authorised the removal of the entire service from Falmouth to Plymouth. Falmouth at once began to wilt. But Plymouth proved ill-prepared for the service, and the ships soon returned. The *Bristol Mirror* reported the celebrations that followed in Falmouth: 'several hogsheads of beer were given away to the populace; some brilliant displays of fireworks took place and bonfires blazed in every direction'.

Yet the brief removal was a warning. In 1815 the world changed in ways that were not at once apparent. Over the coming decades the unseen currents that had suddenly produced Falmouth two centuries earlier were beginning to alter their flow. The free-trading, devil-may-care days were coming to an end. In 1823, partly to give work to the large number of signed-off seamen, the Admiralty took over control of the Falmouth Packets. Civil ships like Bull's *Duke of Marlborough* continued to operate for several more years but as they retired or were sold, they were replaced by naval ships.

The Admiralty introduced their own vessels – ten-gun brigs which were low-sided and wet. They were humorously dubbed 'bathing-machines' by the head of the Post Office; but the men aboard them knew better. They called them 'coffin-ships'. When Edward Pellew first saw them, he cast his seaman's gaze over them and growled: 'they will drown their crews'. Within a decade, nine of these ships had been lost, several without trace in the vastness of the Atlantic; nearly 300 died. To the people of Falmouth, long used to the mysterious whims of the sea, such a loss suggested the work of malignant forces.

The Admiralty also began to experiment with steam power. Early use was a failure – the ships needed constant bunkers, they ran out of coal, the boilers failed, the paddles gave out. But as each problem arose, a solution was found. A hulk was towed into Falmouth to store coal for shipping and also to service various points in the outposts of British territory to the south. Passage-time was reduced and in 1832 the Packet route from Falmouth to Lisbon – the most important, the busiest and the most lucrative – was taken over by steam.

Falmouth's naval agent had long begrudged the Packet commanders their maverick ways, their invented uniforms and their crews free from the press. Gloating in the success of the new steamships, he wrote from Falmouth to the lords of the Admiralty: 'A strange opinion is entertained by these Hired Commanders that they possess a vested right in the Packet Service, of which no power ought to dispossess them.' In particular, he told them, John Bull and the *Duke of*

Marlborough had prolonged their right to operate by some eight years.

John Bull retired. He sold the *Duke of Marlborough* and moved ashore for good, to Marlborough House. For nineteen years he lived there, with its handpainted wallpapers, its distant views of the open sea and the smuggling tunnel that was said to link its cellars with the beach at Swanpool. Steam trails now ran along the horizon, as ships pushed up and down the Channel, bypassing Falmouth.

First to go was the task of victualling and repairing the Packet ships. Then the routes themselves. Liverpool took over the North American Packets and Southampton those for the West Indies. Railways linked these ports and their seaways, bringing track right to the gunwales of waiting ships. Far-off Falmouth with its wind advantage now counted for nothing. The Mediterranean steam service was transferred to London, and although to begin with the steamers took in Falmouth as they passed, they soon set their course far to the south, for Ushant and into the Bay of Biscay, unaffected by the westerlies that hit them full on the nose.

In Falmouth, the effect was immediate. The numbers of poor rose visibly. Those who could, emigrated and the population, which until then had always grown, now levelled out. The local paper was full of reports of Falmouth's demise: 'the condition of the pavements would disgrace any fishing town'. From the harbour, it was a dismal sight: 'Nothing is seen but the blackened and filthy backs of low and irregular hovels.' Its position on the water, the source of its rapid expansion, now proved a curse. Overcrowding, rotting fish-waste and ships from the hot south combined to breed epidemics; by the late 1840s infant mortality and cholera deaths were the highest in Cornwall.

One morning in the spring of 1851, when in London the new technological age was being celebrated at the 'Great Exhibition of the Works of Industry of all Continents', the last Packet ship sailed into Falmouth: 'She brought only a small parcel of letters,' reported the *Royal Cornwall Gazette*, 'and but three packets of diamonds ... This is the last vessel on this station as a packet.' Just weeks later, on the first day of June, Captain John Bull spoke his last words: 'Glorious first of June ... Lord Howe's victory ...'

Falmouth still possesses a model of Bull's *Duke of Marlborough*, presented to him at the height of his career in 1812. I first saw the ship in the old Maritime Museum, a couple of rooms hidden away up an alley in Bell's Court, itself little changed from the days when it housed the Packet office. On a cold day in January I go to seek it out in the new museum, a hangar of a building erected on reclaimed land in front of the Killigrew Monument. The ship stands proud, eighteen inches high, and wonderfully detailed behind a sheet of plate-glass. I kneel down to examine it at eye level.

On the deck, probing through open ports, are seven brass cannon. I follow the line of the hull forward, to where the bowsprit pushes out to a jibboom, and on again to a flying jibboom – enabling headsails to be set over half the hull's length ahead of the bows. A mass of twine faithfully matches the ship's miles of hemp rigging and I follow that too, up from the pin-racks at the foot of the mast, up from the cleats and the chain-plates, up through the first yards to the royals, and then from the futtocks up to the topmasts, converging like an orchestral high-note at the soaring, match-thin tops.

Looked at now, the Falmouth Packets, built for speed, appear as a triumph of technology. This model remains the most detailed record of their rig. Every stay and every knot, every fastening and band and tie, and every joint and curve of the ship's frame and timbers stands at the apex of tens of thousands of sea miles, centuries of trial and test, of experiment and revision. Seeing it here like a stuffed animal, I am still struck by a hollow feeling of awe.

When he retired, John Bull sold the *Duke of Marlborough* to a trading company. In 1836 she was sheltering from a gale in Torbay when her cable parted. She was driven ashore. When she struck, the stays tore from their plates and the mainmast flopped against the rocks. The mate scrambled up it to safety but the rest of the crew gazed up in horror, too terrified to do the same. Over the coming hours, as the *Duke of Marlborough* broke up, each one of those men drowned.

Beside the model of the *Duke of Marlborough* is a smaller object. Gleaming in the museum's halogen lights, its back studded with holes and its gait curiously delicate, stands John Bull's silver pig.

CHAPTER 25

Through the slow hot weeks of June and July 1863 the people of Falmouth prepared for a grand celebration. *The Falmouth Packet and Cornwall Advertiser* had little doubt about its significance. What was coming would not only place the port back to the fore of national importance but would propel it to new levels of prosperity. It was, they suggested, nothing less than 'the greatest event that has ever occurred in the annals of Falmouth, from the first house-warming of the then newly-founded town of "Penny-come-quick"'.

After days of indifferent weather, the morning of 21 July dawned cloudless. From outlying villages, by omnibus and on foot, in punt and yawl across the harbour, the crowds converged on Falmouth. At ten o'clock the mayor left Green Bank at the head of a procession which followed the High Street past the Market Strand, along Market Street and Church Street, Arwenack Street and out towards the docks. Beside the mayor walked the chain-wearing and uniformed officers, the aldermen, councillors, sergeants-at-mace, the coastguards and police, then the town's tradespeople, a sizeable host of clergymen and ministers, as well as members of the Ancient Order of Foresters and the Independent Order of Oddfellows. The band of the Royal Marines followed them, accompanied by the band of the 1st South Devon and

Exeter Rifles (and the Oddfellows band). They played marching tunes, rousing the carnival spirits of the crowd which
stretched behind them for well over a mile.

The procession passed beneath dozens of green arches,
built for the occasion and hung with swags of flowers and
bound by foliage. The shops had decked out their windows
with national flags, and lines of bunting, and fizzing stars
made from gas jets. Like a schoolmaster in a party hat, the
Custom House compromised its authority and joined in,
winding its Doric columns with garlands and bunting.
Opposite it, Messrs G.C. Fox & Co. had picked from the
various Fox gardens a dazzling display of blooms to brighten
its brick and bay-windowed front.

Most impressive of all the arches was the one outside
Arwenack Manor. The old Killigrew estate had passed,
through several tenuous kin-links, to Lord Wodehouse
whose important life meant that, regrettably, he was unable
to come to Cornwall for the celebrations. He had, though,
instructed his stewards to create something suitable, and they
had managed to outdo all the other displays. For a day, the
town was visited by the ghost of its founder, the original John
Killigrew who 300 years previously was rebuilding his shoreside house here with fortress-like embellishments. Arwenack's
stewards raised a Gothic arch, topped with battlements and
suggesting in its grandeur the gateway to 'an ancient stronghold'. The whole was wrapped with ivy and topped by a
single Union flag. The *West Briton*'s glowing description
makes it sound less like a triumphal arch than a version of
Arwenack's own ivy-clad ruins, which stood unnoticed just
yards from the processional route.

But it was not a day for warnings, nor one on which to
highlight the shady areas of Falmouth's sea-shaped past. The
West Briton glossed the memory of the Killigrews – 'one of

PHILIP MARSDEN

the oldest and most deservedly popular of our old Cornish families'.

On pressed the mayoral procession, past Bar Pool and out to Graving Dock Number One where a brand-new wharfside shed had been laid out with eleven rows of tables and place-settings for 500 guests ('the comfort of the guests was further greatly promoted by every one being provided with a chair'). The shed's walls were hung with flowers and foliage and several landscape paintings and photographs.

The mayor mounted the dais; the guests fell silent. 'It has devolved on me,' he began, 'as the chief magistrate to perform the gratifying and delegated duty of bidding you welcome on this auspicious day to celebrate the completion and opening of the Cornwall railway at this, its legitimate terminus.'

Just outside the shed lay the brand-new station of Falmouth Docks, now accommodating between its platforms the port's first train. It had just ferried two carriages of dignitaries down from the main line at Truro and now it sat garlanded and adorned, like a sacred cow from far-off Hindustan.

The first railway had reached Cornwall some years earlier, followed by Brunel's bow-tube bridge across the Tamar in 1859. Falmouth, of course, was its natural destination: 'The undertaking could never realise either the expectations of the public nor the hopes of the shareholders until it had reached the borders of the Fal and clutched with its iron grasp the haven *par excellence* of Cornwall.'

Alfred Fox, as chairman of the Falmouth Docks Company, made a brief speech in which he called the arrival of the railway 'exceedingly gratifying'. He added that a providential sign lay in the 74-foot whale that had recently washed up on the coast.

The chairman of the Cornwall Railway Company then stood before the crowd: 'I reciprocate with all my heart the

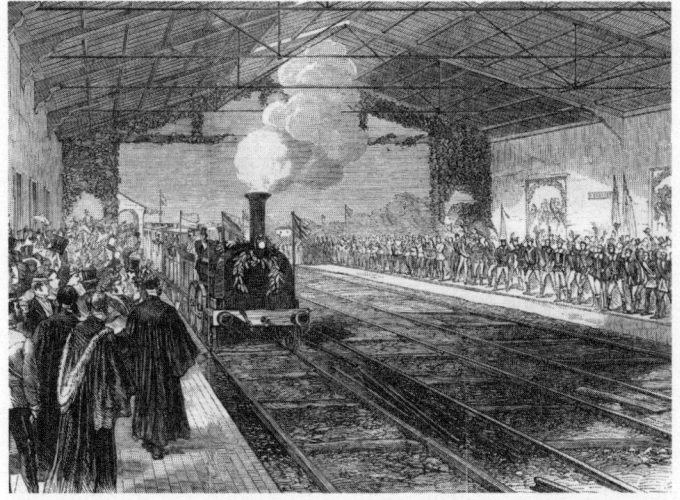

Falmouth's first train.

congratulations you have tendered to us.' He spoke of the difficulties of winning approval to add Falmouth to the rail network: 'They have been great – they have been multiplied – they have been of a most harassing character. Many and many a time has the alternative been pressed on the Cornwall board – not whether they would hasten their works to Falmouth, and arrive here at an earlier period, but whether we could reasonably hope to reach Falmouth at all.'

He did not dwell on this dark suggestion but added his own puff to the day's optimism: 'I am proud and happy to say that we have at last reached the important object of our desires – the attainment of the legitimate terminus of the railway to the town and port of Falmouth.' (Loud cheers.) He ended by repeating the cry that he had heard as he arrived in the town. Someone had shouted at the train: 'Better late than never.' (A laugh.)

It was supposed locally that one of the main reasons for the loss of the Packet service was that Falmouth lacked the necessary rail-link. The *West Briton* was not alone in believing that the arrival of the railway would now restore the port's former importance. 'We may confidently anticipate that Falmouth will become what her position and great natural capabilities pre-eminently qualify her to be – the mail-packet station and general free warehousing port for all England.' The *Illustrated London News* believed Falmouth's advantages were under-valued. Its beauty was 'inferior only to the Bay of Naples while its potential as a port now promised, with the arrival of the railway, to make it '*the Dover of the Atlantic*'.

With such appetising thoughts, the chosen five hundred – pleased to find that each had their own chair – sat down to a feast of nine savoury jellies, four beef dishes, wild boar and lamb, tongue, liver pâté, venison pâté, pigeons in aspic, crab, salads, fromage de cochon, meringues, crème à la vanille, Charlotte à la Russe, Puits d'amour, Tipsy cakes, Gâteau de Savoie, many other sweets and a selection of seven fruits. As the hours of the afternoon drifted past in that improvised banqueting hall, inserted as it was between the sea and the new train track, each citizen could imagine themselves once again a part of the expanding world, linked now to the iron capillaries of commerce, and offering access to the seaways of the Atlantic.

But the Packet service, or anything else to match its global significance, never returned to Falmouth.

*   *   *

The sailing ship did not die with the coming of steam, at least not at once. In fact, through the middle decades of the nineteenth century, the building of merchant sailing ships boomed. In 1860 4.2 million tons of UK shipping was registered of which only about a tenth used steam. Sailing ships could carry bigger cargoes further and faster than their coal-powered equivalent – and would continue to do so for another thirty years. Composite hull construction, in which iron frames were used to stiffen the wooden hulls, meant ships could grow longer than ever before. Masts sprang up to power these elongated hulls – colonnades of four, five and six carrying more than twenty sails between them. The greatest sailing ships ever built emerged during these years and the fastest of them – the clippers – could sail 400 miles in a day.

The bulk of merchant shipping, though, was much smaller. Cutters and brigs and schooners hopped round the coast, sailing materials and manufactured goods from port to port, and in some cases, as on the creeks of the Fal, from village to village. Carts would come from several miles inland to load and unload on the strand. It was these ships with their fore-and-aft rig that in terms of form and function – and sheer numbers – represented the triumph of thousands of years of sail-driven transport.

'The fore-and-aft rig,' wrote Joseph Conrad, 'in its simplicity and the beauty of its aspect under every angle of vision is, I believe, unapproachable.' Such craft he considered to be 'birds of the sea, whose swimming is like flying ... One laughs with sheer pleasure at a smart piece of manoeuvring.'

Towards the end of his book *The Sailing Ship*, R.C. Anderson places an arresting illustration in the margins. He sets a coasting barque of the early twentieth century alongside a sixteenth-century three-master. The modern ship sports a few more topsails, the lateen sail aft has become a mizzen, the spritsail has leapt up on top of the bowsprit and multiplied into headsails – but the overall plan, the structure and the power of the rig, is identical. Life had changed utterly in those 400 years, yet the agent of so much of that change, the vehicle for ambitions, freight and weapons, had remained essentially the same. The last square-rigger to operate a commercial voyage in Britain was the *Waterwitch* of Fowey in 1936, but fore-and-aft schooners carried on plying their coastal trade until about 1960.

In the final decades of the nineteenth century, Falmouth harbour still bristled with masts. It was the first port for returning ships – 'Falmouth for orders' was the last command given to a thousand traders as they sailed out of Bombay, New York, Kingston or Buenos Aires. At Falmouth, they would be told where the best prices were, whether to sail north for Liverpool or Glasgow or up the Channel to London or Rotterdam. But after Messrs G.C. Fox & Co. ran a telegraph cable down to the Lizard in 1856, it was no longer necessary to go in to Falmouth at all.

Its former importance never returned. The Packet ships now bypassed it, before the entire service was made redundant by fast passenger steamers carrying the mails, and by copper wire. There were times in the coming years when Falmouth harbour was mentioned as a possible site for a naval port, or a terminal for transatlantic liners, and more recently for a major container terminal which would transform it into a Harwich or Felixstowe of the West Country. Nothing came of any of these ideas. Despite its natural attributes, its deep-water channels, Falmouth has remained a minor port, far from the population centres that drive commerce, and used primarily for bunkers and repairs, and the laying-up of ships with nowhere else to go, waiting for contracts or for breaking up.

In 1871, a few years after the arrival of the railway, work
began on a new pier in Falmouth. It would eventually push
out further than the town quays, the original stone-built
jetties in front of the Custom House. The pier was catering
for the demands of a new age, the growing number of visitors
whose engagement with the sea was oddly passive after
centuries of action. They liked to look at it, and their willing-
ness to pay to do so soon supported a small fleet of pleasure
steamers.

The pier was built at Market Strand, formerly Smithwick
Creek, where the town had its origins and above whose stony
inlet stood the original lime-kiln. Countless landings were
made here before that, untold centuries of groundings and
gravings and repairs carried out as the tide retreated and left
vessels clear to work, bilge-down, on the shingle. As they
began the pier towards the end of the summer of 1871, waiting for the equinoctial springs to dig the piles deep into the
seabed, something appeared which caused the workforce to
pause. Soon the town's learned gentlemen had gathered at
the site to discuss it.

Later that year at the annual meeting of the Royal
Institution of Cornwall, Mr H. Mitchell Whitley read out a
short paper entitled: 'The Sub-Marine Forest at Market
Strand, Falmouth'. Beneath the water and a thin covering of
sand, lay a forest floor, a mass of semi-decomposed hazel and
oak, beech and birch. In the mud were the remains, too, of
the ferns and flag-irises that had once sprouted there. The
people of Falmouth could now look out into the harbour, at
the traffic of boats and the mooring buoys, and imagine it as
man first saw it, in the early Mesolithic age, as a wooded
swamp. The find at Market Strand was a reminder that the
permanence of the coast is an illusion created by the brevity
of our lives.

Between the two castles of St Mawes and Pendennis is a place that suggests a landscape even older than that. The Admiralty chart shows the contours thickening here, dropping to a gully twenty or thirty fathoms beneath the surface. Large ships enter the harbour along this channel, leaving the buoys of the East and West Narrows on each side, secure in the knowledge that although the land is not far away, the seabed is far beneath them. And for a moment in *Liberty*, I always have the sense at this point not so much of crossing over deep water as of soaring high above a gorge, looking down a cliff to a river rushing through frost-covered boulders towards a shoreline out of sight over the horizon.

EPILOGUE

A boy is holding a model yacht. He is in a boat-shed at Little Falmouth, the yard just upstream from Flushing where a dog-leg in the shoreline has allowed for centuries of ship-building. He is clutching the brand-new hull in both hands. The keel reaches down below his waist and the mast rises high over his head, and although the sails half-block his face, he is grinning behind it, with the irrepressible joy of a long-promised gift.

The two old men are talking, the one who made the model, the other who commissioned it for his grandson and whose own boat, the pea-green gaff-rigged *Ratona* built in this same yard in 1927, is being prepared for the season. The old men are talking first about the boy and the model, then about *Ratona*'s new throat-halyard and the wear-points on the old, and the hanks of the jib, and cleats and blocks and shrouds and the brass fastenings for the mainsheet track. Each man speaks slowly, dwelling on the details, turning the words over in his mouth with an expansiveness that goes far beyond what is necessary.

From behind the model's sails, I see the boat-builder's fingers idly tapping the surface of the workbench as he talks. Each fingertip is short-nailed and hardened like an old chisel. The sunlight glows behind his head, falling through a row of small and dusty panes. It falls on the butcher's block of the

Little Falmouth boatyard.

bench and the tobacco-tins of clips and screws and dowels, on the brushes and paint-pots and varnish jars whose lips hang with honey-like drippings, and I am thinking: *I could stand here for days just looking and still not see everything.*

The sediment of centuries of sail-craft has settled in this shed, thick on the floor underfoot, in soft shavings and planings, in the random timbers that have built up against the wall, laid against each other until the purpose of the first ones, with their half-hidden arrangements of bands and blocks and lanyard, has long since been forgotten or is no longer even understood. It is in the paint test-daubs and wall-swabbings, the strings of shackles and coils of stay-wire, and in the ceiling where sweeps and spars and topsail-yards lie dormant on the beams alongside sets of numbered moulds, whose sectional form contains the hull-shape of long-gone gigs or punts.

We leave the shed and walk up through the yard. *Ratona* is leaning against the sea wall, waiting for her mast to be stepped. I feel uneasy about seeing her out of the water, her keel exposed and all her usual grace and lightness gone. My grandfather pauses and runs his hand over the rudder and along the sharp edges of the antifouling and the boot-line – red, white and the Buckingham green of her topsides.

'Splendid job,' he mutters. 'Splendid.'

I carry the model boat like a prize. We take it back to St Mawes and for weeks afterwards I row after it across the harbour. I tack it back and forth between the quay and Amsterdam Point, in imitation of the racing boats that jostle at the start-line of the regattas. One evening, in a fresh northerly, I set the sails for a long reach out towards Carrick Nath, and have a job catching up with it, as it heads out towards the headland and the open sea beyond.

And now it is March, forty years later, and I am walking beneath a set of pines, looking down the cliff to the white surf and thinking of all the other March days when the first sharp light of spring has quickened my pulse. I am leaving the harbour, moving inland, to our rundown farmhouse on the Upper Fal. I am rowing out to *Liberty*, rolling back the cover, folding the ridge-pole. I am heading past Amsterdam Point with the tiller in the small of my back, and the village to starboard and its whitewashed walls and rows of windows spreading up and out from the crook of the quay. I am passing the rounded walls of St Mawes Castle, and the English Heritage flag fish-tailing in the breeze, and the East Narrows buoy with the submarine cliff far beneath it, and the West Narrows buoy, and beyond that, shadowed and somehow diminished in the brightness of the afternoon, Falmouth and its skyline of masts and funnels and cranes.

I am heading away from the open sea, pushing north across the wide basin of the Carrick Roads, almost empty in mid-March but for the salvage tug, the *Anglian Princess*, and the oyster fleet, hauling their dredges through the cultch, and powered by nothing more than trimmed-down headsails and a half-hoisted main. I am pressing up past St Just and Messack Point, towards the shadowy line of Restronguet Point and the holm oaks at Pill. Looked at from here, the land looks continuous, without any sign of where the river leads in. But now, coming closer, watching a pair of red-breasted merganser rise and skid away from me, I see the gap opening up at Turnaware. I am entering a much narrower channel, the wooded sides no more than a couple of hundred yards apart. I am looking astern, watching the nearby point close like a lock gate and shut out the flat horizon far to the south. The last thing visible down there, some three miles away, is the silhouette of Pendennis, the distant crown of its Tudor castle, and the point itself stretching out and narrowing to a fingertip. The distortion of light upon the sea creates a mirage and, just for a moment, defying the natural order, the land appears not to reach the level of the water, but to hover above it.

Even after several miles, the river still winds between slopes of sessile oak. The tide is falling; drifts of brown leaves and mulch slide down past the hull. I slow the boat, aware of the mud banks emerging from the ebbing stream. As the main Fal swings round to the north, with the thrill of seeing a lover in a crowd, I spot among the tree-tops the roofline of the farmhouse. At the same time, beneath *Liberty*'s hull, I catch sight of the bottom, flecks of old cockle-shell and darker clumps of weed. With the sailor's aversion to the seabed, I jam down the helm and head back downriver.

The muddy creeks are no place for a heavy-hulled boat like *Liberty* and a few days later, with a lack of sentiment which surprises me, I put her on the market. For weeks after we move in, I do little more than cut back the growth of thorn and ivy and elder that surrounds the house. The backdrop to my work is a tussocky paddock, a hedge of Kea plums and a ploughed field sloping upwards to the sky. Do I miss the sea? To begin with I am too excited by the rise and fall of the land, the copses and hedgerows, the peaty smell of the soil, the owls at night, the finches and thrushes in the morning. But one day checking references in the Cornwall Record Office, I find a manuscript plan of the fields around the house – *ink on linen, 1794*. Beside one of the fields is written the word *Quay*. I go back at once and follow the thick creek-side hedge round to the north-western tip, and begin to hack. I topple the rust-coloured stalks of last year's fern, and reach a barrier of bramble and haw and fallen oak.

Already I can see the shape of a cutting, dropping down towards the shore. On hands and knees, I crawl through it. When I stand again, elbowing aside the tangle of growth, I can see rock-steps leading down to a tiny, natural landing place, and the channel arcing in towards it. Within days, I have bought an old coble with cutch-brown sails and now she sits there, moored fore and aft, and floats for a couple of hours each side of high water. When the tides and the winds are right, I can sail downriver to the place where it opens out into the Carrick Roads, and point the bows south towards the flat horizon, and the open sea.

ACKNOWLEDGEMENTS

Many thanks to: Angela Broome and staff of the RIC Courtney Library and to Margaret Morgan of the Royal Cornwall Museum, the staff of the Cornwall Record Office, the Bartlett Library at the National Maritime Museum Cornwall, the Cornish Studies Library in Redruth, Falmouth Library, Truro Library, Cornwall Libraries HQ Store, Falmouth Art Gallery, the London Library, the Rare Books and Manuscripts Room of the British Library, Robin Harcourt-Williams of Hatfield House Library, Dr Williams's Library at Holborn, National Maritime Museum Library at Greenwich, Matthew Imms and staff at the Prints and Drawings Room of Tate Britain, the Pepys Library at Magdalene College, Cambridge, and the Duke Humfrey Room at the Bodleian Library. To Alexander Hoare, Clive Preston, Clem Cecil, Jane Turnbull and Brian Perman, Charles Fox, Tony Pawlyn, Peter Gilson, Matthew Connolly, Anthony Hobson, Will Hobson, and to Charlotte, as always, for unfailing support and candid criticism. Thanks too to Jonathan A. Glenn, for permission to use his translation of *The Seafarer*.

NOTES

APC – Acts of the Privy Council
CRO – Cornwall Record Office
CSP – Calendar of State Papers
HMC – Historical Manuscripts Commission
JRIC – Journal of the Royal Institution of Cornwall (NS – New Series)
MM – Mariner's Mirror
RIC – Royal Institution of Cornwall (Courtney Library)

As this book took me in ever more surprising directions, I found myself struggling to hold its course, adjusting sail to accommodate the freshening breeze of curiosity, while countering the weather helm produced by the weight of references and reading. Certain books spent more time beside me than others – either on my own desk or on those in the various libraries that I grew to know well. Barry Cunliffe's *Facing the Ocean* was an early favourite, as was Philip Payton's *Cornwall: A History* which produced a number of characters who were unknown to me. A.L. Rowse's *Tudor Cornwall* set its vibrant tones over preliminary research into the Killigrew story, as well as providing many sources. Martin Lister Killigrew's chronicle of the Killigrew family in *JRIC* (vols III and IX by R.N. Worth and H.M. Jeffrey respectively) was also used for every section that dealt with the Killigrews. The works of Boase – *Collectanea Cornubiensia* and, with Courtney, *Bibliotheca Cornubiensis* vols I–III, each one a towering work of Victorian scholarship – provided references for every aspect of Cornish history. Susan Gay's *Old Falmouth* was a loyal companion not only for the Killigrews but also for the later days of the Packet Service. James Whetter's *A History of Falmouth* was the starting point for Falmouth after the Restoration. Photocopies from the bound volumes of the *JRIC* filled a great many files. N.A.M. Rodger's incomparable two volumes of maritime history (*Safeguard* and *Command*) were a first stop for all naval matters. A subscription to *British History Online* provided access to many of the state papers (and reduced the need for too many trips to London), while through a subscription to the London Library, I had electronic access to the online archive *JSTOR* and its thousand academic titles, and to the *Oxford Dictionary of National Biography*, all of which, like Killigrew's Lizard light nearly four hundred years earlier, helped to dispel a little of the darkness from the stretch of Cornish coast below my study window.

Chapter 1

The Conrad quote is from the memoir of his life on ships, *The Mirror of the Sea* (section xxxvi), a work often overlooked in favour of his fiction. He describes his own relationship with the sea as 'something too great for words'. The previous section (xxxv) contains a sustained reflection about the sea: 'Faithful to no race after the manner of the kindly earth, receiving no impress from valour and toil and self-sacrifice, recognising no finality of dominion, the sea has never adopted the cause of its masters.' Basil Greenhill writes of the 'age of collaboration' in the opening sentences of *The Merchant Schooners* (p. 1). *Ratona* passed to an uncle following the death of my grandfather; after some years he sold her to a classic-boat enthusiast in Falmouth. She now spends the summer months not far from the Prince of Wales Pier and whenever I take the ferry to Falmouth I can see her at her mooring, low in her topsides and plain in her rig, and painted in a slightly different shade of green.

Chapter 2

For the early saints of the Fal, G.H. Doble gives a very thorough and scholarly account in his series *The Saints of Cornwall* (vol. 3). He finds close parallels between the saints and place names of the Fal estuary and those of the Brittany coast. See also Bowen, *Saints, Seaways and Settlements*.

The story of Glasney is told, in part, in Roddis's *History of Penryn*, Thurstan Peter's *History of Glasney* and in Whetter's *History of Glasney*. Vincent's *Abstract of the Glasney Cartulary* is a translation from the Latin of the Glasney Cartulary in which the story of the founding of the college is told. Over the years Glasney College became a centre for the Cornish language. The only complete surviving work of Cornish medieval literature was believed to have been written there. The *Ordinalia* (Bodleian Library *MSS. Bodley* 791) is a three-thousand-line trilogy of biblical plays, from the beginning of the world to the Crucifixion, and one of the earliest of its kind in Britain. Such is the fluency and beauty of the Cornish script that, when I saw it in the Duke Humfrey reading room of the Bodleian, I couldn't help thinking of all the hundreds of other Cornish manuscripts, now lost, that must have been written at Glasney. The case for the *Ordinalia*'s Glasney provenance rests mainly on the occurrence in it of twenty-four Cornish place names, most of them from the Penryn area. When the First Temple was completed at Jerusalem, Solomon awarded to the masons and carpenters 'the wood of Penryn wholly, / And all the water-courses', the 'Parish of

Budock and the Carrack Ruan' ('seal rock', now known as Black Rock), and the estate of 'Arwenack', owned by the Killigrews and containing the open shoreline from which, following the destruction of Glasney in the mid-sixteenth century, the port of Falmouth would begin to grow (Berresford Ellis, *The Cornish Language*, pp. 38–40, Bakere, *The Cornish 'Ordinalia'*).

Chapter 3

The rise of the port of Falmouth depended on the natural assets of the harbour as a whole – that is, the entire network of estuaries and creeks centred on the broad basin of the Carrick Roads. The Lizard peninsula to the south helps break up the Atlantic swells, while Pendennis Point offers further protection. Being a drowned valley the estuary is also one of the deepest natural harbours in the world. The combination of ample water, shelter and high-sided creeks provided seafarers with all they could wish for in a harbour. 'This harbour of Falmouth, as mariners tell us, is in all respects the largest and safest haven for ships that this Island of Britain affordeth' (Gilbert, *Parochial History*, vol. II, p. 1). John Leland (*Itinerary VII*, p. 119) says that it is 'very notable and famous' on account of the depth of the Carrick Roads, and is 'in a manner, the most principal [harbour] of all Britain'. In Michael Drayton's *Polybion: A Chorographical Description of Great Britain* (1622), a rambling poem of rhymed alexandrines, Falmouth is described as the only place in Cornwall free from Neptune's rage (see Treneer, *The Sea*, p. 226). Descriptions of perfect harbours often resemble Falmouth. Weary Aeneas and his followers find such a place on the Libyan coast (Virgil, *Aeneid*, Book I, 157–222). The harbour described in Thomas More's *Utopia*, Book II, p. 1, bears some relation to Falmouth, with its shelter and the single rock in its entrance. The reputation of the estuary as a haven was known in earlier periods. Ptolemy calls it the 'Cenia', and the early map of the British Isles by Nicholas Germanus (made in Rome 1478–90) gives it this name. 'Falemua' appears on Fra Mauro's map of about 1500.

Henry VIII proposed four castles to defend the Fal estuary. John Leland's visit to the estuary in 1540 coincided with the building of St Mawes Castle. On his map of the Fal he adds a castle to Trefusis point and one at Gyllyngvase; these were only plans and were never built. On Pendennis there is not yet any contemporary building, nothing but a prehistoric ditch.

The brasses of John and Elizabeth Killigrew beside the chancel of St Budock church are discussed with extensive genealogical notes in Dunkin's *Monumental Brasses* (pp. 36–8). Much of the knowledge about the Killigrews comes from the manuscript written by Martin Lister Killigrew in the 1730s (see note on Chapter 12 below). The manuscript is reproduced in *JRIC*, vol. III, p. 269 (Worth, 'The Family'), or at least a version of it. Further letters and manuscript documents by Lister Killigrew were assembled by Fox in *JRIC*, vol. XIII; amendments from other versions, with a full bibliographic study of them were written by Jeffrey, 'Two Historical Sketches', *JRIC*, vol. IX, p. 182. None of the originals survive.

The order of the Privy Council to John Killigrew on his reappointment as governor of Pendennis Castle (that he 'diligently, faithfullie and truly kepe, save', etc.) is from APC, 19 April 1554. For the early years of Pendennis Castle, see also Oliver, *Pendennis*, pp. 1–10. Further mentions of the Killigrews in the APC during the reign of Queen Mary concern their piracy: July 1555 (Killigrew pirate apprehended), December 1555 (a Spaniard's complaint of 'dyvers wrongs done unto him by oone John Killigrewe'), June 1556

(John Killigrew and his son sent for and bound by the Council, then put in the Fleet Prison), January 1557 (Peter Killigrew 'a pirate' in the tower … '150 crowns found on his woman'). From CSP Venetian: 21 July 1556 (an account of the capture of Peter Killigrew and others), 18 August 1556 (claims of their torture in the Tower of London). In CSP Dom Series Mary I (pp. 228–35) are details of Peter and other Killigrews' cross-Channel subversions and piracies in 1556. See also McDermott, *England* (pp. 40–41). For the building of Arwenack and a general account of the Killigrews during this period, see Worth, 'The Family' and Jeffrey, 'Two Historical Sketches', also Croghan, *Arwenack*, *Falmouth*.

The quote from Andrews is in his *Elizabethan Privateering* (p. 16). Mathew's 'Cornish and Welsh Pirates' gives a detailed account of West Country pirates. The papers of Charles Henderson (*Henderson MSS* in the RIC Courtney Library) contain details of the numerous land transactions of the Killigrews in the sixteenth century – the first John Killigrew mainly buying land in the middle of the sixteenth century, and his descendants mainly selling it.

Chapter 4

Lord Burghley's copy of Saxton's *Atlas*, in which is bound the Map of Falmouth Haven (Folio 9), is in the British Library (Royal MS. 18. D.III). The map is discussed by Jeffrey in *JRIC*, vol. IX, 'On a map of part of the parishes of Budock and Mylor'. I am grateful to the late Peter Gilson for discussions about the Burghley Map and other matters of Falmouth's history. He told me that as a young man he passed the days of a convalescence drawing a meticulous copy of the Burghley Map. For the life of Henry Killigrew, and a good deal of Killigrew background, see Miller, *Sir Henry Killigrew*, also Hasler, *The Commons* (Killigrew entry). Andrews's

Elizabethan Privateering is the best source for privateering at this time (p. 42 for 'shite on thy commissions'), and also Andrews, 'The English Seaman'.

The development of ship-based technology in the fifteenth and sixteenth centuries – of hull shape, rigging pattern and on-board ordnance – is a vast and intriguing subject complicated by the paucity of either material or documentary evidence. N.A.M. Rodger makes a good revisionist case against the orthodoxies of Sir Julian Corbett in his essay 'Guns and Sails'; see also the relevant sections of Rodger's *Safeguard* and Alan McGowan's *The Ship*, R.C. Anderson's *The Sailing Ship*, Landstrom's *The Ship*, and Laird Clowes's *Sailing Ships*. I also consulted a great number of articles in the *Mariner's Mirror*, including: R. Morton Nance, 'The Ships of the Renaissance' (*MM*, XLI, 1955, Part I, no. 3 and Part II, no. 4), R.C. Anderson, 'Early Books on Shipbuilding and Rigging' (*MM*, X, 1924, no. 1), Richard Barker, 'A Manuscript on Shipbuilding Copied by Newton' (*MM*, LXXX, 1994, no. 1), Geoffrey Palmer, 'The Dreadnought Revolution of the Sixteenth Century' (*MM*, LXXXII, 1996, no. 3).

Chapter 5

Fragments of Ancient English Shipwrightry is in the Pepys Library, Magdalene College, Cambridge (PL2820). A summary of its contents can be seen in Knighton, *Catalogue* (vol. 5, ii, Manuscripts). It was William Borough, of the Devon maritime family, and himself a maker of maps, who compared Matthew Baker with Vitruvius and Dürer. For John Davis on Baker, see Johnston, *Making Mathematical Practice*, p. 165. The mystique of ship design and hull shape persisted for a long time (even now, the debates of racing yachtsmen reveal it as far from an exact science). The French too were trying to optimise their fleet and in 1697 Paul Hoste published a treatise on ship design: 'It cannot be denied that the art of constructing ships, which is so necessary to the state, is the least perfect of all the arts ...' He recognised that great efforts had been made by very learned people to develop theories and rules but concluded that 'their ships are not better than those that were built without knowledge of reading or writing ... in a word, the constructors of the present day agree with the ancients, that *it is not yet known what the sea requires* [his italics]' (quoted by Fincham, *History of Naval Architecture*, p. xvi).

The quote from Thomas Fuller, regarding nautical imagery and the 'wit-combats' of Ben Jonson and William Shakespeare, is discussed in Honigmann, 'The First Performances' (p. 139).

The full importance of Hakluyt's work and his dedication to it (at least as understood by himself) can be seen in his 'Preface to the Reader' in the *Principal Navigations* (1599–1600 edition): 'Having for the benefit and honour of my Countrey zealously bestowed so many yeres, so much traveile and cost, to bring Antiquities smothered and buried in darke silence, to light, and to preserve certain memorable exploits of late yeeres by our English nation atchieved, from the greedy and devouring jawes of oblivion: to gather likewise and as it were incorporate into one body the torne and scattered lines of our ancient and late Navigations by Sea ...'

As well as the ship designs of Baker, and the ocean-crossing zeal stirred by Hakluyt, the 1570s and 1580s saw great advances in the navigation skills of English sailors. It is D.W. Waters (*Art of Navigation*, pp. 131–2) who makes the claim for the importance of the translation of Euclid. As well as writing the preface to the English Euclid, John Dee was also working on his four-volume *A British Complement on the Perfect Art of Navigation* (of which only one volume survives):

'the most significant work on navigation of his time' (Park and Daston, *Cambridge History*, p. 487). Yet for the ordinary mariner, it was probably William Bourne and his *Regiment for the Sea* (1574) which had the greatest effect. Bourne breached the elitism and secrecy that until then had surrounded the techniques and study of navigation, and placed them in the hands of seafarers. *A Regiment for the Sea* went into ten different editions, plus three in Dutch. It was part of the steady decentralisation of knowledge and power that followed the Reformation, away from libraries and Latin and great feudal landowners, a process that helped shape English seafaring into something aggressive, privately owned and free from government control (see Taylor, *A Regiment for the Sea*).

Chapter 6

The comparison between Plymouth and Falmouth is in the Kerrier section of Carew's *Survey of Cornwall*, a book which is both engaging to read and one of the most valuable of all sources of Cornish history. Although published in 1602, Carew confesses in his dedicatory note that it is an 'ill-husbanded Survey, long since begun, a great while discontinued, lately reviewed, and now hastily finished'. A.L. Rowse (*Tudor Cornwall*) considers it 'a very delightful book' (p. 19), though tires of Carew's 'pleasant and ambling' poetry and his interest in fishing: 'like most fishermen, he was a bore about fishing' (*Tudor Cornwall*, p. 423).

The only documentary evidence I could find linking the Killigrews in Cornwall in any way with the mini-Renaissance of the time were, first, an entry in the diaries of John Dee. In September 1582 the 'second' John Killigrew called on Dee for some legal help with his latest mischief (plundering a ship called the *Marie*, see below). This encounter indicates perhaps only how small the Elizabethan world was, rather

than any interest in metaphysical inquiry on the part of
Killigrew (in return for his help, Killigrew promised Dee
some fish, Dee, *Diaries*, p. 46). The only other link, equally
tenuous, was some letters which appear to be between a ward
of John Killigrew and Thomas Digges (Johnson, 'Two
Treatises', pp. 141–5). Digges wrote a series of letters to a
'JA', which was probably John Arundell. At the time there
were some seventeen living John Arundel/Arundells of note
but it was supposed that this friend of Digges was Sir John
Arundell of Tolverne, an estate on the Upper Fal. Because his
two uncles were deemed 'idiots', Arundell had been brought
up as a ward of John Killigrew (see Chynoweth, *Tudor
Cornwall*, p. 77) at Arwenack. Later it was this John Arundell
who carried news of the death of Sir Richard Grenville and
the loss of the *Revenge* back to England when he landed at
Falmouth in the *Tiger*. His son lost the family's money in an
attempt to discover an island off America called Old Brasil
(see Lysons, *General and Parochial History*, vol. 3, pp. 99–112).
Over the years the Arundells of Tolverne, itself a wooded and
forgotten corner of the Fal, slipped further from prominence
(see O'Toole, *The Roseland*, p. 52). Our own farm, near
Tolverne, was lived in until the 1980s by a family called
Rundle, a depletion in all probability of 'Arundell'. See also
Arundell Papers at the Cornwall Record Office (CRO
AR/17-AR/50).

For the Killigrews' substantial representation in the parliaments of Elizabeth I, I have used P.W. Hasler's three-volume
The Commons 1558–1603. For the story of Anthony Bourne
and its context, see Rowse, *Grenville* (pp. 146–7), while the
description of Killigrew as 'proud as Ammon' etc. is quoted
in Rodger, *Safeguard* (p. 345). The taking of the *Marie* is
reassembled mainly from *Acts of the Privy Council* (1581–2):
28 January 1581 (by new date 1582) ('complainte made by

Spanish Ambassador' against Sir John Killigrew that the *Marie* was 'boarded and carried away'); 13 March 1581/2 (the Privy Council told that Sir John Killigrew was now in London and 'secretlie lurked in some place' and that the ship had been taken to Ireland 'and most of the men cast overboarde'). See also *State Papers Dom. Eliz.* 152, no. 5, 153, no. 37. There is also a story of Lady Killigrew's involvement in this piracy, or one similar (Gilbert, *Parochial History*, vol. 2, p. 7 and reproduced and embellished in numerous studies of women pirates). She and her accomplices were sentenced to death for murder, and all but she were executed. Dubious details help to undermine the credibility of this story, including confusion with a subsequent Killigrew (see note on Chapter 7 below).

Sir John Killigrew's will offered generous legacies to his servants, to his daughter, £5 to the poor of Budock parish and £20 for the erection of the brass monument to his father. But in fact he left debts so far in excess of his assets that despite ever more desperate schemes, his son never escaped them (*Copy Will of Sir John Killigrew* 28 February 1584, Henderson MSS, Cal 8, item 1745, RIC Courtney Library) – £10,000 is the figure quoted, which cost his heir 'by forfeitures and advantages taken from him, £20,000' (HMC *Salisbury*, vol. 11, p. 376). His brother Sir Henry Killigrew tried to help and was 'prodigal towards him to the point of folly' (Miller, *Sir Henry*, p. 233). The rakish progress of his son, the 'third' John Killigrew, can be traced in the APC from 1587 onwards : 29 October 1587, 1 April 1588 (unpaid debts of £440); 3 September 1588 (arrest warrant); 20 November 1588 (complaint of the Danish merchant against him, and issuing of a *capiendum utlegetum*, allowing him to be taken by force); 1 December 1588 (general order to all mayors, sheriffs and bailiffs to apprehend him); 20 April

1589 (only now dismissed as vice-admiral of Cornwall for 'commiting divers outrages, disorders, ryots and misbehaviours'); 6 July 1589 (request to the Solicitor General for the 'writ of rebellion'); 19 October 1589 (warrant for him to be detained at Arwenack). Then, oddly, there is nothing until early January 1595. It is at this time, with the Spanish threat at its height again in Cornwall, that rumours of Killigrew's treachery begin to accumulate in the records (see Oliver, *Pendennis*, pp. 11–19). Mentions of the 'third' John Killigrew occur too in the Cecil papers at Hatfield House (HMC *Salisbury*). HMC *Salisbury*, vol. 13 (p. 431) reveals him seizing two ships in 1590. An outline of the charges against him in 1595 appears in HMC *Salisbury*, vol. 5, pp. 519–20, and subsequently in vol. 8, pp. 58–60. In 1598 he is imprisoned and in June writes to Sir Robert Cecil complaining of conditions (HMC *Salisbury*, vol. 8, p. 190).

Chapter 7

Wilson Knight's *The Shakespearian Tempest* examines Shakespeare's use of the sea in his work. On p. 10 he suggests that 'it is probable that Shakespeare never went to sea, save crossing the Thames by boat'. The quotes from Van Linschoten and from Anne Treneer both come from Treneer's *The Sea* (p. 122). James Anthony Froude was Regius Professor of Modern History and wrote of 'the bark of the English water-dogs' in the opening chapter of his *English Seamen*. John Killigrew's letters from prison, as well as the reporting of more of his misdeeds are in: HMC *Salisbury*, vol. 8, pp. 191, 303–4, 337, vol. 11, pp. 151, 376, 497, vol. 12, pp. 484–5, 548, vol. 16, p. 73 and vol. 24, p. 19. For the progress of Sir Nicholas Parker as governor of Pendennis, see Oliver, *Pendennis*, pp. 16–19. The 'debauching' of Jane Killigrew is in Worth, 'Family', p. 272.

For James I's treatment of the Navy, see Oppenheim, 'Royal Navy' (pp. 473–82). The general climate of corruption during the reign of James I is examined in detail in Peck, *Court Patronage and Corruption*. Raleigh's visit to Falmouth and his suggestion to Killigrew to build a port is mentioned in a number of sources, including Gay's *Old Falmouth*, each saying little more than that he called into Falmouth on his return from Guinea (presumably his first visit there, and not his disastrous second when his son was killed and he returned to face his own execution). A pamphlet in the Cornwall Studies Library goes into more detail (*Scenes of Old Falmouth*, C822/912 1922), unsourced though it is. When he visited Arwenack, it says, Raleigh had with him twenty-two captains and gentlemen, and also the son of the King of Aramaia as a pledge that his father would be a servant of the Queen of England. Raleigh described 'a mountain of chrystal like a white church of exceeding height. There falleth over it a mighty river, which falleth to the ground with a terrible noise and clamour, as if 1000 great balls were knocked one against another.' One can do no more than speculate how, on such evenings at Arwenack, mariners like Raleigh brought ashore something of the promise of new lands across the sea, or spoke of a coming age of ocean-going vessels, thus seeding the idea of a port to serve them at Smithwick. Permission for the four inns at Smithwick, the decision from which Falmouth would grow, is in APC 1613–14, pp. 33, 261–2. The Killigrew cup can be seen in Penryn Museum. Jane Killigrew's tarnished reputation made it easy to attach to her, in popular lore, the charge of piracy (see note on the taking of the *Marie* above). For John Killigrew's case to expand his Smithwick settlement, and the local resistance against it, see the correspondence between John Killigrew and Sir Richard Buller in the RIC Courtney Library (1617 RIC-HC/4/90//1–2). In *JRIC*, vol. IX, Jeffrey's 'Early Topography' is the only surviving version of the 1615 map (opp. p. 148). Jeffrey gives a good account of Falmouth at the time of its conception.

John Killigrew's main ally in the circles of King James's court was his cousin, Sir Robert Killigrew. Sir Robert was the grandson of the original John Killigrew whose brass likeness lies beneath the chancel carpet of St Budock church, and who sent his younger sons Henry and William to London. As William's son, Robert picked up seats in the Commons in several elections, eased himself into the court of James I and was knighted. He was a friend of John Donne and Sir Francis Bacon (and was married to Bacon's niece). He sponsored and indulged his own scientific and medical enquiries. Yet he clearly displayed some of the untamed passions of his Cornish cousins. He angered James I by duelling, physically attacked a committee chairman in the House of Commons and when his patron Sir Thomas Overbury was arrested and put in the Tower of London, Killigrew himself was briefly thrown into the Fleet Prison for talking at his jail window. He was known to be something of an amateur apothecary and never quite escaped the suggestion that it was he who had passed powders to Overbury through the bars, a dose intended to make him ill enough for a pardon, but which actually killed him. James's court was quick to forgive and, with royal favour restored, John and Sir Robert Killigrew set about turning the family's prospects. Sir Robert was appointed governor-for-life of Pendennis Castle the following year, in 1614. See Hasler, *The Commons* (Robert Killigrew entry), *CSP Domestic Series*, 13 May 1613, 7 July 1614, 6 October 1615, 7 January 1618, 31 October 1618, and Oliver, *Pendennis*, p. 22.

Chapter 8

For wrecks around the Lizard, see Larn and Carter, *Cornish Shipwrecks*, pp. 51–138. The earliest surviving record of Cornish light-keeping comes from near Land's End. A four-teenth-century manuscript describes how a certain Richard the Hermit was responsible for a beacon on the summit of Carn Brae. The manuscript (a pouch of ivory-covered vellum dated 25 September 1396 and crusted with the seal of the Prior of St Michael's Mount) is not in the Cornwall Record Office, as a number of sources suggest, but at the RIC Courtney Library (HA/8/1). It grants the right to levy a toll for beaconage and affirms it with the authority of the diocese. The report of the murder of another hermit at Carn Brae some years later suggests the resistance by local seamen to paying levies, and why such written rights might have been needed.

In his *Essays* (p. 172), Charles Henderson claims that the Killigrew plan for a light on the Lizard went back earlier, to 1570 and the success of the 'second' John Killigrew in obtain-ing a patent from the Lord High Admiral. Killigrew ambi-tions for their Cornish fiefdom were clearly deeper-seated than their more profligate activities suggest, running in parallel to the felonies which, until the seventeenth century, undid each one of them. The 'fourth' John's efforts to force a levy to be paid involved a joint campaign with Sir Dudley Carleton, Ambassador to The Hague. If Carleton could persuade the Dutch merchants to pay the levy for his Lizard light, Killigrew would share the proceeds with him. Despite the Dutch having lost £100,000 to the reefs of the Lizard in a decade, the campaign failed. The correspondence regard-ing the lighthouse, including letters from Killigrew and Carleton, is reproduced in *JRIC*, vol. VI, 1879, p. 319, Fox, 'The Lizard Lighthouses' (the original correspondence does not survive). For the general history of lighthouses, see Hague and Christie, *Lighthouses* and Wryde, *British Lighthouses*, which discusses the dispute between James I and Trinity House (p. 62).

Chapter 9

For Killigrew's efforts to build his lighthouse, to maintain it and to levy a toll from passing ships, see *JRIC*, vol. VI, p. 319, Fox, 'The Lizard Lighthouses'. Sir William Monson's defence of Killigrew's light is in CSP Dom. James I, 4 February 1623, and reproduced in Waters, *Art of Navigation*, pp. 565–7 (appendix no. 22). The West Country pirates in North Africa and the rise in piracy off the West Country during the 1620s are covered in Senior, *A Nation of Pirates*, Gray, 'Turks, Moors' and Whetter, *History of Falmouth* (Chapter 1).

Chapter 10

John Selden's *Mare Clausum* was considered such a critical part of Charles I's rule that he ordered that 'a copy should be kept in the Council chest, another in the Court of Exchequer, and a third in the Court of Admiralty' (Wheatley's note on *The Diary of Samuel Pepys*, 17 April 1663). The copy of the translation of *Mare Clausum* in the British Library was owned by Charles Killigrew and bears his signature (probably the son of Thomas Killigrew, see Chapter 11 below). The building of the *Sovereign of the Seas* is covered in Anderson, 'The Royal Sovereign', in Rodger, *Safeguard* (pp. 388–9) and in Pett, *Autobiography* (pp. xci–xcviii, 207–10). A rare first-hand account of her building has been left by a man from Penryn, Peter Mundy (see Chapter 13), who spoke of 'her spacious lofty stately stern, whereon is expressed all that art and cost can do in carving and gilding' (Mundy, *Travels*, vol. IV, p. 35). See also Heywood, *A True Description*. For another picture of the striking mismatch between early Stuart patronage and maritime matters, I would recommend James I's visit to Woolwich in May 1609 during the building of his own piece of nautical folly, the *Prince Royal*. Like *Sovereign of the Seas*, the *Prince Royal* proved more showy than seaworthy (the bill for her decoration survives, *Pipe Office Declared Account No. 2249*, which exceeded £1,300; the original budget for the entire ship was £7,000 – the final bill £20,000). A dispute had broken out about the use of certain timbers and the King himself travelled to the dock to preside over an inquiry. One faction – including the elderly Matthew Baker – argued that the timbers were not fit for shipbuilding. On the other side was the shipwright in charge, Phineas Pett, and many of the corrupt and senior officers of the Navy. The King inspected the timbers and announced that the cross-grain was not in the wood but in those who had chosen to criticise Pett. Eleven years after the launch, the Navy Commissioners reported on the *Prince Royal*. 'Her weakness', they concluded, 'is so great that all we can do unto her at this time with above £500 charge will but make her ride afloat'. The cause of her decay? Her poor timbers. See Pett, *Autobiography* (pp. 7–85), Oppenheim, 'Royal Navy' (pp. 487–94), Anderson, '*Prince Royal*', *MM*, vol. III and Rodger, *Safeguard* (pp. 386–8).

Whitley ('Note on the Destruction') dispels the long-held idea that Sir John Killigrew burnt Arwenack himself (not least by stating that, in 1646, he had been dead for ten years), and reproduces documents from the Public Record Office that prove the account of its destruction here. Oliver (*Pendennis*, pp. 28–67) gives a full and well-sourced account of the siege of Pendennis. The letter 'Dear wiffe ...' is from the sheriff of Cornwall (quoted in Oliver, p. 31). Coate, *Cornwall in the Great Civil War*, provides an overview of the subject.

Chapter 11

The full and very wordy charter of the town of Falmouth (the parchment roll is nine feet long) was published in the nineteenth century: *The Charter of the Town of Falmouth, In the County of Cornwall: With Two Subsequent Acts of Parliament Appertaining Thereto* Falmouth 1863. For Peter Killigrew, see Worth, 'Family'. Whetter, *History* is the best general source for the first years of Falmouth's official existence.

The various connections between the Killigrews and Charles II are explained in Dasent, *Private Life*, Fraser, *King Charles II* and Harbage, *Thomas Killigrew*. For the theatrical careers of Henry, Thomas and Charles Killigrew, see under Killigrew in Highfill, *A Biographical Dictionary*. For the expansion of seaborne trade throughout this period, Ralph Davis ('Merchant Shipping') is an excellent source. By late in the seventeenth century, he calculated, other than those in the agricultural sector, about one in five of the country's workers was involved in building ships, maintaining or supplying them.

Hendrick Dankerts enjoyed the patronage of both Charles II and his brother James, Duke of York. A number of his fine landscapes remain in the Royal Collection, one containing a hidden panel which when slid open reveals a naked woman, thought to have been Nell Gwyn, though now believed to be another of his mistresses, Barbara Villiers, Lady Castlemaine (*The Times*, 2 May 2007). In Penryn, there is a popular belief that Nell was from a local family, related perhaps to the unfortunate Daniel Gwin, first agent of Falmouth's Packet Station (see Chapter 12 below). 'The most shameful incident in the history of the fleet' is from Callender, *Naval Side* (p. 117). Pepys gives a candid view of Pett at the inquiry following the loss of ships on the Medway (*Diary*, 19 June 1667, 22 October 1667). The lines of Andrew Marvell are from *The last Instructions to a Painter, About the Dutch Wars* 1667. For the launch of Falmouth's first large ship, see *CSP Dom. Series* 1667–8, p. 563.

Chapter 12

Greenville Collins became known in Charles II's court circles when he was shipwrecked off Russia in 1676 on a quest to find a north-west route to China. His navigational skills were highly regarded, and he was commissioned by the King to carry out the most thorough survey to date of the coast of Britain and to produce a set of reliable charts. He sailed from harbour to harbour in *Merlin*, a small, eight-gun ship which, given the Falmouth chart's dedication to Sir Peter Killigrew, must have spent some time at anchor off Arwenack. Bryan Rogers (Whetter, *Cornish Weather*, pp. 37–42) fulfilled his ambitions in becoming the most successful merchant in the West Country. He and not the Killigrews was the first beneficiary of Falmouth's rise. But he too was undone by the capricious nature of sea-based trade. Shipwreck and privateers eroded his capital and he died a 'mere beggar'. The duplicity of his protégé Robert Corker helped his downfall. Corker had befriended Rogers's wife (constantly grieving for the death of each of their ten children), but when Rogers died she was pushed out of their house by Corker who also managed to succeed Rogers as head of Falmouth Corporation (see Whetter, *History*, pp. 48–62, Whetter, *Cornish Weather*, pp. 31–6, Whetter, 'Daniel Gwin' and Worth, 'Family'). Corker's brother, Thomas, left Falmouth and ended up in West Africa where he married the daughter of the Ya Kumba house of Sierra Leone and together they produced a slave-trading dynasty of some note (Lovejoy, *Transformations in Slavery*). Thomas Corker was said to have returned to Falmouth in 1700 with 45 ounces of gold, a great number of elephant tusks and several slaves, one of whom was baptised in Falmouth's church of King Charles the Martyr (Bob Dunstan, 'Falmouth's Famous Past' series, *Falmouth Packet*, 1967).

Martin Lister Killigrew's manuscript is tinged with a sense of squandered opportunity. Clearly he has relied to a degree on family anecdote, particularly for the earlier generations, and coloured the account with his own grief. Yet when set against other sources, state papers and contemporary letters, his opinions are invariably verified (see Worth, 'Family' and Jeffrey, 'Two historical sketches').

At the beginning of *Old Falmouth* (pp. 1–2), Susan Gay recalls the Falmouth of her childhood in the mid-nineteenth century and her fascination at the hints of a great maritime past, a fascination that matured into her own historical research (using many sources that are now lost) and her book: 'the old walled garden in which we played, with the little pointed shells in the gravel paths, the great box-borders enclosing beds of Nile lilies in full bloom, the myrtles, and the mingled scent of flowers, and rope, and which came in whiffs from the old sheds near the entrance-pillars to the rope-walk, with their two great stone walls. That was the Killigrew entrance-gate …'

The letters written by Martin Lister Killigrew to his agent in Falmouth, Abraham Hall, regarding the building of the pyramid, are reproduced in Fox, 'Further Killigrew MSS'. Here too is a transcription of the document that was sealed into the stonework when the monument was re-erected (a copy of which was placed at the Arwenack Manor office).

Chapter 13

Peter Mundy's *Travels* are published in five volumes by the Hakluyt Society, and copiously edited and footnoted by

Lt-Col. Sir Richard Carnac Temple. See also June Palmer's exhaustive study of Penryn (*People of Penryn*, p. 28) for the probable site of his house. It is a measure of the range of Mundy's travels that he was one of the only outsiders to leave a record not only of the building of the *Sovereign of the Seas* but also of the Taj Mahal. Mundy added a number of notes and essays to his *Travels*, in which his untutored curiosity is evident. He had clearly read many of the astronomers of the day – Abraham von Franckenberg, Johann Hevelius, Nicolas Copernicus, Albert Linemann. He debates the loss and gaining of a day by respective travellers travelling east and west and compares observations of the shady areas of the moons with his own observations of the eye of a fly (*Travels of Peter Mundy*, vol. 4). Dorothy Carrington includes Peter Mundy in her anthology, *Traveller's Eye* (pp. 178–9): 'His insatiable appetite for information, his eye for detail, his desire for accuracy, would have made him in modern times a first-rate scientist ... each strange item in the surprising world he had inherited is described with a spontaneous brilliance seldom to be found in modern writing.'

The quote regarding Charles II's encouragement of oceanic trade comes from Williamson's *The Ocean* (p. 177). Falmouth's role as a global stepping stone in the seventeenth and eighteenth centuries is well illustrated by there now being fourteen Falmouths worldwide, mainly in the US but also in Canada and Australia, including Tasmania.

The note on the hiding-place of Avery's treasure is in the Cornwall Record Office (CRO J/2277). It was deposited along with a hoard of papers from the Hawkins family of Trewithen but no other details are known. His story is told in Johnson (*Pirates*, pp. 23–40) and in Fox (*King of the Pirates*). In *British Piracy* (Baer, pp. 365–8) there is an interesting analysis of popular ballads relating to Avery that track the glamourisation of his reputation. They started on the London streets as soon as he had mutinied at La Coruña in 1694, while in the 1770s 'bold Captain Avery' appeared, and in the decades after the Napoleonic Wars a ballad was published in Bristol entitled 'Captain Ivory, the Bold English Pirate'. The letter from Mr St Lo is in *CSP Dom. Series* 1700–1702, p. 216.

Chapter 14

From a description of Falmouth in Southey, *Letters from England*, pp. 6–7: 'Everybody is in a hurry here; either they are going off in the Packets, and are hastening their preparations to embark; or they have just arrived, and are impatient to be on the road homeward. Every now-and-then a carriage rattles up to the door with a rapidity which makes the very house shake. The man who cleans the boots is running in one direction, the barber with his powder-bag in another; here goes the barber's boy with his hot water and razors; there comes the clean linen from the washer-woman; and the hall is full of porters and sailors bringing in luggage, or bearing it away; now you hear a horn blow because the post is coming in, and in the middle of the night you are awakened by another because it is going out.' Robert Southey passed through Falmouth in 1795, and later used his impressions in the above passage, written under the pseudonym Don Manuel Alvarez Espriella. The story of the Packet service at Falmouth was first told in full by A.H. Norway (*History*), who wished to correct the imbalance between the celebrated heroics of the Royal Navy and the unsung bravery of Packet commanders and crew. Robinson (*Carrying British Mails*) gives a good general account of the service at Falmouth and other Packet stations around the coast. See also Philbrick, *The Packet Service*. But the starting point for research into

Falmouth's Packet service is Pawlyn's *The Falmouth Packets*.
For Daniel Gwin, see Whetter's article 'Daniel Gwin'.
Beckford's ten days in Falmouth are chronicled in a series of
letters reproduced in Chapman, *The Travel-Diaries* (vol. 2,
pp. 5–17).

Chapter 15

The three volumes of Samuel Kelly's journals are kept at the
Cornwall Record Office (CRO X92). Crosbie Garstin's
edited version was published in 1925 (Garstin, *Samuel Kelly*).
A more recent edition (Cornish Classics, Truro 2005)
contains an introduction by the maritime historian Tony
Pawlyn, who points out the value of such a memoir: 'The
great naval commanders of those times have had their measure of praise; their portraits hang in galleries, their swords in
museums, their names are glorified on the signs of public
houses, but little has been said of the humble merchant
masters who kept trade alive through those critical years,
driving their ill-found, undermanned little brigs and snows
about the world undaunted by the swarms of privateers' (p.
11). Such were the risks, so grim the conditions, and so spare
the rewards that it is hard now to understand their motivation beyond the possibility that for most mariners being at
sea became an end in itself. A brief, handwritten family tree
of the Kellys (CRO DDX.92) explains that Samuel married
an Ellen Jose of St Ives.

Chapter 16

An account of the sinking of the *Royal George* is in Hepper,
British Warship Losses. The quote from Commodore Byron
(grandfather of the poet) provides the title for Cock's very
good essay on copper sheathing (Cock, 'The Finest
Invention', *MM*, 2001). The Susser Archive contains much

useful material on the history of Jewish communities in Britain and particularly in south-west England (http://www. jewishgen.org/jcr-uk/susser). It includes a transcript of the tombstones in Falmouth's Jewish cemetery and an account too of Samuel Hayne, a Customs officer, who alleges that Jews, and particularly 'Levi the Jew', were involved with Sir Peter Killigrew in Falmouth in defrauding the Customs (see Hayne, *Susser Archive*, Chapter 2, Part I, online, and also Susser, *The Jews*). The story of Barnet Levy is told by his grandson Israel Solomon (*Records*). Naggar (*Jewish Pedlars*) has a good account of Zender Falmouth and the Cornish pedlars. I also used Endelman, *The Jews*. In Gay, *Old Falmouth* (pp. 144–72, 197–208) is an account of many of the prominent Falmouth families. The Acadian Indians had resisted the English rule of their land that followed the Treaty of Utrecht. Those who arrived in Falmouth in 1756 were settled in Penryn, where smallpox killed about a quarter of them; sixty-seven are buried in the graveyard of St Gluvias (see *Falmouth Packet archives* online: http://www.falmouth.packet. archives.dial.pipex.com/id163.htm).

Chapter 17

The quote about the number of sects is from Warner's 1808 *A Tour through Cornwall* (p. 114): 'Falmouth, perhaps, contains a greater proportion of persons adhering to different religious sects, than any other town of its size in the kingdom, and (what is equally remarkable, and well deserving the attention of high priests and zealots,) all living in harmony and charity together.' The Jews, he says, 'form a considerable part of its population' while the Quakers are 'still more numerous'. Warner's previous roaming around Britain give his assessment of Falmouth's religious diversity some authority. He also wrote of Falmouth's quayside activity, as he witnessed the boarding of troops for Spain: 'Never was a scene of greater hurry or animation, or one that more irresistibly carried the imagination along with it.'

John Wesley's two visits to Falmouth are recorded in his journal (Wesley, *Journal*, 4 July 1745, 2 August 1755). I am grateful to Charles Fox for allowing me to inspect his extensive collection of Fox family papers, letters and published works. The individual testimonies come from Lower's *Record of the Sufferings of Quakers in Cornwall*. In the Cornwall Record Office (CRO AD447) is the account of Edward Fox trying to restore the prize money. See also Pallett, *Come-to-Good*, and Keast, 'History'.

Chapter 18

For the story of Thomas Pellow (the spelling is a variation of Pellew), see Pellow, *Adventures* and also Giles Milton's study of Pellow and other Europeans in captivity in the Maghreb at the time (*White Gold*). The two main sources for Pellew are Northcote Parkinson's *Edward Pellew* and Osler's *The life*. In the National Maritime Museum, Greenwich (AGC/P/13) is an account of the battle between the *Nymphe* and the *Cléopâtre*. For the same engagement, see also James, *Naval History*, vol. 1, pp. 96–9.

Chapter 19

For a view of Flushing at this time, see the early chapters of James Silk Buckingham, *Autobiography*, vol. I, also Philbrick, *The Packet Captains* and Pawlyn, *The Falmouth Packets. Journey into Cornwall 1795* is bound in an ivory-coloured parchment slip and kept in the Cornwall Record Office (AD 43/I) – it is described as 'probably' by Mr Guillibard. The smuggling that accompanied the Packet service was part of a general permissiveness for contraband that characterised Falmouth throughout the eighteenth century and into the nineteenth. It was estimated that smuggled goods passing through Falmouth would have raised in dues twice what the whole of Cornwall paid in land tax (see Turner, *Buckingham*, pp. 43–4). In a letter from Edward Pellew to Edward Hawke Locker, 13 February 1811, he is dismissive of the heroic rescue: 'Why do you ask me to relate the wreck of the *Dutton*?' He then gives a brief account of what happened on the *Dutton*, before confessing to an episode of intense emotion and ordering Locker to secrecy about it: 'No more have I to say except that I felt more pleasure in giving to a mother's arms a dear little infant only three weeks old, than I ever felt in my life, and both were saved. The struggle she had to entrust me with the bantling was a scene I cannot describe, nor need you, and consequently, you will never let this be visible.' Parkinson, *Edward Pellew* and Osler, *The Life* were the main sources for this chapter.

Chapter 20
The bound editions of *The Cornwall Gazette & Falmouth Packet* (from 7 March 1801) are at the RIC Courtney Library. See also Elvins, 'Cornwall's Newspaper War'. For Joseph Emidy, McGrady, *Music and Musicians* is the best source. Buckingham (*Autobiography*, vol. I, pp. 165–72) provides the fullest first-hand account of Emidy. From newspaper reports and advertisements, Richard McGrady has pieced together a list of Emidy's compositions which include two symphonies, three violin concertos, a horn concerto and variations on a Grecian air. Vladimir Nabokov suggested the area south of Lake Chad as the origin of Pushkin's African great-grandfather, as did Hugh Barnes in *Gannibal*, but like Emidy's early life, it is unlikely that any more information will ever be available.

Chapter 21

Philbrick's *Packet Captains*, Gay's *Old Falmouth*, Pawlyn's *Falmouth Packets* and Norway's *History* were used as sources for Flushing, which for naval officers and Packet captains in the eighteenth century was favoured over Falmouth as a place to live. For James Silk Buckingham, the main sources are his two-volume *Autobiography* and Turner's biography, *James Silk Buckingham*. His own writings are voluminous and come mainly from his Tolstoyan later life in which he wrote and lectured on morality, principles and how to live a better life (for a selection of his work, see Buckingham, *Outline Sketch*). His early attraction to the sea is described by his biographer (Turner, *James Silk Buckingham*, p. 49): 'It was the romance of sea-life that caught the boy's fancy. Falconer's *The Shipwreck* seized his imagination, and Dibdin's sea songs were music to his soul.' The evening with Nelson, Pellew and Coghlan offers an enticing scene (Buckingham, *Autobiography*, pp. 135–6). The young Coghlan had come to the attention of Pellew some years earlier, also in Plymouth, during Pellew's rescue of the *Dutton*. Impressed by his courage, Pellew put him on the quarterdeck of his *Indefatigable* and so began one of the more colourful naval careers of the period. In 1800 Pellew had sent him in a small cutter to board and take a French gun-brig at Port Louis from amongst a number of French ships and three shore batteries. Although wounded, Coghlan and his men succeeded in capturing the ship. He served for some years in the Bahamas before joining Pellew again as his flag captain in the Mediterranean in 1812 (Buckingham says of Coghlan that he was 'a fire-eater of sorts, who had done more daring things than any man of his rank and length of service'). Buckingham recalls the occasion as being between 1798 and 1800, but it was possibly later: Nelson was briefly second-in-command of the Channel Fleet early in 1801, when Pellew and Coghlan were also engaged in the Channel.

Chapter 22

Buckingham's *Autobiography* and Turner's *James Silk Buckingham* are the main sources for this chapter. William Pickersgill's portrait of Buckingham and his wife, now hanging at the Royal Geographical Society, was used as the poster image for *The Lure of the East: British Orientalist Painting* exhibition at Tate Britain in 2008. The anthology of his work (Buckingham, *Outline Sketch*) ends with an index of the 300 UK towns in which he lectured; it also quotes the figure for the number of lectures he made in those places (neither figure includes his years of lecturing in the US): 3,593 in all.

Chapter 23

James Hamilton in his *Turner: A Life* identifies the zest with which Turner travelled and sketched on his 1811 tour of the West Country: 'No corner seems to have been turned on the journey without his jotting down the view. The majority of these are no brief notations, but delicate evocations in which his pencil barely strokes the paper, of ships at anchor or villages falling down into the sea.' See also Bailey's *Standing in the Sun* and Smiles's *Light into Colour*.

A transcription of the torrent of verse that tumbled into Turner's notebooks and his copy of Cotman's *Itinerary* during the summer of 1811 is published in Wilton's *Painting and Poetry*. Wilton appears to struggle with conveying the work's appeal which is, he says, 'surprisingly lucid, though it never attains consistent readability for more than a line or two at a time'.

Ruskin's essay is the introduction to Turner's *The Harbours of England*; for anyone interested in boats, it is sheer pleasure from start to finish. The literature of the sea is constrained by the fact that seamen tend to be men of action, neither reflective by nature nor generally disposed to expressing their thoughts through the written word; likewise the experience of ships and the sea by men of letters is rarely participatory, or even that considered. In the nineteenth century Conrad and Melville were the obvious exceptions. Ruskin too, in a rather different way, can be added to the list. I am grateful to Matthew Imms of Tate Britain, who was cataloguing Turner's sketchbooks. We spent a happy afternoon in the Prints and Drawings reading room identifying Cornish headlands and villages from Turner's faint sketches. See Hamilton, *Turner: The Late Seascapes* for discussion of *The Fighting Temeraire* and his marine work in later life, also Hawes, 'Turner's *Fighting Temeraire*'.

Chapter 24

Falmouth Guide 1815 is in the Cornish Studies Library (Rare Books Store 914.2378). Cyrus Redding travelled through Cornwall in the early 1840s, and leaves a gloomy portrait of Falmouth which 'consists of a narrow ill-built street, running parallel with the harbour, which may now and then be seen close by at the end of some narrow opening among the houses, or down a low and dingy passage' (*Illustrated Itinerary*, p. 131). For Truro Sessions, see CRO QS/1/8/102.

In *Old Falmouth*, Susan Gay speaks of the bypassing of Falmouth by shipping in the late nineteenth century, of the surprise that 'a harbour so large and so secure could at this date remain so silent and at times so empty of ships' (p. 4). Pawlyn's *The Falmouth Packets*, Philbrick's *History Around the Fal*, 5 and Whetter's *Falmouth and the Loss* give good accounts of Falmouth's loss of the Packet service. The sources for John

Bull include Pawlyn, *Falmouth Packets*, Beck, *Captain John Bull* and Philbrick, *Packet Captains*.

Chapter 25

A special edition of the *West Briton and Cornwall Advertiser* was published on Saturday, 22 August 1863, with a very full account of the celebrations surrounding the arrival of the railway at Falmouth. *Illustrated London News* ran a report in its issue of 4 September 1863 (pp. 239–41) entitled 'Completion of the Cornwall Railway'. As well as a half-page illustration of the arrival of the train in Falmouth, it ran a full-page one of the harbour. Now that the railway had put it in touch with other places it predicted many would take advantage of its 'sanitary excellence', commending the town to its readers for its air quality and climate: 'Instances have not been wanting of invalids on their way to Madeira stopping here by preference.'

Conrad's reflection on the fore-and-aft rig is from *Mirror of the Sea* (section VIII). Basil Greenhill (*Merchant Schooners*) provides an elegiac and expert study of the demise of sailing ships as carriers of freight, and see also Bouquet, *West Country Sail*. For the sub-tidal timber exposed in the building of the Prince of Wales pier, see *JRIC*, vol. III, 1871, Whitley, 'The Sub-Marine Forest'.

BIBLIOGRAPHY

Anderson, R.C., 'The *Royal Sovereign* of 1637', *MM*, vol. III, 1913

Anderson, R.C., 'The *Prince Royal* and Other Ships of James I', *MM*, vol. III, 1913

Anderson, R.C., *The Sailing Ship: Six Thousand Years of History*, New York 1926

Andrews, Kenneth, *Elizabethan Privateering: English Privateering During the Spanish War 1685–1603*, Cambridge 1964

Andrews, Kenneth, 'The English Seaman of the Sixteenth Century', *MM*, vol. LXVIII, 1982, no. 3

Andrews, Kenneth, *Trade, Plunder and Settlement: Maritime Enterprise and the Genesis of the British Empire, 1480–1630*, Cambridge 1984

Baer, Joel H. (ed.), *British Piracy in the Golden Age: History and Interpretation, 1660–1730*, London 2007

Bailey, Anthony, *Standing in the Sun: A Life of J.M.W. Turner*, London 1997

Bakere, Jane A., *The Cornish 'Ordinalia': A Critical Study*, Cardiff 1980

Barnes, Hugh, *Gannibal: The Moor of Petersburg*, London 2005

Beck, John, *Captain John Bull*, Exeter 1995

Boase, G.C., *Collectanea Cornubiensia: a collection of biographical and topographical notes relating to the county of Cornwall*, Truro 1890

Boase, G.C., with W.P. Courtney, *Bibliotheca Cornubiensis: a catalogue of the writings, both manuscript and printed, of Cornishmen and of works relating to the county of Cornwall*, vols I–III, London 1882

Bouquet, Michael, *West Country Sail: Merchant Shipping 1840–1960*, Newton Abbot 1971

Bowen, E.G., *Saints, Seaways and Settlements in the Celtic Lands*, Cardiff 1977

Buckingham, James Silk, *Autobiography of James Silk Buckingham, including his travels, adventures, speculations, successes and failures*, London 1855

Buckingham, James Silk, *National Evils and Practical Remedies, with the plan of a model town, accompanied by an examination of some important moral and political problems*, London 1849

Buckingham, James Silk, *Outline Sketch of the voyages, travels, writings and public labours of James Silk Buckingham*, London (undated)

Buckingham, James Silk, *Travels in Assyria, Medina, and Persia*, London 1830

Callender, Geoffrey and F.H. Hinsley, *The Naval Side of British History 1485–1945*, London 1940

Carew, Richard, *Survey of Cornwall 1602*

Carnsew, William, 'William Carnsew's Diary', *JRIC* NS, VIII, 1978

Carrington, Dorothy, *Traveller's Eye: An Anthology*, London 1947

Chapman, Guy (ed.), *The Travel-Diaries of William Beckford of Fonthill*, Cambridge 1928

Chynoweth, John, *Tudor Cornwall*, Stroud 2002

Coate, Mary, *Cornwall in the Great Civil War and Interregnum 1642–1660: A Social and Political Study*, Oxford 1933

Cock, Randolph, 'The Finest Invention in the World': The Royal Navy's Early Trials of Copper Sheathing, 1708–1770', *MM*, vol. 87, no. 4, 2001

Conrad, Joseph, *The Mirror of the Sea*, London 1906

Croghan, David, *Arwenack, Falmouth: A History and a Plan*, Cambridge 1978

Cunliffe, Barry, *Facing the Ocean: The Atlantic and its People*, Oxford 2001

Dasent, A.I., *The Private Life of Charles II*, London 1927

Davis, Ralph, 'Merchant Shipping in the Economy of the late 17th Century', *Economic History Review*, IX, 1956

Davis, Ralph, *The Rise of the English Shipping Industry in the Seventeenth and Eighteenth Centuries*, London 1962

Dee, John, *The Diaries of John Dee* (ed. Edward Fenton), London 1998

Doble, G.H., *The Saints of Cornwall: Part 3, Saints of the Fal and its Neighbourhood*, Lampeter 1997

Dunkin, E.H.W., *Monumental Brasses of Cornwall*, London 1882

Ellis, Peter Berresford, *The Cornish Language and its Literature*, London 1974

Elvins, Brian, 'Cornwall's Newspaper War: The Political Rivalry between the *Royal Cornwall Gazette* and the *West Briton*, 1810–1831', *Cornish Studies*, second series, 9, 2001

Endelman, Todd M., *The Jews of Britain 1656 to 2000*, California 2002

Enys, Valentine, *Cornwall, the Canaries and the Atlantic: The Letter Book of Valentine Enys 1704–1719* (ed. June Palmer), Exeter 1997

A Falmouth Guide: Containing a Concise Account of the History, Trade, Port, and Public Establishments of Falmouth … being a Complete Directory to Strangers, Going Abroad in the Packets, Falmouth 1815

Fincham, J., *A History of Naval Architecture: to which is prefixed, an Introductory Dissertation on the Application of Mathematical Science to the Art of Naval Construction*, London 1851

Fox, E.T., *King of the Pirates: The Swashbuckling Life of Henry Every*, Stroud 2008

Fox, George, *An Autobiography*, London 1904

Fox, Howard, 'The Lizard Lighthouses', *JRIC*, vol. VI, 1879

Fox, Howard, 'Further Killigrew MSS. relating to the Killigrew pyramid or monument at Falmouth, and other matters', *JRIC*, vol. XIII, 1895

Fraser, Antonia, *King Charles II*, London 1989

Froude, James Anthony, *English Seamen in the Sixteenth Century – Lectures delivered at Oxford, Easter terms 1893–4*, London 1896

Garstin, Crosbie (ed.), *Samuel Kelly: An Eighteenth-Century Seaman*, London 1925

Gay, Susan E., *Old Falmouth: the story of the town from the days of the Killigrews to the earliest part of the 19th century*, London 1903

Gilbert, Davies, *The Parochial History of Cornwall Founded on the Manuscript Histories of Mr Hals and Mr Tonkin*, 4 vols, London 1838

Gray, Todd, 'Turks, Moors and the Cornish Fishermen: Piracy in the Early Seventeenth Century', *JRIC*, NS Part 4, 1990

Gray, Todd, *Early Stuart Mariners and Shipping: The Maritime Surveys of Devon and Cornwall 1619–1635*, Exeter 1990

Greenhill, Basil, *The Merchant Schooners: A survey of the history of the fore and aft rigged merchant sailing ships of England and Wales in the years 1870–1940 with something of their previous history and subsequent fate*, London 1951

Hague, D.B. and R. Christie, *Lighthouses: Their Architecture, History and Archaeology*, Cardigan 1975

Hakluyt, Richard, *The Principal Navigations: voyages, traffiques and discoveries of the English nation, made by sea or overland, to the remote and farthest distant quarters of the earth, at any time within the compasse of these 1600 yeres*, 3 vols, London 1599–1600

Hamilton, James, *Turner: A Life*, London 1998

Hamilton, James, *Turner: The Late Seascapes*, Manchester 2003

Harbage, A., *Thomas Killigrew: Cavalier Dramatist 1612–83*, Oxford 1930

Hasler, P.W. (ed.), *The Commons 1558–1603*, London 1981

Hawes, L., 'Turner's *Fighting Temeraire*', *Art Quarterly*, XXXV, 1972

Henderson, Charles, *Essays in Cornish History*, Oxford 1935

Hepper, David, *British Warship Losses in the Age of Sail 1650–1859*, Rotherfield, East Sussex 1994

Heywood, Thomas, *A True Description of his Majesties Royall and most stately Ship called the Soveraign of the Seas, built at Wolwitch in Kent 1637 With the names of all the prime Officers in Her, who were appointed by his Majesty since the time of her launching at Wolwitch. Also a briefe Addition to the first printed Coppy, worthy of your observation and Reading*, (second edition) London 1638

Highfill, Philip H., *A Biographical Dictionary of Actors, Actresses, Musicians, Dancers, Managers & Other Stage Personnel in London 1660–1800*, Illinois 1973–93

Honigmann, E.A.J., 'The First Performances of Shakespeare's *Sonnets*', in *Shakespeare Performed: Essays in Honor of R.A. Foakes* (ed. Grace Ioppolo), New Jersey 2000

James, William, *Naval History of Great Britain*, 6 vols, London 1837

Jeffrey, H.M., 'Early Topography of Falmouth', *JRIC*, vol. IX, 1886

Jeffrey, H.M., 'Emendations of passages in the itinerary of Worcester, which refer to Falmouth Haven and Glasney College', *JRIC*, vol. IX, 1886

Jeffrey, H.M., 'On a map of part of the parishes of Budock and Mylor, drawn about A.D. 1580, with a notice of Arwenack house', *JRIC*, vol. IX, 1886

Jeffrey, H.M., 'A map of the river Fal and its tributatries from a survey made in 1597, by Baptista Boazio', *JRIC*, vol. IX, 1886

Jeffrey, H.M., 'On the early acceptation of the name of Falmouth', *JRIC*, vol. IX, 1886

Jeffrey, H.M., 'Two historical sketches of the Killigrew family of Arwenack, composed by Martin Lister Killigrew, in 1737–8, and known as the Killigrew MS. and the Falmouth MS.', *JRIC*, vol. IX, 1886

Johnson, Charles, *Pirates: A General History of the Robberies and Murders of the Most Notorious Pirates*, London 1998

Johnson, Francis R., 'Two Treatises by Thomas Digges', *The Review of English Studies*, New Series, vol. 9, no. 34, May 1958

Johnston, Stephen, *Making Mathematical Practice: Gentlemen, Practitioners and Artisans in Elizabethan England*, PhD thesis, Cambridge 1994

Keast, John, 'History of the Society of Friends in Cornwall', MSS intended for publication, in Cornwall Centre, Rare Books Store 289.64237

Kelly, Samuel, 'Manuscript Journals of Life and Voyages (3 volumes) 1764–1795', Cornwall Record Office, CRO X92

Knight, G. Wilson, *The Shakespearian Tempest*, London 1940

Knighton, C.S., *Catalogue of the Pepys Library at Magdalene College Cambridge*, volume 5, ii, Manuscripts (Modern), Woodbridge, Suffolk 1987

Laird Clowes, G.S., *Sailing Ships: their history and development, as illustrated by the collection of ship-models in the Science Museum*, London 1932

Lambert, Andrew D., *War at Sea in the Age of Sail, 1650–1850*, London 2000

Landstrom, Bjorn, *The Ship*, London 1961

Larn, Richard and Clive Carter, *Cornish Shipwrecks: the South Coast*, Newton Abbot 1969

Leland, John, *The Itinerary of John Leland the Antiquary*, Oxford 1770

Linzey, Richard, *Fortress Falmouth: A Conservation Plan for the Historic Defences of Falmouth Haven*, Bristol 2000

Lovejoy, Paul E., *Transformations in Slavery: A History of Slavery in Africa*, Cambridge 2000

Lower, Thomas, *Record of the Sufferings of Quakers in Cornwall, 1655–1686 (Documents originally transcribed by, and with an introduction by, Thomas Lower)*, transcribed and edited by Norman Penney, London 1928

Lysons, Daniel and Samuel, *Magna Britannia: a General and Parochial History of the County*, London 1814

March, E.J., *Inshore Craft of Great Britain in the Days of Sail and Oar*, Newton Abbot 1970

Mathew, David, 'The Cornish and Welsh Pirates in the Reign of Elizabeth', *English Historical Review*, vol. 39, no. 155 (July 1924)

McDermott, James, *England and the Spanish Armada: The Necessary Quarrel*, London 2005

McGowan, Alan, *The Ship: Tiller and Whipstaff, The Development of the Sailing Ship 1400–1700*, London 1981

McGrady, Richard, *Music and Musicians in Early Nineteenth-Century Cornwall: The World of Joseph Emidy – Slave, Violinist and Composer*, Exeter 1991

Miller, Amos Calvin, *Sir Henry Killigrew: Elizabethan Soldier and Diplomat*, Leicester 1963

Milton, Giles, *White Gold: The Extraordinary Story of Thomas Pellow and North Africa's One Million European Slaves*, London 2004

Mundy, Peter, *The Travels of Peter Mundy in Europe and Asia, 1608–1667* (ed. Lt-Col. Sir Richard Carnac Temple), vols I–V, Hakluyt Society, Cambridge 1907–36

Naggar, Betty, *Jewish Pedlars and Hawkers 1740–1940*, Camberley 1992

Norway, A.H., *History of the Post-Office Packet Service: Between the Years 1793–1815*, London 1895

Oliver, S. Pasfield, *Pendennis and St Mawes: an historical sketch of two Cornish castles*, London 1875 (facsimile reprint, Redruth 1984)

Olson, Lynette, *Early Monasteries in Cornwall*, London 1989

Oppenheim, M., 'The Royal Navy under James I', *English Historical Review*, 1892

Osler, E., *The Life of Admiral Viscount Exmouth*, London 1835

O'Toole, Laurence, *The Roseland: Between River and Sea*, Padstow 1978

Padfield, Peter, *Maritime Supremacy and the Opening of the Western Mind: Naval Campaigns that Shaped the Modern World 1588–1782*, London 1999

Pallett, Henry, *Come-to-Good and the Early Quakers in Cornwall*, Truro 1996

Palmer, June, *Penryn in the Seventeenth Century*, Truro 1986

Palmer, June, *The People of Penryn in the Eighteenth Century*, Truro 1991

Park, Katharine and Lorraine Daston (eds), *Cambridge History of Science: Early Modern Science*, Cambridge 2006

Parker, Derek, *The West Country and the Sea*, London 1960

Parkinson, C.N., *Edward Pellew, Viscount Exmouth, Admiral of the Red*, London 1934

Pawlyn, Tony, *The Falmouth Packets 1689–1951*, Truro 2003

Payton, Philip, *Cornwall: A History*, Fowey, Cornwall 2004

Peck, Linda Levy, *Court Patronage and Corruption in Early Stuart England*, London 1991

Pellow, Thomas, *The Adventures of Thomas Pellow, mariner, of Penryn, three and twenty years in captivity among the Moors*, London 1890

Pepys, Samuel, *The Diary of Samuel Pepys* (ed. Henry B. Wheatley), 10 vols, London 1893–9

Peter, Thurstan, *The History of Glasney Collegiate Church: Cornwall*, Camborne 1903

Pett, Phineas, *The Autobiography of Phineas Pett* (ed. W.G. Perrin), Navy Records Society, 1918

Philbrick, M.E., *The Packet Captains of Flushing, Cornwall 1689–1815*, Truro 1982

Philbrick, M.E., *John Bull 1798–1832* (*History Around the Fal*, 2), 1983

Philbrick, M.E., *The Packet Service* (*History Around the Fal*, 4), 1986

Pounds, N.J.G., 'Ports and Shipping of the Fal', *JRIC* NS, part 1, 1946

Redding, Cyrus, *An Illustrated Itinerary of the County of Cornwall*, London 1842

Robinson, Howard, *Carrying British Mails Overseas*,
   Liverpool 1964

Rodger, N.A.M., 'Guns and Sails in the First Phase of
   English Colonisation 1500–1650', in *The Oxford History
   of the British Empire* (ed. Nicholas Canny), Oxford 2001

Rodger, N.A.M., *The Safeguard of the Sea: A Naval History of
   Britain 660–1649*, London 1997

Rodger, N.A.M., *The Command of the Ocean: A Naval
   History of Britain 1649–1815*, London 2004

Ronald, Susan, *The Pirate Queen: Queen Elizabeth, her Pirate
   Adventurers and the Dawn of Empire*, New York 2007

Roscarrock, Nicholas, *Nicholas Roscarrock's Lives of the Saints:
   Devon and Cornwall*, Exeter 1992

Rowe, James, *Sixty Years and More: A History of Flushing,
   Cornwall*, Falmouth 1897

Rowse, A.L., *Sir Richard Grenville of the Revenge*, London
   1937

Rowse, A.L., *Tudor Cornwall: Portrait of a Society*, London
   1941

Senior, Clive, *A Nation of Pirates: English Piracy in its
   Heyday*, Newton Abbot 1976

Smiles, Sam, *Light into Colour: Turner in the South West*
   (exhibition catalogue), St Ives 2006

Solomon, Israel, *Records of my Family*, New York 1887

Southey, Robert, *Letters from England by Don Manuel
   Alvarez Espriella*, 3 vols, London 1808

Susser, Bernard, *The Jews of South-West Britain: The Rise and
   Decline of their Medieval and Modern Communities*, Exeter
   1993

Taylor, E.G.R., *Tudor Geography 1485–1583*, London 1930

Taylor, E.G.R. *A Regiment for the Sea and Other Writings on
   Navigation by William Bourne of Gravesend, a Gunner
   (c. 1535–1582)*, Hakluyt Society, Cambridge 1963

Thomas, R., *History of the Town and Harbour of Falmouth*, Falmouth 1827

Treneer, Anne, *The Sea in English Literature: From Beowulf to Donne*, London 1926

Turner, J.M.W., *The Harbours of England* (introduction by John Ruskin), London 1856

Turner, Ralph Edmund, *James Silk Buckingham, 1786–1855: A Social Biography*, London 1934

Vincent, John, 'Abstract of the Glasney Cartulary', *JRIC*, vol. VI, 1878–81

Warner, Oliver, *English Maritime Writing: From Hakluyt to Cook*, London 1958

Warner, Richard, *A Tour through Cornwall in the Autumn of 1808*, Bath/London 1809

Waters, David W., *The Art of Navigation in Elizabethan and Early Stuart Times*, London 1958

Wesley, John, *The Journal of the Revd. John Wesley* (ed. Nehemiah Curnock), 8 vols, London 1909–16

Whall, W.B., *Shakespeare's Sea-Terms Explained*, Bristol 1910

Whetter, James, *Falmouth and the Loss of the Packet Service*, Royal Cornwall Polytechnic Society 1958

Whetter, James, *History of Falmouth 1661–1961*, Gorran, Cornwall 1961

Whetter, James, 'Daniel Gwin – The First Agent of the Falmouth Packet Station', *Old Cornwall Journal*, St Agnes, Cornwall 1964

Whetter, James, 'The Rise of the Port of Falmouth, 1600–1800', from *Ports and Shipping in the South West*, Exeter Papers in Economic History, University of Exeter, 1971

Whetter, James, *The History of Glasney College*, Padstow 1988

Whetter, James, *Cornish Weather and Cornish People in the 17th Century*, Gorran, Cornwall 1991

Whetter, James, *Cornish People in the 18th Century*, Gorran, Cornwall 2000

Whitley, H. Michell, 'The Sub-Marine Forest at Market Strand, Falmouth', *JRIC*, vol. III, 1871

Whitley, H. Michell, 'Note on the Destruction of Arwenack during the Civil War', *JRIC*, vol. IX, 1886–89

Williamson, James A., *The Ocean in English History: Being the Ford Lectures*, Oxford 1941

Wilson, D.G., *Falmouth Haven: The Maritime History of a Great West Country Port*, Stroud 2007

Wilton, Andrew, *Painting and Poetry*, London 1990

Worth, R.N., 'The Family of Killigrew', *JRIC*, vol. III, 1871

Wryde, J. Saxby, *British Lighthouses: Their History and Romance*, London 1913